D1236560

Skepticism and Cognitivism

Skepticism and Cognitivism

A Study in the
Foundations of Knowledge

Oliver A. Johnson

UNIVERSITY OF CALIFORNIA PRESS
Berkeley   Los Angeles   London

University of California Press
Berkeley and Los Angeles, California
University of California Press, Ltd.
London, England

Copyright © 1978 by The Regents of the University of California

ISBN 0-520-03620-4
Library of Congress Catalog Card Number 77-91743

Printed in the United States of America

1 2 3 4 5 6 7 8 9 0

To Carol,
with love and appreciation

Contents

Preface   xi

I. Introduction: The Skeptical Stance   1

1. *Archetypal Skepticism*   1
2. *The Alternative to Skepticism*   4
3. *The Skeptical Tradition*   8
4. *The Varieties of Skepticism*   12
5. *Epistemological Skepticism*   18
6. *Why Skepticism?*   19
7. *Why Not Skepticism?*   22
8. *Plan of the Book*   24

II. Skepticism: The Historical Tradition   26

1. *Historical Sketch of Ancient Skepticism*   27
2. *The Ten Tropes*   30
3. *Analysis of the Skeptical Argument*   34
4. *Evaluation of Ancient Skepticism*   35
5. *Cartesian Doubt*   42
6. *Preliminary Statement of Hume's Skepticism*   45
7. *Hume's Case for Epistemological Skepticism*   46
8. *Hume's "True" Skepticism*   50
9. *Examination of Hume's Arguments for
   Epistemological Skepticism*   55

III. Cartesian Demonology Revived   62

1. General Statement of Lehrer's Skeptical
   Thesis   63
2. The Skeptical Hypothesis   66
3. Explication of the Skeptical Hypothesis   68
4. Preliminary Argument: Can Googols be
   Ignorant?   72
5. The Regress of Ignorant Deceivers   77

IV. Verbal Gestures and the Suspension of Judgment   82

1. Skepticism and Metaskepticism   82
2. The Road to Skepticism   88
3. The "Philosophy" of the Mature
   Pyrrhonic Skeptic   91
4. Can a Pyrrhonist Believe?   97
5. Verbal Gestures and Everyday "Beliefs"   101
6. Verbal Gestures and Philosophical
   "Beliefs"   106
7. Pyrrhonism and Skepticism   112
8. Pyrrhonism—Epistemology or Morality?   115

V. Skepticism by Definition   119

1. Preliminary Statement of Unger's Case
   for Skepticism   120
2. Personal and Impersonal Certainty   123
3. "Contingent" Personal Certainty   127
4. "Logical" Personal Certainty   130
5. The Argument from Emphasis   138
6. Is Certainty a Necessary Condition of
   Knowledge?   144
7. An Alternative Definition of Knowledge   148
8. The Normative Argument from Certainty   150
9. The Argument from the Necessity of
   Clarity   154

10. *The Argument from the Impossibility of Truth*   158

11. *Consequences of Unger's Conclusion about Truth*   165

12. *Unger's Argument: A Final Twist*   168

VI. **Essays in Skepticism**   174

    1. *First Essay in Skepticism*   175
    2. *Evaluation of First Essay in Skepticism*   177
    3. *Second Essay in Skepticism*   198
    4. *Evaluation of Second Essay in Skepticism*   200
    5. *Third Essay in Skepticism*   206

VII. **Skepticism, Cognitivism, and the Foundations of Knowledge**   213

    1. *Who is a Negative Skeptic?*   213
    2. *Circular Arguments*   226
    3. *Logic and the World*   239
    4. *A Qualification*   245
    5. *Is Knowledge that Knowledge Exists Knowledge?*   248
    6. *The Range and Limits of Knowledge*   259
    7. *Belief and Reasonable Belief*   264

Epilogue   268

Notes   271

Index   289

Preface

This book is the product of two activities that, although (to the best of my knowledge) independent of each other, were going on at the same time. The first is of relatively minor importance. In the early years of the present decade, I was writing the manuscript of my book *The Problem of Knowledge* and found to my dismay that the logic of my argument led me straight to skepticism, a conclusion I neither anticipated nor desired. Fortunately, I was able to extricate myself from my predicament, but the argument I used to do so was brief and, I realized, incomplete. At the same time that I was grappling with skepticism, I discovered later, a much more important activity was going on in the field of epistemology. A number of writers were not only concerning themselves with skepticism but also were defending it in a variety of different ways, some of which were novel and quite ingenious. Although I offer some suggestions at the beginning of chapter iii to explain this sudden upsurge of skeptical writing, I do not pretend to be able to account for it in any thoroughly satisfactory way. In any event, my own earlier brush with skepticism, along with the concomitant appearance of a number of skeptical theories, led me to undertake the present work.

I should like to relate an incident about the writing of the book here, if only to illustrate the hazards of the profession. I spent the summer of 1974 working on the manuscript, very often doing my writing in the Ocean Beach Branch of the San Diego Public Library. One day I left my briefcase, containing my handwritten copy of chapter ii, in my unlocked car, in the library parking lot. When I returned, the briefcase was gone, evidently stolen. The next two days my wife and I canvassed the area, including in our search some extraordinary, possible hiding places, but with no success. Just as I was ready to resign myself to rewriting the missing manuscript pages, the briefcase was found, scarcely a hundred feet from where it had been stolen, but carefully concealed. When I opened it, I found nothing to be missing, probably because the only item of marketable value it contained was the Loeb Classical Library set of the works of Sextus Empiricus.

In the course of the book I have quoted at some length from publications of the Clarendon Press, Harvard University Press, Routledge and Kegan Paul, and from *The Philosophical Forum*. I should like to express my appreciation to these publishing houses and this journal for the use in my book of materials published by them.

Many people have helped me with this book, in many ways. My colleagues at UCR and elsewhere have always proved willing to argue with me and have rescued me from many a grievous error. My students have been helpful, not just through their endurance, but particularly through the clarity of their vision of things which have been invisible to me. Clara Dean has been her usual cooperative and efficient self, in typing, in beautiful accuracy, more drafts of the manuscript than I care any longer to recollect. Cheryl Giuliano, of The University of California Press, has, through her copy-editing skills, managed to smooth off many of the sharp edges of what reached her hands in a decidedly rough state. It is hard to express my appreciation to my children and especially to my wife, to whom I dedicate the book, because their contributions, though usually (but not always) intangible, have been of a kind that, at the beginning, made the book possible and, in the end, have made it real. Finally, my gratitude goes to the anonymous benefactor who retrieved my lost manuscript. To all the people who have contributed to the book during the last five years I offer my most sincere thanks.

Riverside   Oliver A. Johnson
March 11, 1978

I Introduction: The Skeptical Stance

1 Archetypal Skepticism

In the closing scene of his dialogue *Cratylus*, Plato pictures the young philosopher Cratylus bidding farewell to Socrates before departing from Athens on a journey into the country. In his final words to Socrates, with whom he has been discussing the nature of names, Cratylus expresses his sympathy for the doctrines of Heraclitus, in particular for the Heraclitean notion of the eternal flux of things. Socrates, whose misgivings about the philosophy of Heraclitus are apparent, offers his friend counsel, urging him not to be too easily persuaded by such views but to reflect further on the nature of reality while he is still young and of an age to learn. With this Cratylus departs.

We know almost nothing of the later career of Cratylus, but the comments made by Aristotle about his life and activities, tantalizingly brief though they are, indicate that he profited little from the advice given him by Socrates. In the course of a discussion of earlier Greek philosophers who advanced sensationalistic theories of knowledge, Aristotle notes that the implications of this kind of epistemology were carried through to their most extreme conclusion by the followers of Heraclitus, in particular, by Cratylus. According to Aristotle's account:

...because [the sensationalists] saw that all this world of nature is in movement, and that about that which changes no true statement can be made, they said that of course, regarding that which everywhere in every respect is changing, nothing could truly be affirmed. It was this belief that blossomed into the most extreme of the views above mentioned, that of the professed Heracliteans, such as was held by Cratylus, who finally did not think it right to say anything but only moved his finger.[1]

Aristotle's all-too-brief intellectual biography of Cratylus is at once intriguing and frustrating. So many questions arise for which we have no answers. Is it literally true that Cratylus gave up speech in favor of finger wiggling? Did he do this altogether, or only when he was in the company of philosophers? How long did it go on, for a short time only or for most of his life? What, if anything, did he think as he performed his manual manipulations? We have, in Aristotle's account, the picture of an extremely unusual human being, one whom many of us would probably describe as foolish, although some might take issue, calling him a wise man indeed. Still most of us would probably agree that if he took his philosophical conclusions and the physical behavior that resulted from them seriously, Cratylus must have been an individual not only of strong conviction but of equally strong will. Beyond that we would surely pity him his existence, for few of us would find happiness, or even contentment, in a life of silence.

For philosophers, Cratylus's idiosyncratic conduct gives rise to two further questions. First, what is the meaning or significance of his lapse into finger wiggling silence? To this question Aristotle offers a plausible, and almost certainly correct, answer. Cratylus refused to speak because he had come to the conclusion that it was impossible to make true assertions about the nature of anything. But to conclude that truth lies beyond our grasp is to embrace skepticism, or the thesis that we can know nothing. Although we have no record in Cratylus's own words acknowledging his acceptance of the skeptical thesis, we do have, if Aristotle is to be believed, dramatic evidence of his personal adoption of the skeptical stance in the physical activity into which he ultimately retreated. In the apparent conviction that philosophy is more than merely an intellectual exercise, Cratylus, by accepting a life of silence, seems to have put into practice the consequences to which he felt driven by the philosophical doctrine that nothing can be known. He thus succeeded in earning for himself the title of "archetypal skeptic."

The second philosophical question raised by the skepticism of Cratylus and its consequences in practice concerns the reasoning that led him to the conclusion that reality is unknowable. Again, Aristotle offers an explanation of this reasoning, but it is much too brief to be satisfying. The primary source of Cratylus's skepticism lay in the Heraclitean metaphysical notion of eternal flux, coupled with the epistemological view that knowledge must take its rise from sensation. It is reasonable to agree with Aristotle regarding the philosophical foundations from which Cratylus derived his skeptical conclusion, and, indeed, most scholars have done so.[2] Nevertheless, one would like to be able to follow the line of his argument in detail, grasping the precise steps that led him from his original premises to his final conclusion. But this, unfortunately, we can never do. We are left only to speculate. Making use of the scant historical information we have, we can nevertheless offer one conjecture about the philosophical antecedents of the skepticism of Cratylus which seems at least plausible: that whatever the nature and extent of his debt to Heraclitus, Cratylus could easily have come under the *direct* influence of Gorgias, who lived in Athens at the same time he did.

My reason for suggesting a possible connection between Cratylus and Gorgias is obvious: Although classified by historians of philosophy among the sophists, Gorgias must also be recognized as one of the most thoroughgoing skeptics in the Western tradition. Though we have little direct information about him—beyond a few fragments his writings have all been lost—we do have, particularly in the works of Sextus Empiricus, a clear and forceful account of the extreme form of skepticism he advocated. Sextus writes:

> Gorgias of Leontini belonged to the same party as those who abolish the criterion [of truth], although he did not adopt the same line of attack as Protagoras. For in his book entitled *Concerning the Non-existent* or *Concerning Nature* he tries to establish successively three main points—firstly, that nothing exists; secondly, that even if anything exists it is inapprehensible by man; thirdly, that even if anything is apprehensible, yet of a surety it is inexpressible and incommunicable to one's neighbour.[3]

That the name of Gorgias must be added to that of Cratylus among the earliest and most radical exponents of skepticism is clear from his second and third points, while his first point places him among the extremely thin historical ranks of metaphysical nihilists. It is not to my purpose here to concern myself with a critical examination of the arguments by which Gorgias tried to support his nihilism and skepticism.[4] I have referred to him mainly in order to call attention to his final thesis that even if anything could be known, this knowledge could neither be expressed nor communicated. May we not have in this thesis a philosophical doctrine whose practical application found its ultimate expression in the fingerwiggling of Cratylus?

2   The Alternative to Skepticism

Although skepticism is of ancient origin, relatively few philosophers in the Western tradition have followed in the path marked out by Gorgias and Cratylus. Rather most have rejected skepticism in favor of an epistemology based on the conviction that, however limited its scope, knowledge does exist. There are things we can know. Perhaps because of its very dominance in the tradition, this standard, positive view of knowledge, unlike skepticism, has never been given a name. Although the lack of nomenclature for the alternative to skepticism raises no theoretical difficulties, it poses a troublesome practical problem for one writing on the subject; namely, that he must employ awkward and lengthy locutions to identify the view. Such complications can, however, be avoided by the simple expedient of coining a term to identify it. This is what I propose to do. Whether I shall be successful in my endeavor is, nevertheless, a moot point, for others have tried to do this before with a notable lack of success. Before offering the term I shall use in this book to identify antiskeptical epistemologies, I should like to make a few comments on some of these earlier efforts.

Skeptics themselves have never experienced any difficulty in tagging their opponents. Almost from the beginning they have referred to them as "dogmatists." The term is liberally sprinkled through the writings of the earliest skeptic whose works remain extant, Sextus Empiricus. Although he used it as a general designation to characterize any epistemologist who claimed to know anything, Sextus applied it particularly to the Stoics, who represented the school of positive philosophy most opposed to skepticism during his own time. The term has, for perhaps obvious reasons, remained popular among writers of the skeptical persuasion. Hume, for example, made use of it. And in our own day Keith Lehrer can write: "The skeptic has been mistreated. Sophisticated epistemologies have been developed in defense of dogmatic knowledge claims."[5]

Should we follow the skeptics in using the term *dogmatism* to identify antiskeptical epistemologies? Before we write the suggestion off as obvious question-begging name-calling, I think we should at least recognize that its etymological roots are innocent. The ancient Greek word from which our word *dogma* is derived meant, according to the Oxford English Dictionary, "that which seems to one, opinion, tenet, decree." Sextus at least, writing as he did in Greek, might very well have been using the term in a straightforward descriptive sense to designate schools of philosophy (like the Stoics) which held positive opinions or tenets about the nature of reality. Hardly so, however, the moderns, for dogmatism has long since taken on overtones that have destroyed its original Greek meaning, turning it into a pejorative term to refer to a belief held without, and generally in opposition to, reason. Given its present connotations, dogmatism is a term whose offensiveness renders it totally inappropriate for use in serious philosophical debate to designate an antiskeptical epistemology. So I shall have to seek elsewhere for a distinctive designation for such a view.

A number of other candidates might be suggested. An obvious term to employ would be *gnosticism*, from the Greek word for knowledge; but this term has been rendered virtually unusable for our purposes by its long history of unfortunate and misleading associations and connotations. Turning from Greek to Latin, we might employ a term derived from the verb "to know" (*scire*); namely, "scitism." For some time I considered coining such a word and using it —there is some precedent here, for according to the OED, the term *sciture* is an obsolete English word for "knowledge"— until I became convinced that there is good reason why the word has become obsolete; it is simply a verbal barbarism. Another term that has recently been used in the literature is *rationalism*.[6] Its inadequacy should be apparent, however, for it is much too limited in its connotations, being associated with one particular, historical conception of knowledge, to be employed as a general term to designate *all* theories that hold knowledge to be possible.

After a great deal of discussion of the problem with my colleagues and students—which gave rise to a number of fascinating and sometimes ingenious suggestions regarding nomenclature—I have finally settled on a term, again derived from Latin, which I think aptly and felicitously describes all general, positive epistemologies. This is *cognitivism.*[7] One who claims that knowledge exists, thus, would be a "cognitivist." The appropriateness of the word for our purposes is verified by dictionary definitions. For example, after the word *cognition,* Webster's Third New International Dictionary offers the definition "the act or process of knowing in the broadest sense." And the OED in definition of the word *cognitive* writes: "Of or pertaining to cognition, or to the action or process of knowing." There is some precedent in the philosophical literature as well for using this term to designate a view affirming the possibility of knowledge. A generation ago the logical empiricists, in developing the implications of their verifiability principle, concluded that the "propositions" of normative ethics, being incapable of empirical verification, could be neither true nor false, hence could not constitute legitimate items of knowledge. This view of ethics came to be known (among other things) as "ethical noncognitivism." Opponents of the empiricists, who rose to defend the knowledge-status of normative ethics, responded by referring to themselves as "ethical cognitivists." The terminological proposal I am making here is to broaden the range of application of the term *cognitivism* by dropping the adjective *ethical,* so that cognitivism becomes the view that affirms the possibility of knowledge in general.

Having found a term to give to the view held by antiskeptical, positive epistemologists—and having given it coequal standing with its negative counterpart, skepticism, in the title of this book—I must add an important qualification. Although I shall attempt to reach a decision between skepticism and cognitivism in the book, and although it will be clear throughout the argument that I am very much concerned with cognitivism as well as with skepticism, I shall nevertheless concentrate my main attention in the course of the discussions that follow on skepticism rather than on cognitivism. Most of the book, thus, will be devoted to a critical examination of skepticism, in a wide variety of its forms. My use of cognitivism, at least until the final chapter, will be mainly that of a foil against which to contrast the theories offered by the skeptics.

3 The Skeptical Tradition

It is evident from the careers of Gorgias and Cratylus that the skeptical stance was one taken up by philosophers early in Western history. And it has proved perennially attractive to a small proportion of those who have succeeded them. Although one cannot speak of a "school" of skeptical philosophy persisting down through the ages, it is still possible to trace the course of what may reasonably be referred to as "the skeptical tradition." By no means continuous, and with periods of relative quiescence as well as activity, skepticism, as a negative answer to the question Is knowledge possible? has remained an option accepted by certain epistemologists right up to the present day, being defended with vigor and considerable dialectical skill by a number of contemporary writers.

Any attempt to describe the range of skepticism in Western philosophy and list exhaustively the names of its adherents would be a task far beyond the scope of this inquiry, whose main purpose is to offer an analytical and critical study of skepticism as an epistemological position, rather than to survey its history. Nevertheless, as a background for the discussions to follow, I shall devote a few paragraphs here to a brief sketch of the skeptical tradition, mentioning the names of the most prominent figures who have been associated with it since the period of classical Greek thought.

Following the Alexandrian epoch, throughout the Hellenistic and early Roman periods, skepticism was, with Stoicism and Epicureanism, one of the three main schools of philosophy in the ancient world. A great number of writers and teachers flourished under its banner, many of whom we know only by name, their works having been lost. Perhaps the most prominent among this host were (in rough order of their dates) Pyrrho, Timon, Arcesilaus, Carneades, Aenesidemus, and Sextus Empiricus. (I shall have more to say about these classical skeptics and their views in §1 of the next chapter.)

With the rise of Christianity, skepticism went into decline and remained generally quiescent for well over a thousand years. Although certain medieval thinkers (e.g., Nicholas of Cusa and William of Ockham) have on occasion been described in the literature as skeptics, their views regarding the nature and possibility of knowledge would seem to justify so labeling them only in the most marginal way. However, the religious and cultural upheavals characteristic of the Reformation and Renaissance, with their destructive effects on the established intellectual framework and major institutions of Western society, brought with them a renewed interest in the skeptical answer to the question of knowledge. The sixteenth century witnessed a Latin translation of Sextus's *Against the Mathematicians* by Gentian Hervet, with a preface containing a strong reaffirmation and defense of skepticism by the translator, a book bearing the title *Why Nothing Can Be Known* by the Iberian philosopher Francisco Sanchez, and Michel de Montaigne's well-known *Apology for Raymond Sebond*, which is filled with arguments defending skepticism.

The skeptical tradition continued to retain its vitality throughout the period of early modern philosophy. From the seventeenth century the names of three French writers should be mentioned (although the first two leaned strongly in the direction of what I shall call "mitigated" skepticism)—Pierre Gassendi, who early in his career wrote a defense of skepticism entitled *Dissertations in the Form of Paradoxes Against the Aristotelians;* Simon Foucher, who attacked Descartes's

9

notion of knowledge through clear and distinct ideas as well as the rationalism of the later Cartesians; and Pierre Bayle, who in his *Historical and Critical Dictionary* used the biographies of certain (often obscure) historical figures as the springboard for a very powerful dialectical defense of an extreme form of skepticism. Modern skepticism reached its apex, however, in the eighteenth century, in the figure of one of the greatest philosophers in Western history, David Hume. (Since I shall examine Hume's skepticism at some length in chapter ii, I shall not add anything more about him here.) Following the publication of Kant's *Critique of Pure Reason*, which had its impetus in its author's endeavor to find an answer to Humean skepticism, the ranks of avowed skeptics in the Western tradition thinned almost to the vanishing point. From the nineteenth century one might mention the Danish religious fideist, Søren Kierkegaard, who denigrated reason to make way for the "leap of faith," and from the early twentieth century the American, George Santayana, particularly in his book *Scepticism and Animal Faith*. But neither of these writers is a major figure in the philosophical tradition, although Kierkegaard has had a substantial, indirect influence on recent and contemporary philosophy.

Looking back over the brief sketch I have just given of the skeptical tradition, one might be tempted to conclude that skepticism is not of great importance in the history of Western philosophy. Nor would such an evaluation be totally without justice. Certainly it must be granted that—with the obvious exception of David Hume—the monumental figures in the history of philosophy are not to be found enrolled among the ranks of the avowed skeptics. Indeed, I think it safe to say that few professional philosophers today would be able even to identify all (or perhaps even most) of the names I have included in my historical sketch. (This remark, I hasten to add, is not meant to downgrade the people on my list, many of whom have other claims to historical significance, but only to point out that they do not stand in the foremost ranks of philosophers.)

At this point, therefore, we might pause to ask the question: If skepticism represents, as my last remarks seem to indicate, a minor strain in the history of philosophy, how can one justify devoting the major part of a book to its critical examination? I should like to offer three responses to this question. (1) Skepticism offers a solution (albeit a negative one) to a whole set of the most fundamental and difficult problems of philosophy, problems that have exercised the minds of the greatest thinkers in the tradition from Plato to Wittgenstein. These problems can be summed up as those concerning the nature, sources, justification, limits, and possibility of human knowledge. Furthermore, skepticism is not simply a theoretically possible solution to these problems—one that philosophers must take into account simply to avoid overlooking a remote, bare logical option. On the contrary, as I shall illustrate in greater detail in §5, throughout history skepticism has proved to be the (often desolate) refuge into which certain philosophers have found themselves driven by an apparently inexorable logic, in their very attempts to provide a basis for the claim that we truly do know something. (2) Historically, skepticism has been an important goad in motivating positive epistemologists to develop theories capable of justifying our claims to know. The determination to avoid, or to find an alternative to, skepticism was partially, if not primarily, responsible for the production of many of the major contributions to Western epistemology, including writings of such diverse philosophers as Plato, Augustine, Descartes, and Kant. The *indirect* influence of skepticism on the history of thought may indeed by adjudged of greater significance than the direct contributions of the skeptics themselves. (3) Even if there had been no skeptical tradition and no historical writers who adopted the skeptical stance, an examination of skepticism could still be justified at this particular time, for explicit skepticism, which has been relatively quiescent since Hume, is now enjoying a resurgence. Just within the last decade several epistemologists have offered quite diverse arguments in its defense. Nor have these been writings on the fringe of philosophy, of literary or sociological interest only. On the contrary, they are the products of competent professional epistemologists, well versed not only in the skeptical tradition itself but also in the techniques of modern analytic argument. Their writings are important to epistemology and deserve a thorough critical study.

4   The Varieties of Skepticism

I have referred to skepticism as the view that "we know nothing" or that "knowledge is impossible." Before going further we need to clarify this conception and to define it more precisely.[8] Perhaps the best way to go about doing this is indirectly, by considering the meaning of the central notion with which the theory is concerned; namely, knowledge. What is it the skeptics are denying when they claim that knowledge does not exist? What is knowledge? Without probing variations of detail in the definitions of knowledge epistemologists have offered (which do not affect the main issue), for our present purposes we can accept as a working definition the classical conception of knowledge as justified true belief. If one is to *know*, what he believes—or asserts, claims, affirms, accepts—must be true; it must accurately describe or articulate the nature of the world or some part thereof, for we cannot know what is false. But truth, though a necessary condition, is not a sufficient condition of knowledge, for we may believe or assert what is in fact true simply by accident; in such a case we should not be said to know. Before we can claim knowledge, we must establish that what we believe or assert is true; we must, that is, justify the truth of our belief or assertion. If we can do that, but only if we can, can we legitimately conclude that we know. Now skepticism, in holding that we know nothing, claims that nothing we believe, or no assertion we make, succeeds in fulfilling these conditions of knowledge.

The definition of skepticism I have just given is "idealized," in that it depicts the view in a pure form, as the logical denial of the generally accepted theory that we do know something; namely, cognitivism. But, as we shall see later, only a portion of the philosophers who are usually classified as skeptics hold the theory in the pure or idealized form that I have just described. Others tend to modify their negative claim to some degree, drawing back from the extreme of flatly denying that anything can be known. To use the term that has become standard, they espouse mitigated skepticism (also referred to as "limited" or "partial" skepticism) rather than "total" (or "extreme") skepticism. Of course, we are left with a problem; because it seems safe to say that, to some degree, all (or most) of us are mitigated skeptics. Most of us would, I think, draw limits to human knowledge, admitting that there are things we do not know, even that we cannot know. But if everyone is a mitigated skeptic, to speak of mitigated skepticism as a special philosophical position held by a fairly small minority within the Western tradition is simply misleading. The term denotes no distinctive view at all. The problem can, I believe, be resolved by noting that the issue really turns on a question of degree. Within certain general boundaries—which are, admittedly, quite vague—one can acknowledge our ignorance of things without earning the title of (mitigated) skeptic. Just because all of us are "skeptical" about certain things, it does not mean that we are all *skeptics* (even in the mitigated sense). However, the denial of knowledge beyond a certain point does land one within the skeptical camp. Where this point lies, or where the dividing line should be drawn, is a matter about which philosophers do not all agree. Was Kant a (mitigated) skeptic because he denied knowledge of things-in-themselves? Some philosophers have said so; most have said not. The best we can do on this issue, I think, is to accept the historical consensus. Some philosophers have generally been deemed skeptical enough to be classified as such, and others have not. But there can always be disagreement on the proper classification in specific cases.

Or, to raise a related but somewhat different problem,

should a philosopher be classified as a skeptic if it can be, or has been, shown that his epistemological assumptions, when pursued to their ultimate conclusions, lead to skepticism, even though he himself did not realize or intend this, and as a result, believed himself to be a cognitivist? Among those who could fall into this category we might include such philosophers as Locke or Wittgenstein. In the discussions that follow, I shall not adopt such a procedure but rather shall limit my inquiries into skepticism to the writings of those who have been explicit skeptics; that is, those who have deliberately and openly claimed to embrace and defend the skeptical point of view.

Since many skeptics have mitigated their negative claims in some way, but often in different ways from others, it might be worthwhile to sort out the major variations that appear in the literature. If we accept the term *mitigated skepticism* as a name for the general view that denies knowledge in a very major and important sense, without going to the extreme of denying its existence altogether, we can discover several different forms that this denial might take. (It does not follow that anyone who falls within one—or even more than one— of the categories I shall list below would be labeled a mitigated skeptic; the qualifying remarks I have made above apply here.) These categories overlap in many ways; often a person falls within one of the categories because he is a skeptic according to another.

a. "Subject area" skepticism: It is common for philosophers to deny knowledge within certain subject-matter areas. Thus we have religious, ethical, historical, scientific, metaphysical skepticism, etc. Examples of philosophers who have been skeptical of knowledge within one or more of these areas are too numerous to require mention. Nor need such skepticism, unless it embraced a significantly large number of different subject areas, render one a mitigated skeptic, as the term is usually applied.

b. "Specific object" skepticism: This is the view that denies knowledge of certain objects, or kinds of objects. Examples would be the denial that we can know that God, matter, other minds, causal connections, etcetera, exist. Again, examples are common.

c. "Faculty" skepticism: This is the denial of our ability to gain knowledge through the employment of some specific faculty or capacity we are held to possess. Thus, we have skepticism about reason or skepticism about the senses, etc. Rationalists, for example, tend toward skepticism about the senses, and empiricists tend toward skepticism about reason; both tend toward skepticism about intuition or revelation, etcetera.

But another kind of distinction regarding forms of skepticism needs to be made between what I shall call "methodological" and "theoretical" (or "terminal") skepticism.[9] The methodological skeptic is one who uses the technique of doubt as a device to aid him in his quest for knowledge, in contrast to the theoretical skeptic for whom skepticism represents the theory or position on which he takes his stand. The methodological skeptic, par excellence, is of course Descartes. Needless to say, a methodological skeptic should not be classified among the skeptics, for if he is successful in his aim, his methodological skepticism has cognitivism as its final result.

A final, very important distinction must be made before we can form a clear conception of the nature of skepticism. This distinction, which I have sloughed over in the formulations I have given of the skeptical thesis earlier in the chapter, is between what may be termed "contingent" (or "a posteriori") skepticism and "logical" (or "a priori") skepticism. The difference between the two can be illustrated by different formulations of the skeptical thesis. "We know nothing" or "Knowledge does not exist" typifies contingent skepticism; "We *can* know nothing" or "Knowledge is *impossible*" exemplifies logical skepticism. The distinction between the two is plain: Contingent skepticism asserts merely the nonexistence of knowledge as a matter of fact, whereas logical skepticism asserts its necessary nonexistence. According to contingent

15

skepticism, although we do not know now, we may know in the future, but, according to logical skepticism, we shall never know—because we cannot know.

Although it is a view that has been held, contingent skepticism is not a theory to which we need devote major consideration. There are several reasons for this. The first is historical; few skeptics of consequence in the tradition have espoused it. (There is a notable exception, which we shall discuss in chapter iv.) Its lack of adherents can be accounted for if one appreciates what its adequate defense demands. The claim that no one knows anything, if this were held to be a contingent fact, would, unless it were purely gratuitous, have to be based on evidence. One making it would have had to conduct an extensive, if not exhaustive, survey of human beliefs, finding that none of these satisfied the conditions necessary to qualify as an item of knowledge. (The situation would be like that of the naturalist who formulates the generalization that no swans are black, basing his claim on an extensive survey of the world's swan population.) Although it is true that many skeptics have originally been led in the direction of skepticism by their recognition that the human beliefs they have encountered do not constitute knowledge, I know of none who has conducted the kind of survey necessary to support his skeptical conclusion as a generalization based on empirical evidence.

There is a good reason why most skeptics have avoided contingent skepticism; it is vulnerable to telling objections. In the first place, it could be overthrown by the appearance of a single counterexample, like the naturalist's generalization about swans. Again, it is hard to see how it could avoid the charge of being self-referentially inconsistent. The statement "No belief that has been found satisfies the conditions to constitute it an item of knowledge," considered as a generalization based on an appeal to evidence, presupposes that the person making it has examined various beliefs and, as the result of his examination, has been able to categorize each of these beliefs either as "knowledge" or "not-knowledge" and, of course, has always placed them in the latter category. Now if the generalization is to be exceptionless, all the beliefs of the contingent skeptic himself would have to be placed in the category of not-knowledge, including his beliefs about the category into which each of the beliefs he is examining should appropriately be placed. But if, on one hand, he does not know that these beliefs all belong in the not-knowledge category, he may be mistaken in placing them there. Some, or maybe even all, might rightfully belong in the knowledge category. If, on the other hand, he does know where they belong, his generalizaton, on which his contingent skepticism rests, has an exception, so breaks down.

However, the essential shortcoming of contingent skepticism lies in the fact that it fails to come to grips with the crucial point at issue between skeptics and cognitivists, whose disagreement is not empirical or factual, but conceptual or logical. The items of knowledge (or things known), whose reality is in dispute, are not empirical objects whose existence can be established, if at all, through an appeal to observable evidence. Although it is true that we can empirically observe a sentence that states a proposition containing an item of knowledge (supposing any such items to exist), we cannot by any empirical means whatsoever verify *that* a given sentence does state such a proposition. If two sentences were put before us and we were told that one stated a proposition containing an item of knowledge and the other did not, we could examine both endlessly, applying to them whatever empirical tests ingenuity could devise, without ever gleaning the slightest clue as to which was which. As epistemologists, whether skeptical or not, have almost all realized, the question of the existence of knowledge cannot be viewed as a contingent issue to be resolved by empirical means. On the contrary, the existence of knowledge, if it does exist, must be established by logical argument; likewise, its nonexistence, if it does not exist, must be established by the same means.[10]

17

5 Epistemological Skepticism

Summarizing the results of the distinctions made in the last section, we can draw the following conclusion: The skepticism that will be our primary concern in this book is *total* (rather than mitigated), *theoretical* (rather than methodological), and *logical* (rather than contingent). The reasons for the last two choices are clear, but some doubt might be raised about our concentrating attention on total rather than mitigated skepticism, considering that many of the philosophers who are traditionally labeled skeptics have mitigated their skepticism, at least to some degree. Several reasons can be given for this decision, including the following: (a) The tradition does include total skeptics. Gorgias appears definitely to be one, and the same can by inference be said of Cratylus. Also, the contemporary defenses of skepticism to which a good part of the book will be devoted include arguments meant to support total skepticism. (b) Total skepticism, for the very reason that it is an extreme position, is epistemologically more important than mitigated skepticism. If it is correct, the boundaries of our possible knowledge are not merely limited, something most of us might be willing to acknowledge, but close in upon us and completely crush us. The goal toward which the intellectual endeavors of the human species—in philosophy, science, indeed in thought in general—have been directed from the beginning of recorded history is proved illusory, so either a new rationale must be found for the exercise of thought, or we must accept, as the only apparent alternative, the death of the intellect. (c) Because it is both more important and more extreme than mitigated skepticism, total skepticism has a wider and deeper interest for philosophers as well. As the stakes raised are higher, so the concerns engaged are broader. If a philosopher asserts that we can know nothing, say, of the existence of God, his views may cause consternation in the ranks of the theologians but hardly raise a ripple among philosophers of science. Or if he asserts that reason alone can never yield knowledge, he cannot expect serious repercussions from the empiricists. But if he asserts that none of us can know anything, he is raising an issue that no philosopher can disregard. Mitigated skepticism, one might say, gives rise to interparty disputes among philosophers, but total skepticism presents a challenge that touches the vital interests of us all. (d) Finally, I believe (and shall try to show later in the book) that total skepticism is in a unique way methodologically fruitful, for implications that are of great importance for epistemology and, as a result, for philosophy as a whole can be generated from it.

For these reasons—and also for the personal reason that I find it a fascinating subject of study—I shall concentrate my attention on total skepticism. (After all, if the total skeptics are right, mitigated skepticism is rendered not only redundant but also, as a theory that holds that *some* knowledge is possible, false as well.) As a descriptive tag to identify the theory of total skepticism, I shall, somewhat apologetically, adopt the term that has become standard in recent literature —*epistemological skepticism*. The problem with this term is obvious. It is meant to serve as a distinctive appellation, to distinguish total skepticism from several more specific types of mitigated skepticism, such as religious, ethical, scientific skepticism, etc. But *all* types of limited skepticism, as the denials of knowledge in some sense, are forms of *epistemological* skepticism. Hence, the adjective *epistemological* serves no function. Nevertheless, since the term is now in general use—I have myself employed it in several places—I shall follow the accepted practice here, although often I shall use only the single word *skepticism* to identify the theory.

6 Why Skepticism?

Why should any serious philosopher come to the conclusion that knowledge is impossible? I think there are two main reasons, both historical and theoretical, which have led philosophers to embrace epistemological skepticism. Because I shall be examining these two reasons at considerable length later in the book, I shall not discuss them in detail here but only sketch out their main lines. I might add that, although some skeptics have concentrated their attention more on one than on the other of the two reasons, they have by no means all done so. Rather, many have combined the two reasons to buttress their case for skepticism.

The first of the reasons rests on the problem of error. One of the discoveries all of us make early on is our liability to error. We believe something only to discover later that we have been mistaken. But when we believed we assumed we knew, an assumption that our subsequent discovery forces us to abandon; for we couldn't have known if our belief was mistaken. Recognizing the prevalence of error in human intellectual affairs, the philosophic mind is not long in coming to entertain the generalization that error may be universal. If we are mistaken sometimes, may it not be possible, the philosopher asks, that we are mistaken always?[11] And if we are always mistaken in what we believe, it follows that we know nothing. The skeptic, in exploiting this argument, begins with the acknowledgment of error and then goes on to try to show that error is universal because we always must be mistaken in what we believe, and therefore that we can never know anything. Or, taking another somewhat more sophisticated tack, he argues the case that although some of our beliefs are not in error, others are, and we cannot distinguish between the two classes of belief. That is to say, we can never conclude of any given belief that it falls within the class of those that are true rather than within the class of those that are false. Therefore, we are precluded from ever legitimately claiming of any belief we hold that it constitutes something we know.

The second reason for accepting skepticism is more difficult to explain briefly, because it rests on considerations that have to be supported by complex and lengthy arguments. At this point I shall limit myself to presenting a simple formulation of the case, to give a preliminary idea of the nature of this skeptical argument, without going into details. The point the skeptics attempt to make, stated in its most general terms, is this: Knowledge is an attainment. It is a goal toward which we are striving in our various beliefs. But it is a goal we cannot possibly reach. That this is so results from the very nature of knowledge itself. Taking the traditional definition of knowledge as justified true belief, it can be shown that no belief we hold can possibly satisfy both of the conditions required by the definition to constitute knowledge.[12]

It might seem that the skeptic would have great difficulty in showing that we cannot establish that any of our beliefs is both true and justified. But any optimism we might have on this score begins to dissipate as soon as we recognize that the two conditions necessary to knowledge are not independent but intimately related to each other, for when it is said that a belief, to qualify as knowledge, must be both justified and true, the definition requires that the belief must be justified *as* true. Or, to put the point in another way, if we assert a thesis as something we know, and then offer reasons in its behalf, the reasons we give, if they are to be good reasons or reasons capable of justifying our belief as something we know, must establish that the belief is true. But even if we understand that to know we must establish the truth of what we believe, we might still question whether such a requirement offers grounds to support the skeptics' case, for are we not able to establish the truth of many of the things we believe? The crux of the question here lies in just what we mean by the phrase "establish the truth of." The skeptical thesis usually takes the following form: To qualify as knowledge a belief must be true and the only grounds on which we can legitimately assert of any given belief that it is true are the reasons we offer in its behalf. We can conclude on the basis of these reasons that the belief is true only if, given the reasons, the belief must be true, for if the belief may be false in spite of the reasons given,

21

the reasons fail to constitute good reasons. But no set of reasons we can offer for any belief can succeed in fulfilling the task required of them, since, whatever the reasons in question should be, they may be accepted as true and the belief itself still, with complete consistency, be denied as false. Hence no reasons can qualify as good reasons, and the truth of none of our beliefs can be successfully justified or established. Such is the second skeptical argument in very brief form; the complex and elaborate argumentation that must accompany it in order to buttress it revolves mainly around the contention that no reason or set of reasons we can offer in support of a belief can successfully establish the belief to be true.

7 Why Not Skepticism?

Despite the arguments that may be offered in its behalf, epistemological skepticism has not drawn large numbers of philosophers into its camp. Why is this true? Why have most philosophers rejected it? Although several different reasons could be given, at least one must certainly be taken into account, a reason so important that it may fairly be called the standard objection to skepticism. This objection (briefly stated) runs along the following lines: The skeptic puts forth a thesis or theory; namely, that nothing can be known. But in advancing this theory he is himself making a knowledge claim, the claim that the theory states. But if, in order to advance the theory that nothing can be known, the skeptic must make a knowledge claim, he contradicts himself. One cannot consistently know that nothing can be known.

It might seem that the standard objection should not trouble the skeptic unduly, for he could easily escape from the contradiction in which it tries to trap him simply by denying that he is claiming to know anything himself when he asserts that nothing can be known. Naturally, he might respond, if nothing can be known, then clearly he cannot know that nothing can be known. But there are dangers in this maneuver, for one might ask the skeptic: "If you do not know that nothing can be known, why do you assert it?" Should the skeptic reply that he does not *know* that nothing can be known but has reasons (perhaps strong reasons) for believing it and that these reasons justify his asserting it, he lays himself open once again to the charge of contradicting himself. In asserting that he has reasons to support his skeptical thesis he is still making a knowledge claim (i.e., he is claiming to know that he does have reasons that support the thesis), thus contradicting the theory he is putting forward. Unless the skeptic can escape this kind of dialectical pursuit, which apparently is capable of forcing him into a vicious regress, he must finally acknowledge that he cannot support his theory at all. But this is to admit that the theory is gratuitous. And a gratuitous theory need hardly claim our allegiance.

I have, as I indicated I would, given only a brief sketch of the standard objection to skepticism here. Clearly the argument, both pro and con, must be pursued much further later. At this point I want only to add that, as we go on to study the various defenses of skepticism, we should keep the standard objection in view, asking ourselves in each instance if the skeptic does (inconsistently) commit himself to making a claim to knowledge or if he succeeds in avoiding the trap leading to self-referential refutation and at the same time manages to present a persuasive case in support of his skeptical thesis.

Summing up the last two sections, I believe the arguments sketched in them (brief as they are) indicate that skepticism is neither an idle theory that philosophers can brush aside with disdain nor a conclusion to which epistemologists must inevitably be led. Rather, I think, if we weigh the issue of the possibility of knowledge objectively and disinterestedly, that we must acknowledge that it is an extraordinarily difficult one to resolve; for a strong case can apparently be made for both skepticism and cognitivism. Can the issue be resolved at all? I shall try to provide an answer to that question before I conclude this book, using the study of skepticism to which much of the book will be devoted to aid me in doing so.

8   Plan of the Book

This book is not meant to be a historical, but an analytical and critical study. So I shall not devote a lot of space in it to a review of the skeptical tradition (nor any space to the standard, cognitivistic tradition). Nevertheless, because I want to examine at least the main arguments that have been offered in support of skepticism in the past, I need to consider the works of the writers who are responsible for them. This I shall do in chapter ii. I shall concentrate my attention first on the ancient skeptics, preferring them over the early modern skeptics mainly because most of the arguments used by the latter are embellished renditions of those originated by the former. The one exception I shall make to this procedure is to examine the views of David Hume, not only because of his philosophical eminence but also and more importantly because he made significant, novel, and in certain respects, ingenious contributions to the literature of skepticism. Also in chapter ii, for reasons that will become obvious there, I shall comment briefly on the *methodological* skepticism of Descartes, who was, of course, not a skeptic but a cognitivist.

The bulk of the book, chapters iii through v, will be devoted to a consideration of three contemporary skeptics. All the works I shall examine have been published within the last decade, and each is quite different in its line of argument from the other two. Although two of the three develop theories that have appeared before in the literature, they make significant alterations in and additions to these themes, and the third presents a case for skepticism which, as far as I know, is quite original. Because the writings in question are the work of accomplished and sophisticated epistemologists, who make use of the tools of modern analysis, they offer what we can, at least at the outset, assume to be as strong a case for skepticism as we can expect to see at this time. In coming to grips with them, we can thus anticipate that we shall be facing twentieth-century skepticism at its best.

In chapter vi I shall offer my own contributions to the skeptical tradition. In doing so not only shall I attempt to develop one particular line of skeptical argument further than has as yet been done but also I shall make my own (I think distinctive) contribution to the literature of skepticism. In formulating my essays in skepticism, I shall try to be self-critical, recognizing the force of the objections that can be made to whatever theses I may advance and attempting to answer these objections as best I can. My aim in doing all this will be to see if it is possible to arrive at a definitive answer to the question: *Is* there any formulation of the skeptical thesis that can hold its own in the forum of philosophical debate?

The final chapter of the book will be devoted to an exploration of certain major issues that have developed in the course of the argument. I shall look at these from the perspectives of both skepticism and cognitivism together. In doing so I shall occupy myself with two main topics: (a) I shall try to examine the foundations of knowledge in a completely general way, pursuing in some detail the logical relationships between skepticism and cognitivism; and (b) I shall consider particularly the implications of skepticism in the effort to determine what value, if any, it has as a methodological device productive of conclusions that are fruitful for epistemology.

II Skepticism: The Historical Tradition

As I said at the end of chapter i, I shall not undertake an extensive survey of the skeptical tradition in Western thought in this book. Rather, I shall focus my attention on the ancient skeptics and on David Hume (with a short digression on Descartes). By so limiting my survey, I shall, of course, leave out of consideration a number of important writers, particularly from the early modern period, people like Montaigne and Bayle. But as I have indicated, the arguments offered by these writers are largely derivative from those of the ancients. In his detailed study of the early modern skeptics, *The History of Scepticism from Erasmus to Descartes*, Richard Popkin states, "thinkers like Montaigne, Mersenne and Gassendi, turned to Sextus for materials to use in dealing with the issues of their age." He also notes that Sanchez was indebted to Arcesilaus, Carneades, and Sextus and describes Bayle as "the great Pyrrhonist."[1] Since my aim in this book is to examine the case for skepticism critically, I think the most effective method for me to employ at the beginning is to concentrate my attention on the thought of its originators. Although the writings of only one of the ancient skeptics (Sextus) have come down to us in more than fragmentary form,[2] we are fortunate in having extant in his work both a historical survey of the thought of his predecessors and an incisive as well as persuasive defense of the skeptical point of view.[3]

But even the attempt to consider critically the full corpus of skeptical thought in the ancient world would be a task far beyond the scope of this book, for that period of time amounts to approximately six hundred years and the contributors are legion. Even to cover fully the materials included in Sextus would require more space than we can afford, for he multiplied arguments and illustrations with bountiful profusion. To give the ancient thinkers their due and at the same time to keep the discussion within bounds, I shall concentrate my attention on certain core arguments that they developed in support of their views, rather than try to come to grips with all of the issues they pursued. These arguments are available to us in clear and reasonably succinct form in Sextus. Before turning to them, however, it may be helpful to offer at least a brief historical account of skepticism in the classical world.

1 Historical Sketch of Ancient Skepticism[4]

The ancient skeptical tradition is an intellectual phenomenon of the Hellenistic and Roman worlds, the third of the three dominant post-Aristotelian "schools" of philosophy vying for centuries with both Stoicism and Epicureanism. Its reputed founder, Pyrrho, accompanied Alexander the Great on his famous military expedition to India and its last major figure, Sextus Empiricus, did not die until well into the third century A.D. To speak of the skeptical "school" of philosophy, however, is misleading for at least two reasons. First, there is no continuous history of skepticism throughout ancient times; rather the skeptical view waxed and waned periodically during these centuries, sometimes apparently disappearing altogether from the intellectual stage. But, more important than these facts, there are two distinct ancient skeptical traditions, which have come to be known in the lit-

erature as Pyrrhonic skepticism—or Pyrrhonism for short—
and Academic skepticism. As its name indicates, Pyrrhonism
is the tradition that stemmed from Pyrrho. About the skeptical philosophy of Pyrrho we do not have much reliable information; however we have numerous anecdotes (some probably apocryphal) concerning his way of life. On the basis of
fragments from his pupil Timon, Eduard Zeller writes of
Pyrrho's philosophy as follows: "The little which is known of
Pyrrho's teaching may be summed up in the three following
statements: We can know nothing as to the nature of things:
Hence the right attitude towards them is to withhold judgment: The necessary result of suspending judgment is imper-
turbability."[5] The main ancient Pyrrhonists include Pyrrho's
student Timon and, centuries later, Aenesidemus and, finally,
Sextus. Academic skepticism, as its name indicates, flour-
ished in the Platonic Academy, after the death of its founder.
Both of its main exponents were heads of the Academy,
Arcesilaus in the third and Carneades in the second century
B.C.[6]

Scholars do not fully agree either on the nature or the
importance of the differences between the two traditions of
ancient skepticism. There is evidence that Timon ridiculed
Arcesilaus—the two were contemporaries in Athens and
knew each other personally—but this is probably attributable
more to professional rivalry and Timon's caustic wit than to
philosophical disagreements between them. Yet Sextus, in his
account of the skeptical tradition, makes a clear distinction
between the followers of Pyrrho, among whom he includes
himself, and the philosophers of the later Academy. In
Chapter 33 of Book I of his *Outlines of Pyrrhonism* (which is
entitled "Wherein Scepticism differs from the Academic Philosophy") he has the following to say: "The adherents of the
New Academy [i.e., Carneades and his pupil Clitomachus],
although they affirm that all things are non-apprehensible,
yet differ from the Sceptics even, as seems probable, in respect of this very statement that all things are non-apprehen-

sible (for they affirm this positively, whereas the Sceptic regards it as possible that some things may be apprehended)."[7] Whether Sextus was fully justified in distinguishing the views of the Academic skeptics from Pyrrhonism in the way he did—and evidence from other ancient sources raises doubts on this point (e.g., see Zeller's summation of Pyrrho's philosophy, above)—it remains true that the skeptical thesis was advanced in two different forms during the classical period. These may be stated in the following ways: (a) Knowledge is impossible and (b) on the question of whether knowledge is or is not possible, as on all other questions, we suspend judgment. Sextus to the contrary, the proponents of the first form of skepticism, (a), will here be considered as authentic skeptics, on the very good grounds that their formulation is an exact statement of the view I defined in the first chapter as "total" or "epistemological" skepticism. It is precisely that theory I am concerned with in this book. But what about the second or "Pyrrhonic" version of skepticism, (b)? Can it legitimately be classified as skepticism? Sextus would certainly claim that it is *more* skeptical than the first version, because, unlike that form, it refrains from committing itself to any "dogmatic" pronouncement about knowledge, either positive or negative. Although it could be argued that the Pyrrhonist, by suspending judgment, offers no theory about knowledge whatsoever, so cannot truly lay claim to the title of skeptic, nevertheless it is important to examine this form of skepticism, for at least three reasons: (1) It was an important strain in ancient skeptical thought; (2) it is defended at length by one of the contemporary skeptics with whom I shall be concerned later in the book; and (3) it apparently offers a way in which the skeptic can escape the trap set by the standard objection to skepticism that I described in §7 of chapter i. Because of the second reason I have just given, I shall reserve my main discussion of this version of scepticism for chapter iv, in which I shall examine the view in the form in which it has recently been defended.

2   The Ten Tropes

Although the ancient skeptics developed numerous arguments aimed at undermining the possibility of knowledge, the essence of these was distilled in ten objections called "Tropes" or "Modes," the purpose of which was to show that we can offer no satisfactory grounds for ever asserting about any object we perceive that we are perceiving it as it actually exists. Because we can never do this we cannot legitimately claim to know—or, at least, we should suspend our judgment about—the real nature of the world. Traditionally attributed to Aenesidemus, the Tropes are presented at length by Sextus, occupying the central portion of Book I of his *Outlines of Pyrrhonism*.[8] Of their importance to ancient skepticism Charlotte Stough has the following to say: "The Ten Tropes . . . constitute a unique systematization of all skeptical arguments known to Greek philosophers."[9] In this section I shall present the ten Tropes in a condensed version, then summarize the logic of the skeptical argument in the following section, concluding my survey of the ancient skeptics with an evaluation of their case in §4.

Trope 1: The variety in animals. The object of the first Trope is to show that because of differences in their origins and bodily structures, different animals receive different impressions from the same objects. Such differences are apparent in all of the sense organs through which impressions are obtained. For example, the eyes of different creatures vary markedly, some being slanted and elongated and others round, some convex and others concave. And so it goes with all of the senses. It is reasonable to conclude, from the fact of these variations, equal differences in the nature of the impressions that the animals in question, including man, receive of the world. There is no justification, therefore, for us to claim that our impressions are more veridical than those of any other animal. As Sextus concludes, "we cannot prefer our own sense-impressions to those of the irrational animals."[10]

Trope 2: The differences in human beings. The second Trope uses the same kind of argumentation as the first but concentrates on humans. That the impressions different individuals receive of the world vary is well attested by the variations in their responses to things. Sextus writes, "Seeing, then, that choice and avoidance depend on pleasure and displeasure, while pleasure and displeasure depend on sensation and sense-impression, whenever some men choose the very things which are avoided by others, it is logical for us to conclude that they are also differently affected by the same things, since otherwise they would all alike have chosen or avoided the same things."[11] Given these differences among human beings, we have no reason to select the impressions of certain individuals (specifically ourselves) and claim these to represent the world as it is, as against the impressions of those who differ from us.

Trope 3: The different structures of the organs of sense. The same line of argument is continued, but the focus is narrowed to the sense organs of a single individual. Here, also, we find divergences. A painting, which appears to be three-dimensional to the eyes, seems flat to the touch; perfume has a pleasant odor but a bad taste; etc. Which of the sense organs give us a true picture of the object itself? And can we say?

Trope 4: The circumstantial conditions. The nature of the impressions we receive is dependent on our subjective state, variations being caused by such things as our physical condition and our emotions. For example, the world appears different to the drunk man than it does to the sober; the warm room of the bath house seems cold to one who has just been in the hot room but hot to one who has just entered from outdoors; to a lover, his mistress, whom everyone else considers ugly, seems beautiful. Nor can we draw a valid distinction between the real world, as viewed by normal people, and the aberrations perceived by those in an abnormal state, because to the abnormal, the normal themselves appear abnormal.

31

We do not, that is, have any acceptable criterion of normality. Hence we cannot conclude that anyone's impressions reveal the world as it really is.

Trope 5: Positions and intervals and locations. The appearances of the objects we perceive vary according to the nature of the circumstances of these objects, as well as their relationships to us. Thus, the same ship seen at a distance appears small and stationary, but viewed from close at hand large and moving; the necks of doves appear different in hue as we observe them from various angles; the oar, which appears straight, becomes bent to our view when thrust in water; etc. From all this Sextus concludes, "while we can, no doubt, state the nature which each object appears to possess as viewed in a certain position or at a certain distance or in a certain place, what its real nature is we are, for the foregoing reasons, unable to declare."[12]

Trope 6: Intermixtures. No object appears to us in isolation but always in some surrounding medium, which affects its appearance. Thus, the color of a person's complexion varies with the temperature, and the nature of a sound with the rarity or density of the atmosphere. Furthermore, our sense organs themselves do not operate in isolation. Our vision, for example, is affected by membranes and liquids in the eyes, our sense of taste by saliva in the mouth. We are unable, in other words, to apprehend any object simply by itself through means of a sense organ functioning in its purity.

Trope 7: The quantities and formations of the underlying objects. The appearances of external objects vary as the objects are perceived in the aggregate or discretely. Thus, on one hand, a goat's horn looks black but goats' horn filings look white; on the other hand, a block of silver looks white but silver filings look black. What, then, is the real color of goats' horns and silver? We cannot say.

Trope 8: The fact of relativity. To know an object as it truly is, one must apprehend it just as it is and not as it is in relation to anything else. But necessarily we perceive all objects in relation to something else, if only in the sense that, in order to perceive them, we must bring them into relation with ourselves as perceivers. So, Sextus concludes:

> When, however, we have thus established that all things are relative, we are plainly left with the conclusion that we shall not be able to state what is the nature of each of the objects in its own real purity, but only what nature it appears to possess in its relative character. Hence it follows that we must suspend judgement concerning the real nature of the objects.[13]

Trope 9: The frequency or rarity of occurrence. Spectacles to which we have grown accustomed we take for granted, but those which rarely occur we greet with amazement. For instance, few take note of the sun, whose rising and setting is a daily phenomenon, yet everyone is stricken with awe by the passage of a comet. But the latter is not nearly so remarkable a spectacle as the former. Hence, our responses to such phenomena are not appropriate to the objects as they really are but depend rather on the frequency with which they appear to us.

Trope 10: The disciplines and customs and laws, the legendary beliefs and the dogmatic convictions. The final Trope differs from the previous ones in being concerned not with the relativity of our sense impressions but with that of our conduct. As Sextus says, this Trope is concerned with ethics, and consists in an enumeration of dozens of examples of ethical relativism. In one society a certain type of conduct is accepted but in another it is condemned, instances of this relativity being found in such practices as homosexuality, adultery, human sacrifice, incest, homicide, etc. According to Sextus these conflicting beliefs about appropriate forms of conduct indicate a lack of agreement concerning the nature of objects. Given the divergencies, we cannot form a reasonable judgment as to the true nature of the objects involved. As he puts it, "since by means of this Mode also so much divergency is shown to exist in objects, we shall not be able to state what character belongs to the object in respect of its real essence, but only what belongs to it in respect of this particular rule of conduct, or law, or habit, and so on with each of the rest."[14]

3   Analysis of the Skeptical Argument

As our brief sketch of the Tropes shows, they are all designed to contribute their bit to a single skeptical conclusion—that we can never know the world as it is in itself but are limited in our apprehensions to the way things appear to us. Each individual Trope—with one exception—concentrates on some aspect or consequence of our sensory experience and, by use of illustrations, makes the point that our impressions cannot accurately represent the nature of independent objects. The exceptional Trope is the eighth, which offers a general argument to support the same conclusion: Every sense impression is, and must be, tainted through its very nature, for all, in order to exist, must be relative to their possessor, the observer, and therefore cannot reveal the nature of their objects in their independent (or nonrelative) reality. Thus, what the other Tropes support piecemeal, the eighth purports to demonstrate conclusively: that it is from the very nature of the case impossible that we should know the world as it really exists. All that remains as the possible objects of our apprehension are phenomena. In reaching this conclusion the skeptics accepted a distinction that was widely held in ancient Greek philosophy (as it is even today)—the dichotomy between appearance (phenomena) and reality (the world). But whereas some ancient philosophers had argued that reality is knowable, the skeptics, through appeal to the Tropes, endeavored to make the case that it is not.

Yet the Tropes alone do not seem capable of establishing a conclusion of such universality. Even though we might grant that they do eliminate the possibility of our knowing reality through the agency of our senses, they do not of themselves make it impossible that we should know it in some other way. Clearly, if the skeptics are to support their denial of objective knowledge, they must supplement their appeal to the Tropes by some additional argument. This, in fact, they do by relying on a thesis that was widely (but not universally) accepted in the ancient world. This thesis, which I shall label the "empiricist assumption," simply asserts that all of our knowledge consists of what we apprehend through our senses. I think it can easily be recognized that the empiricist assumption is implicit throughout the Tropes, and is essential to them, if they are to lead to their intended skeptical outcome. That the empiricist assumption is integral to the epistemology of ancient skepticism is attested to by Sextus, who writes in his book *Against the Logicians*, "every intelligible thing derives its origin and source of confirmation from sensation."[15]

To see the skeptics' argument as a whole, thus, it is necessary to combine the Tropes with the empiricist assumption. We can do this in the following, formal way:

All of our knowledge consists of what we apprehend through our senses [empiricist assumption].

Our senses can provide us no knowledge of reality or of the world as it is in itself but only of phenomena or appearances [evidence of the Tropes].

Therefore, we can have no knowledge of reality or of the world as it is in itself but only of phenomena or appearances [skeptical conclusion].

In the next section I shall examine this argument critically.

4 Evaluation of Ancient Skepticism

The case for skepticism encapsulated in the ten Tropes is subject to criticism on a variety of points. One could, for example, find instances in which the illustrations Sextus offered in

35

support of a Trope are less than convincing. If I were engaged in a detailed study of ancient skepticism, I should have to examine and evaluate such instances at length. But for our purposes here the effort would not justify itself, since its results would not, I think, yield us a definitive, or even persuasive, answer to the central question with which we are concerned: Is the skeptical denial of the possibility of knowledge true or false? Much more rewarding would be a critical examination of the logic of the relationship between the illustrations the skeptics offer and the conclusion they derive from them. We could ask: Is it true, as the skeptics contend, that our sense impressions cannot reveal the nature of the world as it really is, but only as it appears to be? Although this could, I believe, prove to be a more fruitful line of inquiry— we might, for example, argue for the kind of view of sensory-based knowledge that the Stoics defended—I shall not pursue it here, in part because it is not, in my opinion, the most effective way to get to the heart of the question regarding the possibility of knowledge. But even more important—and this is my main reason for not pursuing the argument—I am convinced that the skeptics are correct on this point. Although I shall not defend my agreement with them (leaving that matter in their own good hands and referring the reader to the Tropes themselves), I think that if all our knowledge must consist of what we apprehend through our senses, we can never know the nature of things as they exist in themselves. The deductive argument in which I have cast the skeptics' case, beginning with the empiricist assumption and using the Tropes as evidence, does yield the skeptical conclusion they draw from it.

But a different kind of argument might be offered against the skeptics, aimed at their appearance-reality distinction. One could note that the skeptics' conclusion denies the existence of knowledge of reality *only*, not the existence of knowledge of appearances, or phenomena. On the contrary, the skeptics in general were agreed in holding that we can grasp the way in which things appear to us. To mention a favorite example of theirs, which apparently goes all the way back to Pyrrho, Timon writes in his work *On the Senses*, "I do not assert that honey really is sweet, but that it appears sweet I grant."[16] In this quotation Timon is clearly admitting that he knows *something*; namely, that honey tastes sweet to him. If, however, one were to tax him with having abandoned his skepticism, I do not think he would be greatly disturbed. He would probably respond that my criticism establishes simply that his skepticism is of the (slightly) "mitigated" rather than the total or epistemological type and that, in any event, his interest is not in labels but in the critical philosophical issue of the limitations that must be placed on possible human knowledge. And on this issue his case is made: We cannot know the nature of the world as it is in itself but only as it appears to us to be.[17]

Yet the appearance-reality dichotomy and the issues it generates cannot be written off so quickly. For suppose some antiskeptical cognitivist were to challenge the skeptical view on this point by asserting that he is able to know the nature of reality as it is so is not limited in his knowledge to appearances; that he knows, for example, that honey not only tastes sweet but is actually sweet in itself.[18] How would a skeptic go about responding to him? The answer is evident from the Tropes: he would point out that, while honey tastes sweet to the cognitivist now, it doesn't always, when it is rancid, say, or when he is sick; it doesn't taste sweet to all men; and it doesn't taste sweet to all other sentient animals. For him to prefer his present taste sensations—to claim that they correctly describe the honey—over all the other incompatible sensations is arbitrary and unjustified. But what if the cognitivist is both persistent and dialectically adroit enough to attempt to turn the tables on the skeptic by admitting his contrary evidence and then adding that the honey still is sweet (as he knows it to be), but is also not-sweet (as the others know it to be)? Most of us would, I am sure, reject such a counterargument. And in this we would have the concurrence of the skeptics. But that is not the point. The real issue I am trying to uncover lies in the *grounds* on which we would reject it. These are not far to seek: The honey is not both sweet and not-sweet because it *cannot* be. To assert inconsistent predicates of the same subject is to embrace a self-contradiction.[19]

Although I think the reply to the counterargument I have just given is decisive, that is not my main concern. Rather the point I wish to raise here is this: Is it a reply that the skeptics can legitimately give? Note that it makes a knowledge claim —that no subject can have inconsistent predicates—and that this knowledge claim is made about reality and not about appearances—about real honey and not about the taste of honey.[20] Do not the skeptics, in offering such a reply, abandon their own skeptical thesis that we can have no knowledge of reality? And *must* they not nevertheless do so, because their skeptical thesis itself rests on the assumption that two descriptions of the same subject that are incompatible with each other cannot both describe that subject? In other words, for the skeptics to reach the conclusion that we cannot know reality as it is, they must assume that we have some knowledge of reality as it is. But such an argument is self-refuting.

The same point can be made in a somewhat different way. If, as the skeptic assumes, everything that he can know must consist of what he senses, how can he know that an object (say, honey) cannot have inconsistent characteristics? Appeal to the senses would seem to render just the opposite verdict; for our senses "tell" us that many objects possess inconsistent characteristics. Our eyes tell us that the oar thrust into water is bent, but our fingers tell us that it remains straight; the senses of the man entering the warm room of the bath from the outdoors tell him that it is hot, those of the man entering from the hot room tell him that it is cold; etcetera. If we based our claims regarding what we can know on sense impressions, we should certainly never conclude—as everyone, including the skeptic, does—that an object cannot possess inconsistent characteristics, for many clearly seem to do so—if the evidence of our senses is accepted at face value. To assert, therefore, that they cannot do so, it is necessary to appeal to some other source of knowledge than sense impressions. This source is reason or logic. Our justification for claiming to know that the same subject cannot have inconsistent attributes (that the honey cannot be both sweet and not-sweet) is that we recognize that it is logically impossible for it to have them. This recognition, however, cannot be explained in terms of what we sense, for who ever *observed* a logical impossibility? So we must, if we are to find any force in the skeptics' reasons for rejecting the possibility of any knowledge of reality, admit that we can know things by other than empirical means. But that is to abandon the empiricist assumption, which is an integral part of the skeptics' case. Perhaps before we do so it would be wise to examine the assumption itself in some detail.

The skeptics accept the empiricist assumption; indeed it is (as we have seen) essential to their argument. But is the assumption sound? To try to answer this question let us look again at the logical structure of their argument. To repeat:

All of our knowledge consists of what we apprehend through
    our senses.
Our senses cannot reveal the world as it is.
Therefore, we cannot know the world as it is.

This argument is undoubtedly valid; the conclusion follows logically from the premises. But is it also cogent? Does it provide us good reasons for believing the conclusion to be true? As I have already indicated, I think the skeptics have presented adequate support for the minor premise in the Tropes. This leaves us with the major premise, which is, of course, the empiricist assumption. If the conclusion the skeptics draw is to constitute a thesis that they have good reasons to believe to be true, this premise must also constitute a thesis for whose truth they can offer good reasons. Let us see, therefore, if there is any way in which the skeptics could establish the truth of their major premise.

Theoretically, the truth of the proposition "All of our knowledge consists of what we apprehend through our senses" can be established, *if* the proposition is empirical, a proposition capable in principle of being confirmed or disconfirmed by sense experience. But this is just what it is not. It is a universal proposition, but it is not an empirical generalization. When a naturalist concludes, for example, that all swans are white, he does so on the basis of an empirical study of swans, which never reveals any of a color other than white. But no possible empirical observation of "knowledge" could ever provide any confirmation or disconfirmation of the proposition "All knowledge consists of what we apprehend through our senses." The reason is obvious; unlike the concept "swan," the concept "knowledge" is not empirical in nature. It is intrinsically impossible that we should ever observe knowledge through any of our senses. Because its subject is a nonempirical concept, the proposition must likewise be nonempirical, therefore incapable in principle of being either confirmed or disconfirmed by an appeal to empirical evidence.

To summarize, we can say that for the skeptics, the empiricist assumption must both be something (1) they know to be true (because they use it as a premise in their argument) yet (2) do not gain through any of their senses. But the proposition itself asserts that all knowledge must be "sense-knowledge." Thus it must itself offer an exception to its own pronouncement. It is, in other words, self-referentially self-refuting. It follows that its denial "It is not true that all of our knowledge consists of what we apprehend through our senses" is true, and true necessarily.[21] The demonstration of the falsity of the empiricist assumption undermines the argu-

ment that the skeptics offer in support of their skeptical conclusion. Because the assumption has the consequence of destroying their case, the skeptics must, to save their skepticism, abandon it. But since the assumption is a formulation
of the fundamental reason that prompted them to embrace
skepticism in the first place, their abandonment of it would,
in essence, cut the ground from under their own feet. They
would no longer have any reason for being skeptics. This
dilemma facing the skeptics is basic and, I believe, one that
they were never able to resolve successfully.

The kinds of problems that I have just posed did not go unnoticed by the skeptics themselves. Many (particularly
among the Pyrrhonists) recognized that any attempt they
might make to assert their skeptical theory as a conclusion
they had derived from argument would inevitably lead them
into insuperable logical difficulties. To avoid these entanglements, they felt that the only safe course was to refrain from
asserting their skeptical thesis at all.[22] In place of assertion,
they substituted suspension of judgment. As skeptics, incapable of knowing anything, the only proper attitude for them
to take is to suspend judgment about everything. And this
applies to the skeptical theory itself. Clearly this line of
thought is important and needs to be investigated with care,
for perhaps it may be capable of rescuing the skeptics from
the logical difficulties into which the positive assertion and
defense of their theory seems to lead them. As I noted earlier,
this approach has been revived and defended at length by a
contemporary skeptic so I shall defer further consideration of
it until I turn to his writings in chapter iv.

I should like to conclude my brief criticism and evaluation
of ancient skepticism by emphasizing the problem to which I
have just referred. To anyone who studies the writings of
Sextus it becomes increasingly apparent that there is a deep
ambivalence running through the entire tradition. On the one
hand it is clear that the skeptics not only believed in the truth
of their skeptical thesis but also believed that they had good

reasons for accepting it. As philosophers, furthermore, they were concerned with asserting it; they had an important theory that they wished to lay before the world. On the other hand they recognized the dangers that confronted them if they yielded to their desires. As a result of this conflict we find a constant countertendency at work in them: an urge to hold back, to refrain from taking a positive stand. If only, many of them must have felt, one could somehow state and defend the skeptical position and at the same time not state and defend it! This ambivalence, and an attempt to resolve the dilemma, is clearly revealed in a remarkable passage from Sextus, in his book *Against the Logicians:*

> And again, just as it is not impossible for the man who has ascended to a high place by a ladder to overturn the ladder with his foot after his ascent, so also it is not unlikely that the Sceptic after he has arrived at the demonstration of his thesis by means of the argument proving the non-existence of proof, as it were by a step-ladder, should then abolish this very argument.[23]

Has Sextus correctly applied his ladder metaphor to his own theoretical situation? The analogy between a ladder and an argument is risky, for it must be noted that kicking away a ladder after using it no more destroys the ladder than the abandonment of further argument abolishes an argument after it has been used. The metaphor is more seriously flawed, for a ladder *can* get a climber to a high place, but a *cogent* argument *cannot* get a philosopher to a conclusion proving the nonexistence of proof. One attempting such a feat finds that he simply has no ladder on which to climb.

5 Cartesian Doubt

The death of Sextus marked the end of ancient skepticism, the gap in the tradition extending for well over a thousand years into the beginning of modern times. Although the history of medieval philosophy is filled with controversy and disagreement, no thinker of major stature in the Western world espoused the skeptical cause. The obvious reason for this is almost surely the correct one: as Catholic Christians the medieval philosophers possessed in their faith an unchallenged—and, at least to them, unchallengeable—basis for belief. It remained for the Protestant reformers of the sixteenth century to question this basis for belief, precipitating what Popkin calls the *"crise pyrrhonienne"*[24] of the early seventeenth century. Yet the attack launched by the Protestants against orthodoxy was, after all, only an internecine struggle between antagonists who shared the same metaphysical and theological assumptions. Much more serious was the attack soon to follow, launched originally by the astronomers but joined by scientists of every kind. That religious belief, and the intellectual security it brings, is no longer a possession of the educated mind is a result primarily of the work of Copernicus and his long line of scientific successors. The conflict between science and religion is long since over and has been replaced by others, but in the sixteenth and seventeenth centuries it was waged with fury, producing in its wake a resurgence of skepticism. The works of Sextus were revived and translated, and became the nucleus around which a new case for skepticism was constructed. It was within this context of doubt, uncertainty, and the general denigration of reason that Descartes set out to discover, as he writes in the title of one of his works, "the method of rightly conducting the reason and seeking for truth in the sciences."

Although not a skeptic himself, Descartes nevertheless is responsible for an argument that must be classified among the most imaginative and profound in all the arsenal of skepticism. This argument appears in his first *Meditation*, in which the author, in order to set the stage for his own constructive philosophy, attempts to develop the strongest and most thoroughgoing skeptical case he is capable of devising. The steps in his argument are well known. Beginning with the recognition of error and the consequent dubiousness of many of his beliefs, he undertakes the skeptical endeavor to undermine by progressive steps *all* of his beliefs. The climax of his skeptical argument comes in his novel hypothesis of a powerful and malignant demon that devotes all of its energies to deceiving him.[25] An argument of a type quite unlike those in the earlier skeptical repertoire, the evil demon hypothesis owes much of its strength to its universality. Whereas the Tropes, for example, were limited in the scope of their attack against knowledge, the object of this argument was to destroy in one blow the possibility of our knowing anything at all. Because of its power and imaginativeness, the evil demon argument has become a mainstay of skeptical thought since Descartes. We shall meet it again in the next chapter.

Of course Descartes himself was not convinced by his own skeptical arguments. In the second *Meditation* he replies to them with the most famous of all his philosophical creations —the Cogito argument. No matter how powerful or evil a demon may be, it cannot undermine the truth of his own belief that while he thinks he necessarily exists. In concluding my brief remarks on Descartes I should like to make a comment on this argument. From the text of the *Meditations* it seems clear that Descartes believed he had discovered in his own necessary existence, while thinking, a *first* indubitable truth incapable of being shaken by any deceiver, no matter how powerful. But I wonder what his response would have been had the demon he had created come to life and replied to him in some such manner as this: "The reason why you claim that it is necessarily true that you exist while you are thinking is that it is impossible that you should think and not exist. But what kind of impossibility are you talking about here? Let us suppose that the impossibility is, as it seems to be, the strongest kind of all—logical impossibility. Could I not still cast doubt on your existence simply by arranging, in my unlimited power, that, even though you think, and it is logically impossible that you should think and not exist, nevertheless you do not exist?"

It is not my aim here to defend the demon; indeed, I am as unimpressed by the reply I have put in his mouth as Descartes himself undoubtedly would have been. Nevertheless that reply indirectly makes a point that seems to me to be of considerable interest and importance, and which may have a bearing on our understanding and evaluation of skepticism itself. The point is that the fact of Descartes's own necessary existence, while thinking, was not the *first* truth to escape the demon's deceptiveness, for as the response I have put in the demon's mouth indicates, that truth can be accepted as indubitable only on the assumption that if the denial of a proposition involves a logical impossibility, the proposition must be true. Therefore, one can know, as Descartes claimed he did, that he exists necessarily while thinking only if, in a logically prior sense, he knows something else—that logic is the absolute criterion of truth. There is, and can be, no demon with sufficient power to destroy the laws that logic has laid down.

6 Preliminary Statement of Hume's Skepticism

Although David Hume is generally considered to be the greatest skeptic in the Western tradition, most of those who accept this judgment do so on the basis of the arguments in *A Treatise of Human Nature* that are aimed at undermining our knowledge of the existence of a material world, of selves, and of causal relationships. It would be pointless to deny that Hume's conclusions on these issues are skeptical—for, in an extremely important way, they are—yet they still add up only to a mitigated skepticism rather than to the total or epistemological skepticism with which I am concerned in this book. If Hume had had no more to say about the limitations on our knowledge, I would not be writing about him here. But he did.

Toward the end of Book I of the *Treatise*, in a quite complex and easily misunderstood series of arguments, Hume arrived at the seemingly odd position of first establishing epistemological skepticism, then rejecting it, and finally claiming to be even more of a skeptic than the writers of classical antiquity. It is with these conclusions and with the arguments he uses to support them that I shall be concerned in the remainder of chapter ii. I shall begin by reproducing the argumentation that leads Hume to his initial conclusion about the impossibility of knowledge, which is a clear example of epistemological skepticism.[26] As he later sums up the matter, "the understanding, when it acts alone, and according to its most general principles, entirely subverts itself, and leaves not the lowest degree of evidence in any proposition, either in philosophy or common life."[27] However, he no sooner reaches this conclusion, which he describes as *"total* scepticism,"[28] than he draws back from it, going on to embrace a somewhat different position that he holds to be more skeptical than total skepticism.[29] After describing and explaining this final version of Humean skepticism, I shall then offer some critical comments concerning it, turning lastly to an analysis and evaluation of the arguments he has given in support of his initial view, which, because it is an example of epistemological skepticism, is of primary interest to us here.[30] Although this organization will make the course of the argument somewhat more difficult to follow, it is, I think, responsive to Hume's own line of thought.

7 *Hume's Case for Epistemological Skepticism*

Hume's argument for epistemological skepticism has two parts. Beginning with a recognition of human fallibility and our proneness to error, he goes on to maintain (1) that not one of our judgments constitutes an item of knowledge but only a statement of probability and (2) that the strength of this probability diminishes until it finally disappears, so that we are left ultimately with no reasons whatsoever to offer in support of anything we believe. To make his case as strong as he can, he selects for illustration a discipline in which the claim to know is generally thought to have its greatest support—mathematics. If our belief in the possibility of mathematical knowledge can be shown groundless, he argues, then a fortiori we shall have to abandon any pretence to knowledge elsewhere. Let us turn to look at the two steps of Hume's argument in greater detail.

Suppose someone were to offer a case of simple addition, saying "2 + 2 = 4, and I know this to be so." What Hume wishes to show in the first part of his argument is that no one can be justified in making a claim to knowledge in mathematics, even in so simple a case as this; rather all he can legitimately claim is that 2 + 2 *probably* equals 4. In support of this contention he offers three specific arguments. (1) A mathematician is never completely confident of the correctness of any computation he makes the first time he makes it, regarding the result to be only probable. So he repeats the computation, often several times, and gets others to do it, his confidence in its correctness increasing as the results always agree.[31] (2) Even if it be granted, for purposes of argument, that we can be certain about the results of simple computations (like 2 + 2 = 4), we can have no such assurance about the results of long and complex computations, hence must treat those as being no more than probably true. It follows from this that it should be possible to draw some line separating those computations that constitute knowledge from those that constitute only probability. But no such line can be drawn, so we must conclude that it is impossible for us to say of any increasingly simple computations that, at some precise point, here probability ends and knowledge begins, therefore we must admit that all computations must be regarded as being no more than probable. (3) When we perform a long and complicated addition, consisting of many individual numbers, we are ready to admit that the total we reach is only probable. But we do such a sum by successively adding two individual numbers together. If these successive simple additions were certain, then the final result should be certain also, unless, as Hume says, "the whole can be different from all its parts."[32] Because it is not certain, neither can any of them be.

Since mathematical reasoning, the surest of which humans are capable, can yield only probable results, we can safely conclude the same of all other types of reasoning. Thus Hume draws the general conclusion, which completes the first stage of his argument, that "all knowledge resolves itself into probability."[33]

Hume's object in the second part of his case for skepticism is to destroy this probability, a task he performs through the use of a single argument. I shall state the argument first in his words and then in my own, so that we can have it before us in a quite clear form. He writes:

> In every judgment, which we can form concerning probability, as well as concerning knowledge, we ought always to correct the first judgment, deriv'd from the nature of the object, by another judgment, deriv'd from the nature of the understanding.... Here then arises a new species of probability to correct and regulate the first, and fix its just standard and proportion. As demonstration is subject to the controul of probability, so is probability liable to a new correction by a reflex act of the mind, wherein the nature of our understanding, and our reasoning from the first probability become our objects.
>
> Having thus found in every probability, beside the original uncertainty inherent in the subject, a new uncertainty deriv'd from the weakness of that faculty, which

judges, and having adjusted these two together, we are oblig'd by our reason to add a new doubt deriv'd from the possibility of error in the estimation we make of the truth and fidelity of our faculties. This is a doubt, which immediately occurs to us, and of which, if we wou'd closely pursue our reason, we cannot avoid giving a decision. But this decision, tho' it shou'd be favourable to our preceeding judgment, being founded only on probability, must weaken still further our first evidence, and must itself be weaken'd by a fourth doubt of the same kind, and so on *in infinitum;* till at last there remain nothing of the original probability.[34]

Although it may appear obscure, this argument is quite straightforward. It can be clarified by a simple illustration, my judgment that 2 + 2 = 4. This, as we have already seen, is not something I can legitimately claim to know. Suppose I make the judgment (which is itself only probable) and then (as Hume says in the first sentence of the above quotation we ought always to do) I attempt to confirm or correct it. In order to accomplish this I must evaluate the correctness or cogency of my reasoning process when I made the original addition. But any such evaluation can itself result in no more than a probability judgment, which in turn needs to be confirmed or corrected by a further evaluation (i.e., an evaluation of my reasoning in my evaluation of my original process of reasoning), which is itself only a probability judgment, and so on forever. Thus the probability that I attributed to my original judgment (that 2 + 2 = 4) is gradually diminished until it is totally destroyed. The result, when generalized to cover all judgments, yields epistemological skepticism. So Hume concludes his argument by saying:

When I reflect on the natural fallibility of my judgment, I have less confidence in my opinions, than when I only consider the objects concerning which I reason; and when I proceed still farther, to turn the scrutiny against every successive estimation I make of my faculties, all the rules of logic require a continual diminution, and at last a total extinction of belief and evidence.[35]

8   Hume's "True" Skepticism

Although Hume's argument leads him inexorably to epistemological skepticism, to "a total extinction of belief and evidence," he is not willing to rest there. Immediately after he reaches the conclusion I have just quoted, he writes, "Shou'd it here be ask'd me, whether I sincerely assent to this argument . . . I shou'd reply . . . that neither I, nor any other person was ever sincerely and constantly of that opinion."[36] Why this abrupt rejection of his own conclusion? Hume explains his reversal in the following words:

> Nature, by an absolute and uncontroulable necessity has determin'd us to judge as well as to breathe and feel. . . . Whoever has taken the pains to refute the cavils of this *total* scepticism, has really disputed without an antagonist, and endeavour'd by arguments to establish a faculty, which nature has antecedently implanted in the mind, and render'd unavoidable.[37]

On the surface Hume's two conclusions seem clearly to be incompatible with each other. However, he would insist that they are not incompatible, for in the course of the argument he has changed the subject of discussion. His first, skeptical conclusion is true; knowledge is indeed impossible. But it does not follow from this that he or anyone else will accept such a skeptical conclusion. On the contrary, we believe that we know certain things to be true. We do so because we are so constituted by nature that we must do so. Although he has shown that we can have no rational grounds for belief, Hume wishes to make the case that we still believe because there are psychological causes at work that force us to do so. Thus, although in one sense he rejects epistemological skepticism (as being psychologically impossible of acceptance) in another sense he still maintains it (as being philosophically irrefutable). Philosophically Hume is a total skeptic, but psychologically he is a believer, as indeed we all are.

To arrive at his final position, "true" skepticism, Hume gives his argument one additional twist. Pursuing further his analysis of human nature, he argues that we are so constituted psychologically that we find ourselves at times in a thoughtful mood, in which we gain pleasure from pursuing philosophical issues.

> At the time, therefore, that I am tir'd with amusement and company...I feel my mind all collected within itself, and am naturally *inclin'd* to carry my view into all those subjects, about which I have met with so many disputes in the course of my reading and conversation.... These sentiments spring up naturally in my present disposition; and shou'd I endeavour to banish them, by attaching myself to any other business or diversion, I *feel* I shou'd be a loser in point of pleasure; and this is the origin of my philosophy.[38]

But Hume finds the pursuit of philosophy, entered on with such pleasure, leading him into problems for which he can find no answers, until in despair he admits, "I am confounded with all these questions, and begin to fancy myself in the most deplorable condition imaginable, inviron'd with the deepest darkness."[39] Just as reason betrays him and he finds himself sinking into melancholy, nature comes to his aid. He suddenly loses interest in philosophical issues and feels an urge to thrust disputation from his mind, returning to relaxation and amusement. "I dine, I play a game of back-gammon, I converse, and am merry with my friends.[40] And so the pendulum of Hume's life swings to and fro.

Because we cannot help doing both—thinking and seeking pleasure—Hume concludes that we should try to get as much enjoyment as we can out of each. This is the point of view of the true skeptic. In particular, the true skeptic is a person who, although he philosophizes when he is in the mood to do so, never allows his skeptical conclusions to destroy the pleasure he derives from intellectual activity, a person who also, because he does not take his philosophy seriously, can drop it at will and return to the common pleasures of everyday life.

> The conduct of a man, who studies philosophy in this careless manner, is more truly sceptical than that of one, who feeling in himself an inclination to it, is yet so overwhelm'd with doubts and scruples, as totally to reject it. A true sceptic will be diffident of his philosophical doubts, as well as of his philosophical conviction; and will never refuse any innocent satisfaction, which offers itself, upon account of either of them.[41]

Although Hume is undoubtedly writing autobiographically when he describes the feelings, beliefs, and attitudes that philosophers should properly have regarding their theorizing, I think his analysis of why we sometimes enjoy the activity and at other times find it repugnant strikes a chord of response in all who have devoted much time to it. As a description of the psychology of intellectuals in general, it is, it seems to me, often remarkably perceptive. However, Hume intends more by his argument than merely to describe the psychology of philosophers. He is also attempting to defend true skepticism. He is arguing that because of the duality in our psychological make-up, we *ought* to philosophize when we are so inclined and desist when the activity palls, but in any case enjoy ourselves in whatever we do.

> Nay if we are philosophers, it ought only to be upon sceptical principles, and from an inclination, which we

feel to the employing ourselves after that manner. Where reason is lively, and mixes itself with some propensity, it ought to be assented to. Where it does not, it never can have any title to operate upon us.[42]

I think it is clear that Hume's case for true skepticism, however ingenious it may be, is unacceptable. The root of its failure lies in the fact that one of the presuppositions on which it rests is epistemological skepticism. Hume had already established—to his own satisfaction at least—that knowledge is impossible *before* he undertook the final argument I have just been describing. Indeed, it was his skeptical conclusion about knowledge itself that led him to pursue his inquiry into human psychology. But if we can know nothing, on what basis does Hume make all his subsequent claims about human nature and the activities and attitudes that ought to be pursued by the true skeptic? It is true that he has changed the subject, but it is equally true that he continues to theorize and make claims to knowledge regarding the new subject of his inquiry (i.e., human psychology), thus contradicting the skeptical conclusion he had already reached about the possibility of knowledge. In justifying his concentration on psychology, which led him to his true skepticism, he himself writes, "Human Nature is the only science of man."[43] But a *science*, whatever its subject matter may be, is a theoretical activity whose conclusions are based on reason and evidence.

There is one way in which Hume might get around this objection. He could maintain that nothing he wrote after he reached his skeptical conclusion on page 183 of the *Treatise* is to be regarded as the statement and defense of a theory; that he is not making any knowledge claims at all. Without raising the question of what he might then have been doing if he were not theorizing in the several pages that constitute his discussion of how the true skeptic should act and why, I think it is obvious that indeed Hume was throughout engaged in an activity directed toward an end that his epistemological skepticism had already proscribed. Countless quotations could be cited in support of such a conclusion.[44] To multiply these is really unnecessary, for Hume is himself aware of the contradiction in his reasoning. He writes:

> Shall we, then, establish it for a general maxim, that no refin'd or elaborate reasoning is ever to be receiv'd? Consider well the consequences of such a principle. By this means you cut off entirely all science and philosophy. ...And you expresly contradict yourself; since this maxim must be built on the preceding reasoning, which will be allow'd to be sufficiently refin'd and metaphysical.[45]

These remarks clearly apply to Hume himself. Because he had concluded that no "refin'd and elaborate reasoning" can be received, he was led to embrace epistemological skepticism. Unwilling to rest in that position, however, he then engaged in the same type of reasoning to reach his final conclusion of true skepticism, thus contradicting himself, for if one can know nothing, one cannot know anything about human psychology. That Hume recognized the impossible situation in which he had placed himself is evident from the remark he makes immediately after admitting the contradiction in his own argument (appearing in the quotation just above), for he adds:

> We have, therefore, no choice left but betwixt a false reason and none at all. For my part, I know not what ought to be done in the present case.[46]

To sum up, Hume reached the end of his line on page 183 of the *Treatise*, when he concluded in favor of epistemological skepticism. Everything he wrote beyond that point was added at the expense of self-contradiction. Whether a view similar to his true skepticism could be successfully formu-

lated and defended—a thesis that seems dubious at best—
Hume declared himself ineligible for the task before he ever
embarked on it.

9 Examination of Hume's Arguments for Epistemological Skepticism

Besides being an argument he could not make, Hume's defense of true skepticism is not directly relevant to the issue
with which we are concerned here. So §8 constitutes a digression—though, I think, an interesting and historically important one—from our main task, to which I now return. In this
section I shall examine the two-step argument Hume offered
(in §1 of Part IV of Book I) in defense of epistemological skepticism, taking the two steps and their supporting arguments
in the same order as before (see §7 above).

1. None of our judgments constitutes an item of knowledge but only a statement of probability or, as Hume puts it,
"all knowledge resolves itself into probability."[47] In support
of this thesis Hume offers three arguments, the first, (a),
being that mathematicians consider the results of new computations as being only probable the first time they reach
them, their confidence increasing as they, and others, repeat
them, always obtaining the same answers. Although I hesi-
tate to speak for the mathematicians, I doubt that many
would be impressed by this argument. Though it may be true
that they sometimes react in the way that Hume describes, I
think it is more often than not untrue. If the mathematician
has reached his result by a careful and rigorous application of
the rules of mathematics, why should he doubt its correctness? Hume's real point here should be, not one about the
feelings of mathematicians toward their results, but about the
ever-present possibility of error. That would be a stronger
case. But I think even it will not do. Although theoretically
error is always possible, the possibility in fact reaches a van-

ishing point. Without even being a mathematician, I, for the first time (as far as I know), make the following computation: 10 X 1,000,000 = 10,000,000. I do not consider my result probable, but the correct answer. For there is no reasonable possibility of error here. Nor would my repeating the computation, or having others do so, increase my confidence in its correctness.

Another, internal objection can be made to Hume's argument as well, for in the second step of his case for skepticism, he maintains that every reconsideration we make of a line of reasoning we have engaged in *decreases* its probability, but in this argument he inconsistently holds that it *increases* its probability.

Hume's second argument, (b), is that if we grant we can know that certain simple calculations (e.g., 1 + 1 = 2) are correct but admit that other more complex ones are only probably correct, we should be able to draw a line separating the two types. This, however, we cannot do so we must conclude that all are only probably correct. Hume's argument is clearly a non sequitur. Even if we grant that it may not be possible to draw a line separating those calculations whose results we consider only probable from those we consider definitely correct, it does not follow that *none* can be held correct. Let me illustrate this point by a simple analogy. Suppose someone were to present me with a sheet of paper on which he had marked 100 dots in a horizontal row and asked me to draw a line between the forty-third and forty-fourth dot, counting from the left. I might doubt my ability to do so unerringly, recognizing the possibility that I might miscount. But if he next asked me to draw a line between the first and second dots I would have no hesitation, being sure that I knew where the line should go. Furthermore, even if I could not state precisely at what point in the series of dots my confidence in my correctness gave way to a feeling of probability only, this would generate no doubts about the correct placement of my second line (i.e., the one between the first and second dots). Returning to mathematics, I find no reason for doubting that I know I am correct when I say that $1 + 1 = 2$, even though I have doubts about my results when I engage in long and complex computations.

Hume's final argument, (c), in support of his first thesis is to the effect that every addition would be certain if any were so, because a whole cannot be different from all its parts. But some additions are not certain, therefore none can be so. As I have paraphrased it, Hume's point seems to be this: Suppose we were doing a sum, consisting of very many small numbers. To add these, we should do so by couples, adding another number in our group to each successive sum we attained until we reached our final total. Now, Hume contends, if each of these successive acts of addition were certain, the final result should be certain as well. But it is not, therefore none of them is. That this argument is a non sequitur based on a confusion is fairly clear, and can easily be illustrated. Suppose I am attempting to add a column of fifty single-digit numbers. The first two numbers in the column are 1, but the remaining numbers are randomly mixed from 1 to 9. As I go down the column, adding numbers to each successive sum I reach—and, let us assume, trying to hold these constantly enlarging sums in my memory—it is quite possible that I should make a mistake and that my final result should therefore be incorrect. But does it follow from this that I cannot know that my first sum when I begin to add the column $(1 + 1 = 2)$ is correct? The answer is obvious and would undoubtedly have been so to Hume if he had taken the trouble to test his arguments against actual facts.

I conclude that the three arguments Hume offered in support of the first stage of his case for skepticism end in failure. We may grant that we can establish no more than the probable truth of many of our beliefs, but not one of Hume's arguments proves that this is true of all of our beliefs, in particular of the kind of simple mathematical beliefs, like $2 + 2 = 4$, which were a special object of his skeptical attack. In spite of all the objections he has been able to muster, we can still justly affirm of such mathematical beliefs that we know them to be correct.

2. But let us assume, for purposes of further argument, that Hume did make his first point successfully, showing that all knowledge resolves itself into probability. Can he complete his second step as well, showing that no matter how great the probability may originally have been, it gradually diminishes until "at last there remain nothing of the original probability,"[48] hence that the final result of all reasoning is "a total extinction of belief and evidence."[49] Let us examine his argument supporting this conclusion. An illustration will help. Consider the multiplication I performed a few pages back: $10 \times 1,000,000 = 10,000,000$. The result I then obtained (assuming Hume's first point) was only probable. Since it was not certain, Hume maintains, I ought to correct it, by making another judgment about it. But this judgment will have for its content or subject matter not the numbers I originally multiplied but my thought processes when I performed the multiplication.[50] Now my new judgment, by which I am attempting to correct my original judgment (of multiplying), can be no more than probable, so I must correct it by a further new judgment (with *it* as its subject matter), which, being in turn only probable, requires further correction, and so on, until Hume concludes: "No finite object can subsist under a decrease repeated *in infinitum;* and even the vastest quantity, which can enter into human imagination, must in this manner be reduc'd to nothing."[51]

The first thing that must be said of Hume's conclusion, which I have just quoted, is that it is self-contradictory. If it takes an infinite number of steps to reduce an object to nothing, as Hume's argument requires, then we can never eliminate the object, because the process necessary to produce that result is an infinitely long one. But that is not the main objection to the argument. What is really wrong is that Hume has totally misdescribed what normally happens when we attempt to correct or check judgments we have previously made. Hume may be different from me, but when I review the mental activities I engage in while checking a mathematical calculation I have just completed, I find these activities to consist in my *recalculating the sum.* If I have added a column of numbers and want to be sure my answer is correct I simply *add the column over again* (sometimes working backward from the bottom to the top). Never do I do what Hume claims we must do, i.e., attempt to make the object of my examination the psychological processes I went through when I added the numbers the first time. And I am quite sure that almost everyone—including Hume, if he had really considered what he did in such situations—would agree with what I have just said. So Hume's whole second argument, because it is based on a misconstruction of the facts, is beside the point.

Since neither of the two steps of his argument is anywhere near coercive, I think we have to conclude that the attempt Hume makes to offer a *proof*[52] of epistemological skepticism is a failure. But more can be said on this point, for Hume's case can be shown to be *necessarily* a failure. Hume himself seemed dimly to realize this fact, for at the end of the first stage of his argument he writes: "I had almost said, that this [i.e., the conclusion he had just reached] was certain; but I reflect that it must reduce *itself,* as well as every other reasoning, and from knowledge degenerate into probability."[53] In other words, when Hume applies the result of the first stage of his argument to his own thesis that all knowledge resolves itself into probability, he is forced to conclude that that thesis itself must be only probable. And this he sees. But he should have gone further to recognize that when he applies the result of the second stage of his argument to his own thesis, he must conclude that the thesis is now "reduc'd to nothing." Thus his thesis for epistemological skepticism, as he in part realizes, is logically self-destroying.

I should like to conclude my examination of Hume's skepticism by reproducing, and then commenting briefly on, a famous and often-quoted passage in which he recapitulates, in metaphorical language, the line of argument that he has offered in support of the thesis that knowledge is impossible.

> Reason first appears in possession of the throne, prescribing laws, and imposing maxims, with an absolute sway and authority. Her enemy, therefore, is oblig'd to take shelter under her protection, and by making use of rational arguments to prove the fallaciousness and imbecility of reason, produces, in a manner, a patent under her hand and seal. This patent has at first an authority, proportion'd to the present and immediate authority of reason, from which it is deriv'd. But as it is suppos'd to be contradictory to reason, it gradually diminishes the force of that governing power, and its own at the same time; till at last they both vanish away into nothing, by a regular and just diminution.... Were we to trust entirely to their self-destruction [i.e., the sceptical arguments], that can never take place, 'till they have first subverted all conviction, and have totally destroy'd human reason.[54]

Hume's language is striking, and the picture he draws with it vivid. Nevertheless, if we look behind the facade of the metaphor and try to formulate its message in discursive, argumentative terms, we run into difficulties. Let us suppose, for the sake of argument, that a skeptic has, by use of rational arguments (e.g., like those offered by Hume), reduced his cognitivistic opponent to the point where a single additional argument will demolish him and totally destroy reason. Can the skeptic strike that final, and epistemologically crucial, blow? Can he produce the argument required? If it is not a rational argument, it cannot accomplish his goal, for the cognitivist can brush it aside; but if it is a rational argument, he has not yet reached his goal, for we are left, after it has been delivered, with reason still effective (in the form of the rational argument itself) and thus intact. As the actual situation is uncovered from beneath its metaphorical disguise, we find the skeptic (Hume to the contrary) necessarily and perpetually frustrated, for he can *never* use reason to destroy reason, for that is impossible. Instead, all that he destroys is his own skepticism.

To end this chapter I might note that Hume's metaphor, although couched in the language of politics, is in fact a reverse image of Sextus's metaphor of the skeptic on the ladder.[55] This is appropriate, since the problem the two skeptics face and try to solve through their appeal to metaphors is essentially the same. And, needless to say, their efforts end in equal failure.

III   Cartesian Demonology Revived

Although it could be shown that certain of the epistemological theories developed by modern philosophers lead to skepticism, it does not follow that the originators of these theories would count themselves among the skeptics. Quite the contrary, for very few philosphers since the seventeenth century have explicitly embraced skepticism, that is, until quite recently. But in the last decade there has been a marked resurgence of skepticism in the philosophical literature.[1] In this chapter, and the two that follow, I shall review and examine three of the most prominent of the recent defenses of skepticism. These include the theories of Keith Lehrer, Arne Naess, and Peter Unger.[2]

Before turning to my task, however, I should like to make some preliminary remarks on the general subject of contemporary skepticism. Specifically, I want to consider the question: Why should skepticism be enjoying a revival today, after centuries of relative quiescence? I do not know the answer to this question. Nevertheless, it raises an intriguing issue, one that I think is worth at least a bit of speculation. As possible answers to it, I offer the following suggestions—and I emphasize that these are *no more* than suggestions. (1) The subject of epistemology in general—and, more particularly, that area of epistemology which is concerned with the foundations of knowledge—has in recent years occupied the attention of analytical and critical philosophers on a scale never before witnessed. The journal literature on these topics during the past quarter century is voluminous, and the number of books published legion. It seems reasonable to expect that, as philosophers have probed more deeply into the difficult and even apparently unsolvable problems of knowledge, at least some should finally be driven to a skeptical conclusion. (2) The possibility that some contemporary epistemologists should embrace skepticism is enhanced by the fact that much of modern epistemology, although not explicitly skeptical, rests on foundations which, if pursued to their final implications, seem to lead to skepticism. In particular, this can be said of empiricism. Historically, skepticism has been most fully and explicitly embraced—both in the ancient world and in Hume—by epistemologists who began with empiricist assumptions. In the modern world empiricism has become an increasingly pervasive epistemology among philosophers in the anglo-American tradition, especially in the twentieth century. This is clearly evidenced not only by the popularity recently enjoyed by logical empiricism but also by that of other movements, like pragmatism and ordinary language analysis, for which empiricism has generally provided the epistemological foundation. It could be argued that current skepticism is a natural consequence of the dominant empiricist predisposition of recent epistemology. (3) Finally, an even more general hypothesis, about the state of our culture, could be put forward to explain the current resurgence of skepticism. Some say, just as society changed rapidly in Hellenistic times or during the sixteenth century, civilization today is in a state of radical transformation. Old standards and values are collapsing and nothing has been devised to replace them. And as skepticism in the past flourished during such periods of change and uncertainty, so it is reasonably to be expected that it should do so now.

1   General Statement of Lehrer's Skeptical Thesis[3]

That skepticism is flourishing today is well attested by the bibliographical items I have just listed (in n. 2, above). The first of these, Keith Lehrer's "Why Not Scepticism?" contains an argument for skepticism—he calls it "the sceptical hypothesis"—which, like its Cartesian forebear, is a classic of brevity.[4] In fact it occupies less than fifteen printed lines in his article. Before turning to an examination of this admirably succinct statement of the skeptical thesis—a task that will occupy my attention for the rest of chapter iii—I should like to make a few comments about the scope of the skepticism Lehrer is defending in it, for different remarks he makes about the breadth of his skepticism could give rise to questions. At the beginning of his article Lehrer takes an uncompromising stand in favor of epistemological (total) skepticism, writing:

> The form of scepticism I wish to avow is more radical than traditional sceptics have been wont to defend. Some philosophers have maintained that we do not know about anything beyond some necessary truths and some truths about our own subjective states. But they have not denied that we do know about those matters. I wish to seriously consider a stronger form of scepticism, to wit, that we do not know anything.[5]

Having taken such a radically skeptical stand, however, Lehrer later seems to modify his view somewhat, coming to rest in what is apparently a form of mitigated skepticism. In §IV of his article he considers the antiskeptical thesis that an individual can at least know certain of his beliefs about his own current psychological states to be true (for example, that he is feeling a pain). Lehrer argues, quite convincingly I believe, to the contrary, maintaining that the individual's belief that he is feeling a pain may very well be mistaken, because he is in fact experiencing a different sensation (for example, an itch), which he confuses with a pain. The same argument, Lehrer believes, can be leveled against other similar claims to knowledge, with one exception. As he describes this sole exception:

The argument applies to almost all conscious states with a notable exception. If I believe that I believe something, then the first belief does seem to be one such that it is logically impossible that I should be mistaken. For, it is logically inconsistent to suppose both that I believe that I believe something and that I do not believe anything. It would be tempting to rid oneself of such troublesome cases by saying that it does not make sense to speak of believing that one believes, but I do not believe that such a contention is correct. So, I concede that the set of incorrigible beliefs about one's own conscious states is not null.[6]

One reading this quotation, particularly its last sentence, would, I think, naturally conclude that Lehrer mitigates his skepticism at least to the extent of allowing that we can know that we are in the state of believing something else. But Lehrer has a skeptical response to this conclusion. For a person to know something, he argues, it must be logically impossible that he be in error about it; however, the logical impossibility of error, although a necessary condition of knowledge, is still not a sufficient condition of knowledge. A person may believe a proposition, the truth of the proposition may be logically necessary, yet the person still may not be able legitimately to claim to know the proposition. To justify that claim, it is also necessary that he know that the truth of the proposition is logically necessary. This argument leads Lehrer to conclude:

A sceptic may contend that we do not *know* that anything is logically impossible however strongly convinced we may be. And he may conclude that we do not know that those beliefs are true even where the logical possibility of error is excluded, because we do not know that the logical possibility of error is excluded.[7]

On the basis of the argument just described and the conclusion that he derives from it, it is apparent that Lehrer does not make any real exceptions to his claim that we know nothing. Rather, the skeptical thesis that he sets out to defend is unqualified and total; he is, in other words, an epistemological skeptic. But Lehrer's conclusion, which I have just quoted, raises a question. In it he writes that a skeptic *"may* contend . . . and he *may* conclude" (italics mine) that we cannot legitimately claim to know anything because we cannot know that the logical possibility of error is excluded. Indeed, a skeptic *may* do this, but, unless his contention and conclusion are to be gratuitous, the skeptic must offer some reason for claiming that we are unable to know that the logical possibility of error is excluded. Lehrer believes that he has such a reason; he calls it "the skeptical hypothesis." I shall begin §2 with his statement of this hypothesis.

2 The Skeptical Hypothesis

In §VIII of "Why Not Scepticism?" Lehrer presents his case for skepticism in these terms:

> The sceptical hypothesis might run as follows. There are a group of creatures in another galaxy, call them Googols, whose intellectual capacity is 10^{100} that of men, and who amuse themselves by sending out a peculiar kind of wave that affects our brain in such a way that our beliefs about the world are mostly incorrect. This form of error infects beliefs of every kind, but most of our beliefs, though erroneous, are nevertheless very nearly correct. This allows us to survive and manipulate our environment. However, whether any belief of any man is correct or even nearly correct depends entirely on the whimsy of some Googol rather than on the capacities and faculties of the man. If you are inclined to wonder why the Googols do not know anything, it is because there is another group of men, call them Googolplexes, whose intellectual capacity is 10^{100} that of the Googols,

and who amuse themselves by sending out a peculiar wave that affects the brains of Googols in such a way that...I think you can see how the story goes from here.[8]

Beyond the obvious and, I think, incontestable fact that Lehrer's skeptical hypothesis offers an imaginative and ingenious defense of skepticism, it can still be recognized that its origin lies in the first *Meditation*, for the Googols are the direct intellectual descendants of Descartes's evil demon. Yet in the intervening centuries these awesome creatures have not only developed a more subtle method of deceiving us poor humans but have in addition spawned a formidable and (for them) unfortunate progeny of their own, the Googolplexes.

The embellishments that Lehrer has added to the Cartesian hypothesis deserve a couple of comments. (1) In describing the nature and extent of the deceit practiced on us by the Googols, Lehrer develops his case in important ways beyond that of Descartes. The Googols, he argues, lead us astray but only *slightly* astray. ("Most of our beliefs, though erroneous, are nevertheless very nearly correct.") This modification of the argument allows him to conclude that, even though we know nothing, we are not rendered practically helpless but are still able to survive and manipulate our environment. Furthermore, the Googolian deceit is not universal but selective. Although the Googols deceive us most of the time, occasionally they turn off their subversive waves so that what we believe is in fact true. (2) Presumably, Descartes's evil demon (being very close to omnipotent) was a being who knew many things. In this, however, Lehrer's Googols do not resemble him at all, for they are victims as much as victimizers, their brain processes being distorted as much as our own by a higher order of beings as malicious as themselves, the Googolplexes, whose amusement lies in fooling Googols. Since Descartes never recognized a need to postulate succeeding orders of higher-ranking intellectual deceivers, one may well ask: Why does Lehrer believe this move to be necessary? One of our first orders of business will be to make his reason clear. So let us turn directly to that point, as well as to an explication of other crucial steps in Lehrer's skeptical hypothesis.

3 Explication of the Skeptical Hypothesis

Although ingenious, Lehrer's skeptical hypothesis is truncated. Certain important steps in the argument are unstated, being left for the reader to supply for himself. This is true, in particular, of the further development of the hypothesis beyond the point at which Lehrer himself breaks it off. Although the devise of leaving the argument incomplete undoubtedly enhances its interest, it does throw a certain burden of responsibility on the reader. That Lehrer himself considers this burden to be light is clear from the remark with which he concludes his statement of the hypothesis, "I think you can see how the story goes from here." I agree fully with this remark; when I first read the passage I encountered no difficulty in deciding how the hypothesis should develop beyond the place where Lehrer abruptly halted. Given what had gone before, the line of development seemed natural and obvious to me and would, I believed, seem the same to any other reader. So far there was no problem. However, a difficulty was to arise later, for Lehrer himself has since offered an interpretation of the way the hypothesis should be continued which is inconsistent with my—I think, natural—interpretation.[9] So we are faced with a problem: Just how should the argument of the skeptical hypothesis be understood? How *does* "the story go from here"? To deal with this issue I shall adopt the following procedure: In this section I shall offer my own initial interpretation of the hypothesis, giving my reasons for understanding it in the way that I do. Then in §5 (after discussing a preliminary difficulty in the hypothesis in §4) I shall present Lehrer's new interpretation, comparing it with my own in terms of the text, then evaluating it both as an accurate explication of the original hypothesis and as an argument for skepticism in its own right. In all of this I shall attempt to be as objective as I can, remembering that our final goal is to decide whether Lehrer's skeptical hypothesis, *however* understood, provides a cogent argument for skepticism.

To turn to the specifics of *my* interpretation, two passages in the skeptical hypothesis require elucidation. These are (1) the clause "If you are inclined to wonder why the Googols do not know anything" and (2) the clause (with particular emphasis on the three dots that introduce it) ". . . I think you can see how the story goes from here." I shall discuss each in turn.

The clause "If you are inclined to wonder why the Googols do not know anything," appearing as it does in the middle of Lehrer's argument, probably comes as a shock to most readers. At least it did to me on my first reading of the article, for certainly to that point I had not been inclined to wonder about this question, since I was concerned rather with the issue of whether humans can know anything. The clause thus caused me to pull up short and ask myself: "What is Lehrer's point in introducing it into the argument, and why does he believe that this point must be made?" The answer to my first question is clear: in a somewhat cryptic way, Lehrer is implying in his clause that Googolian ignorance is essential to his case. My second question is harder to answer. Why would the admission that the deceiving Googols themselves possess knowledge undercut Lehrer's skeptical hypothesis? Descartes apparently was not disturbed by this problem, for he at least strongly suggests that his evil demon is far from ignorant. (He describes the demon as being both "très-puissant" and "très-rusé.") I think a clue to the reason why Lehrer should depart from Descartes on this issue is that he is arguing in support of skepticism and that Descartes was (ultimately) arguing against it. Descartes wished to prove that he knew

something; for his purposes, therefore, the demon's possession of knowledge could present no later embarrassments.
Lehrer, on the contrary, hopes to prove that no one can
know anything; if an admission that the Googols know something can provide the basis for a counterargument leading to
the conclusion that humans must then be granted the capacity for knowing something as well, Lehrer is embarrassed indeed, for his skeptical hypothesis collapses.

So we have to ask: Why should an admission by Lehrer
that the Googols are knowers open up the possibility of a
counterargument that would be fatal to his case? After all,
the postulated Googols have been situated in another galaxy;
their knowledge should not contaminate us. With so much
distance separating us from them, surely we could remain
innocent and ignorant however much they might know. Unfortunately, the problem cannot be disposed of so easily. Lehrer himself offers a clue to its difficulty later in the skeptical
hypothesis when he refers to the super-super-intelligent Googolplexes, who amuse themselves by deceiving the Googols,
as "men." Now, if the Googolplexes are human and thus, according to the hypothesis, presumably dwelling among us,
why might not the Googols be doing so also? In this age of
advanced human technology, in which men have already
traveled to the moon and are preparing trips to more distant
planets, it requires little imagination to picture the possibility
of Googols, with an intellectual capacity 10^{100} that of ourselves, having long since made the trip from their galaxy to
our planet and having settled among us. If they have indeed
done so and if their main amusement is deceiving humans,[10]
then it is reasonable to conclude that they will not advertise
their Googolian presence but will instead assume the perfect
camouflage. That is, they will make themselves indistinguishable from everyone else. Perhaps some of our best friends are
Googols. Although its imaginative elucidation can produce
fanciful and comic results, the point is perfectly serious. If the
Googols (like the Googolplexes) are men as well, then, if they

are allowed to know anything, Lehrer's skeptical hypothesis fails. Hence he must argue for Googolian, as well as human, ignorance. (The same thing, obviously, must be said of the Googolplexes also.)

We are led by this conclusion to Lehrer's second crucial clause ". . . I think you can see how the story goes from here." At this point Lehrer breaks off and implicitly invites the reader to complete the argument. But he also gives him guidelines to direct him on his way. The three dots, appearing as they do at the end of an incomplete sentence that, up to the point at which Lehrer breaks it off, repeats the first substantive sentence of the argument, exemplify a literary convention; namely, that the sentence and argument broken off be continued in the same form as the original sentence and argument which they partially repeat. That is to say, the reader is instructed to continue the uncompleted last sentence and, thus, the skeptical hypothesis in the following way:[11] ". . . the Googols' beliefs about the world are mostly incorrect. This form of error infects beliefs of every kind, but most of the Googols' beliefs, though erroneous, are nevertheless very nearly correct. This allows the Googols to survive and manipulate their environment. However, whether any belief of any Googol is correct or even nearly correct depends entirely on the whimsy of some Googolplex rather than on the capacities and faculties of the Googol. If you are inclined to wonder why the Googolplexes do not know anything, it is because there is another group of men, call them super-Googolplexes, whose intellectual capacity is 10^{100} that of the Googolplexes, and who amuse themselves by sending out a peculiar wave that affects the brains of Googolplexes in such a way that . . ." At this point again, the three dots (followed by "I think you can see how the story goes from here") are of crucial significance, for they indicate that the reader should once again return and repeat the argument in the same way but at a higher level, with the super-Googolplexes first deceiving the Googolplexes but then, themselves knowing nothing, being in turn deceived by super-super-Googolplexes, and so on ad infinitum. It is clear from the form of the argument that the heart of Lehrer's skeptical hypothesis lies in its generation of a vicious infinite regress, with the result that no being at any level whatsoever can legitimately be said to know anything.

But it is more than simply form that leads to the conclusion that the essential feature of the skeptical hypothesis is its generation of a vicious regress. Lehrer is arguing for skepticism, the thesis that no one knows anything. As we have already seen, "no one" must mean "no being at all." To subvert knowledge at the ordinary human level, he has appealed to the deceitful activities of beings at a higher level—the Googols—and to subvert knowledge at the Googolian level he has appealed to the deceitful activities of beings at a still higher level—the Googolplexes. The pattern of argument set, its infinite continuation follows. Every level of beings is subverted by beings at a higher level, hence no beings at any level know anything.

4 Preliminary Argument: Can Googols be Ignorant?

Having offered an interpretation of the skeptical hypothesis which I believe to be borne out by its text, I shall, in this section, offer an objection to it. My reason for inserting this argument here, before discussing Lehrer's own (later) interpretation of the hypothesis, is that the objection in question applies to the hypothesis both on my own and on Lehrer's interpretation of it. The point I shall try to make, although preliminary to the central issue raised by the hypothesis, is, I think, important in its own right. It can be formulated by raising the question: Is it possible for the Googols to be successful in their malicious deceit of humans if they themselves are being deceived by the Googolplexes to the same extent that they are attempting to deceive us? My reason for calling this an important issue is that if we must answer the question which I have just raised negatively, the skeptical hypothesis collapses immediately. My reason for calling it a preliminary issue is that, even though we should answer the question positively, our answer will not affect our ultimate evaluation of the hypothesis.

In the following argument I shall try to show that the Googols, if they are deceived by the Googolplexes in the way Lehrer depicts them to be and hence know nothing themselves, cannot successfully practice their own deceit on us humans. I cannot, I believe, demonstrate that my conclusion on this issue is correct; however, I believe that a massive weight of argument can be brought to bear in support of my contention. To set the issue before us, let us describe in some detail the knowledge and ignorance situation, as Lehrer's skeptical hypothesis pictures it. Our purpose in doing this is to answer the question: Can Googols, who know nothing, successfully deceive human beings, or can they not? The first point that needs clarification concerns the nature and extent of the Googols' ignorance. Although the skeptical hypothesis does not speak directly to this issue (having been brought to an end with three dots just before it would appear), we can by extrapolation conclude that the state of Googolian ignorance parallels that of human ignorance, for they are, after all, being deceived by Googolplexes in precisely the same way that they are deceiving us. We can say, then, that most Googolian beliefs are false, but that they are only *slightly* false.[12] Another conclusion we can derive from the hypothesis is that the Googols believe that the method they are using to deceive us (i.e., sending out a peculiar kind of wave that affects our brains) is successfully leading us astray. This conclusion follows from Lehrer's description of the Googols' activity. He writes that they "amuse themselves by sending out a peculiar kind of wave." Their action, in other words, is voluntary and deliberate and aimed at the achievement of an end; their purpose in sending out the waves is to deceive us in order to be amused by our plight. Given this as their motivation, we must conclude that they believe their activities are successfully achieving their purpose, for if they did not believe this, they would change their procedures (e.g., alter the waves they are sending out or perhaps adopt an entirely different program of deceit). Now we can ask: Is the Googolian belief that they are deceiving us true, or is it one of those beliefs (which make up the vast majority of their beliefs) that is false? If on one hand it is true, we are being deceived hence know nothing. On the other hand, if it is false, we are faced with a further problem. Since their belief, if it is false, is (by hypothesis) only slightly false, we need to ask: What could one mean by *slightly* false, in the present context? The belief in question, we must remember, is that the acts performed by the Googols are deceiving us humans. Thus, the falsity of this belief entails the truth of the belief (proposition) that these acts are not deceiving us. It will not do, for example, to contend that the slight falsity of this belief entails only that these acts are not deceiving us in the precise way the Googols believe they are, but rather are deceiving us in a slightly different way, for according to this interpretation, the Googols' belief that their acts are deceiving us would be true, rather than false (which is our present hypothesis). The point I am trying to make here can perhaps be clarified by an old analogy: That the locution "slightly false," when used to describe a belief or proposition, must be understood in the same way as the locution—used, admittedly, in a different context— "slightly pregnant."

The first conclusion we can draw from our argument is that the Googols are in fact deceiving us only if their belief that they are doing so is true. In other words, this belief must not fall among those that are false (the great majority of their beliefs) but rather among the small minority that are true. I reiterate the disparity between false and true Googolian beliefs mainly to reject what would appear to be an easy refutation of Lehrer's contention that we are being deceived by the

Googols, for one might argue: Lehrer's thesis that we know nothing rests on the contention that we are being deceived. But the Googols' belief that they are deceiving us about any given matter is probably false. Hence, we can conclude on statistical grounds alone that the probabilities strongly favor the conclusion that, since we are not being deceived about the matter in question, we do know something. Such a statistical argument is unsatisfactory; for, however much the probabilities may favor the opposite view, it still remains possible that the Googols' belief that they are deceiving us on this particular matter constitutes one of their true beliefs so that what we believe, as a result, is false. Let us turn to a different kind of argument.

I shall try to show that the situation postulated in the skeptical hypothesis—one in which the Googols know nothing and humans know nothing as well—describes a state of affairs that cannot exist. Human beings believe they know a number of things about the world. Now this human belief must be either true or false. But for Lehrer's purposes it cannot be true, because its truth entails the conclusion that humans know a number of things,[13] and that conclusion destroys skepticism. So it must be false. The reason for its falsity, if it is to be considered false, is that the Googols are deceiving us on this point.[14] And as I have just shown, the Googols *must* deceive us on this point, for if they did not, we should possess knowledge. To bring the argument down to specifics let us consider some particular proposition, *p*. I believe *p* to be true and claim to know that it is true because I have established it to be so. However, I still know nothing because *p* is false. The reason why *p* is false, and the only reason why it can be false, is that the Googols are deceiving me. Now let us consider this situation from the side of the Googols. As they sit watching me as I set about to establish that *p* is true, they must either remain inactive, thus permitting me to know something, or go to work deceiving me. We assume that they go to work by sending out their brain waves. We can conclude that, for reasons I have given before, they believe they are successful in their subversive operation. And in this they are right. Their deceitful activities have distorted my mental processes so that I cannot know p because p is false. Thus I know nothing—but the *Googols* know something. They believe they have deceived me, they have reasons to justify their belief, and the belief is true. So for me (as a human) to know nothing, the Googols must know something. However, we have forgotten the Googolplexes, who are at the same time watching the Googols. As they see the Googols giving their reasons to justify their belief that they are deceiving me, they realize that unless they subvert this belief, the Googols will know something (i.e., that they are deceiving me). So the Googolplexes immediately set to work, sending out *their* brain waves to distort the Googols' minds, with the result that the Googols' belief that they are deceiving me, although supported by reasons, nevertheless is false. By this quick action of the Googolplexes, Googolian ignorance is preserved; they know nothing. But this ignorance is preserved at a cost, for if the Googolian belief that they are deceiving me about p is false, then I am not being deceived. Since the only grounds on which it can be denied that I know p is that the Googols are deceiving me, we can conclude that I *do* know p. Humans may know nothing or Googols may know nothing but Googols who know nothing *cannot* deceive humans so that they know nothing either. The two cannot both be ignorant together.

I believe this argument is sufficient to refute Lehrer's skeptical hypothesis. If by the hypothesis either humans or Googols must know something, it cannot be the case that all beings are ignorant. However, as I indicated earlier, the heart of the hypothesis lies elsewhere, in the infinite regress of deceivers who are themselves simultaneously being deceived. This is the most original and ingenious feature of Lehrer's case for skepticism. I return to it now.

5 *The Regress of Ignorant Deceivers*

The skeptical hypothesis is an attempt to explain why no one
—not humans, nor Googols, etc.—knows anything. Like Descartes's demon, the various higher levels of deceivers are postulated in order to *undermine* the knowledge pretensions of
beings on the level immediately below them. The hypothesis
is advanced because it is deemed necessary as a way in which
to undermine these pretensions; otherwise it would not only
be fanciful, not to say bizarre, but strictly gratuitous. The
point I am concerned with here can be put in another way:
Humans believe many things. For these beliefs we very often
offer reasons. And some of the reasons we offer are conclusive; they establish that the belief in question is true. (For
example, we believe that some of our beliefs are true and proceed to demonstrate the truth of this belief.) Such beliefs constitute things we know . . . *unless*. At this point the Googols
enter the picture. The only way, according to the skeptical
hypothesis, that *all* human beliefs can be subverted, leaving
us in total ignorance, is to put the Googols to work. For the
accomplishment of this goal, the Googols are indispensable.

But to impoverish the entire universe of knowledge (the
skeptics' goal) the Googols' beliefs must be subverted as well.
Hence Lehrer's introduction of the Googolplexes. For the
skeptical hypothesis, the Googolplexes are as necessary, as
subverters of Googols, as the Googols are necessary, as subverters of humans. Etc., etc. So Lehrer breaks the hypothesis
off with the remark ". . . I think you can see how the story
goes from here." As this concluding quotation makes clear,
and as the logic of the argument as I have just described it
confirms, the essence of the skeptical hypothesis lies in the
vicious infinite regress that it generates. I reemphasize this
point (which I have already made) because Lehrer, since writing "Why Not Scepticism?" has rejected the interpretation of
his skeptical hypothesis that I have just given, interpreting it

in a different way. I think that in doing so he has himself mis-interpreted his own argument, and to no purpose. To see why this is true, we shall have to examine the alternative account that he gives.

Lehrer's new interpretation is to the effect that the move he makes from the Googols to the Googolplexes *completes* his skeptical hypothesis. If this is correct, then the point of the hypothesis is not, as I have pictured it to be, to generate a vicious regress at all. Rather its object is to establish only that humans and Googols know nothing. Such a conclusion, thus, must be sufficient to make the case for skepticism. In Lehrer's words:

> The argument I gave to show that human beings are agnoite *can* be modified to show that the Googols are agnoite too. For all they know they might be manipulated by the Googolplexes. The move from the Googols to the Googolplexes *completes* my argument. Once it is conceded that for all we know the Googols manipulate us, and hence we are agnoite, and moreover, that for all the Googols know, the Googolplexes manipulate them, and hence they are agnoite, we have met the objection.[15]

I should like to make two comments concerning Lehrer's new interpretation and defense of the skeptical hypothesis. (1) I invite the reader to compare the claim Lehrer makes in it that the move from the Googols to the Googolplexes completes his argument with the statement with which he ends the skep-tical hypothesis "...I think you can see how the story goes from here." As I have already argued, the incomplete sen-tence that precedes this conclusion, and that repeats almost exactly the wording Lehrer used earlier in the hypothesis, simply substituting Googols for humans as those deceived and Googolplexes for Googols as those deceiving, *invites* the reader first to complete the sentence for himself, in the *same terms* with which the earlier sentence is completed, and then to continue with his repetition of the rest of the hypothesis, with appropriate substitutions. Furthermore, since such a repetition breaks the hypothesis off in the middle of a sentence (which would now begin with the words "If you are inclined to wonder why the Googolplexes do not know anything . . ."), it invites the reader to repeat the round once again in the same terms, but at a higher level. And so on, ad infinitum. My contention all along has been that the form in which the hypothesis is set up, in particular the literary conventions it uses, offers an unambiguous entry into an endless regress. (2) All appearances to the contrary, let us concede for the sake of argument that Lehrer (as he contends in the quotation above) did not intend to generate an infinite regress in his skeptical hypothesis but to complete his argument with the step in which the Googolplexes deceive the Googols with the result that they know nothing. The *only* reason Lehrer offers in his original argument for concluding that humans know nothing is that they are deceived by Googols; hence, if such deceit were not assumed, the skeptical hypothesis would collapse. Exactly the same thing can be said of the Googols' lack of knowledge. Only because they are deceived by the Googolplexes can Lehrer conclude that they lack knowledge also. So we come to the Googolplexes. Are they or are they not devoid of knowledge as well? Given the argument that has gone before, if they are to be considered without knowledge, they *must* be deceived by a still higher order of being. But if they are not so deceived, hence are not devoid of knowledge, we are forced to conclude that the universe contains beings who *do* know something. Furthermore, these beings who would then know something are referred to in the hypothesis as men. And even if they are not men, the crucial difficulty would remain for Lehrer—of *knowers* in the universe. (That Lehrer must consider the existence of *any* being who possesses knowledge sufficient to destroy his hypothesis is implied by his postulation of the Googolplexes, who are required to undermine the knowledge pretensions of the Googols.) So the claim Lehrer makes in his new interpretation of the skeptical hypothesis—that the move from the Googols to the Googolplexes completes his argument—leads to failure. The hypothesis either generates a vicious regress or it accomplishes nothing.

So we come to the final stage in our scrutiny of the skeptical hypothesis—an examination of the vicious regress, which is the mark of originality in Lehrer's case for skepticism, setting it apart particularly from its intellectual forebear, the Cartesian evil demon theory. Can the fact that the hypothesis generates such a regress establish the skeptical conclusion that knowledge is impossible?

To resolve our question we need to look more closely at how the regress works. In particular we need to be sure that it is, in fact, vicious, for there are benign regresses. We can say at the outset that the regress generated by the skeptical hypothesis is infinite. If, as Lehrer's case requires, no being whatsoever can know anything, we cannot, once we have made the move from humans to Googols and from Googols to Googolplexes, halt the further movement of the argument from level to ever higher level before infinity, for should we ever do so we would be saddled with beings who deceive but are not themselves deceived, hence know something. Granted that the regress generated is infinite, we can now turn to the question: Is it vicious as well? Or may it be benign?

These two kinds of infinite regress can be distinguished from each other, as far as the question of knowledge is concerned, in the following way: If, to establish the truth of any proposition, A, one must establish, as a necessary condition, the truth of an infinite number of propositions B . . . n, the regress is vicious, because one is, as a consequence, logically incapable of ever establishing the truth of A. If this consequence is not entailed, the regress that can be generated, although infinite, is nevertheless benign. Now the proposition whose truth the skeptical hypothesis is designed to establish is that no being knows anything. And the argument offered is that all beings at any given level are deceived by beings at the next higher level. That the regress thus generated is infinite we have already seen; that it is vicious, as well, is apparent, since, should we bring it to a halt at any level, we contradict the original proposition that no being knows anything, because we are left with a being that is not deceived hence knows something. To establish the truth of the original proposition, we *must* generate an infinite ascending series of deceivers. But—and this is the crux—it is now obvious that it is *not* the truth of the thesis of cognitivism but rather the truth of the thesis of skepticism which, in order to be established, logically requires a never-ending argument. Ironically, the vicious regress that Lehrer generates by his skeptical hypothesis fails altogether in damaging cognitivism but succeeds brilliantly in destroying skepticism.

IV Verbal Gestures and the Suspension of Judgment

In §1 of chapter ii I noted that the ancient skeptics developed two somewhat different traditions, which have come to be known in the literature as Academic skepticism and Pyrrhonic skepticism (or Pyrrhonism). My discussion of ancient skepticism in that chapter concentrated primarily on the first of these traditions. I deferred detailed consideration of the second tradition mainly because it has been reformulated and defended by one of the contemporary exponents of skepticism. This chapter will be devoted to an exposition, analysis, and evaluation of Pyrrhonism in its modernized version. The skeptic whose work will be studied is Arne Naess.

1 Skepticism and Metaskepticism

In his book *Scepticism*[1] Naess makes no claim to be offering an original contribution to the literature of skepticism. Rather he admits he has a quite modest purpose in mind, to devote himself simply to the exposition, clarification, and defense of Pyrrhonism, as expounded by Sextus Empiricus in his *Outlines of Pyrrhonism*. At least, so Naess explains his aims in the foreword to *Scepticism:*

The present work attempts to give a concise account of sceptical philosophy in its most radical and important form [i.e., Pyrrhonism]. In it will be found attempts to remedy certain weaknesses in the traditional ways of describing this philosophy, and answers offered to certain arguments that have been brought against it.[2]

With this disclaimer of originality before us, we might ask ourselves: Why study Naess as a contemporary exponent of skepticism at all? If his book does not go beyond the Pyrrhonism of Sextus, perhaps it would have been more appropriate for us to have examined the view in its original form. I think, in fact, that Naess is too modest in the claims he makes for himself. *Scepticism* does offer us a number of advances beyond *Outlines of Pyrrhonism*, some of them of considerable importance and some so closely associated with contemporary philosophical discussion that the book's formulation of Pyrrhonic skepticism is more relevant to the issues of current epistemological discussion than any statement of that view written in an earlier era. The main ways Naess has developed Pyrrhonism beyond Sextus and placed it within the context of modern thought and epistemology seem to me to be the following:

1. His systematization of Pyrrhonism. Perhaps Sextus's greatest contribution to ancient skepticism (beyond the fact that he alone left to history a written *corpus* that is still extant) lay in his systematic articulation of a point of view that Pyrrho had never developed in any organized way. But as a systematizer, Sextus still leaves a good bit to be desired, as I think anyone who has read his works will readily acknowledge. In his book Naess carries much further the work of systematization that Sextus had begun. As a result one is able, by reading him, to grasp more clearly and completely what it is that the Pyrrhonists, as self-proclaimed skeptics, are and are not maintaining. However, an important caveat must be noted here. When I say that Naess systematizes Pyrrhonism I do not mean to imply that he attempts to formulate it as a

system of philosophy. To interpret him in such a way would be to beg a critical question against him, for one of the most important points he wishes to make in his book is that Pyrrhonism is *not* a system of philosophy. In saying that Naess systematizes Pyrrhonism, then, I mean only to point up his well-developed formal organization of the Pyrrhonic version of skepticism.

2. His elaboration of the ethical implications of Pyrrhonism. In the ancient tradition, the goal of Pyrrhonic skepticism was held to be the suspension of judgment. However, this was only the epistemological, not the ethical or final goal. The ultimate goal, for which the suspension of judgment was held to be a necessary condition, was *ataraxia*, or peace of mind. Naess is very concerned with the question: Can a person who follows the Pyrrhonic way of life attain peace of mind? Indeed he devotes an entire chapter to this problem, putting the issue in the setting of contemporary psychological literature. In this chapter (iii), which he entitles "Scepticism and Positive Mental Health," he notes six criteria of positive mental health which have been developed by recent psychologists and tries to evaluate the "peace of mind" striven for by the Pyrrhonist in terms of them.[3] Although this is an important issue—indeed, for the Pyrrhonist, all-important—it is not directly relevant to the epistemological problem of skepticism, which is my concern here. Consequently I shall not take it into consideration in my evaluation of Pyrrhonism as an epistemological point of view; however, I shall return to it for a few brief remarks at the end of the chapter.

3. His formulation and defense of skepticism within the context of contemporary epistemological thought, in particular, the common-sense, ordinary language views that have played a prominent role in recent anglo-American philosophy. Naess devotes a good portion of two chapters (iv and v) to an analysis and criticism of several recent views concerning the nature and possibility of knowledge, and to showing the extent to which his conception of Pyrrhonism is compatible with them and the ways in which it diverges from

them. Although these discussions perform a valuable function in that they attempt to relate skepticism both termino-
logically and conceptually to contemporary epistemology,
they do not impinge directly on my interest in the critical
evaluation of skepticism. So I shall limit my concern with
them here to points that have a direct bearing on the issue of
whether Naess's articulation of Pyrrhonism, as a tradition in
ancient thought that can have relevance for philosophers
today, constitutes a viable point of view in epistemology.

4. His concern with Pyrrhonism as an attitude toward
knowledge that anyone can adopt. Naess devotes Chapter II,
entitled "The Psychological Possibility of Scepticism," to
what he considers to be the most serious problem confronting
the Pyrrhonist; namely, the question of whether it is psychologically possible for anyone to follow a way of life in which
he suspends his judgment on every issue he faces. More point-
edly, he raises and attempts to answer the question: Assuming that all of us, in order to live our lives, must believe certain things, can any sense be given to the notion of belief that
will allow a person to believe in a manner necessary to carry
on his everyday practical affairs and yet remain in a state of
Pyrrhonic suspension of judgment? In his discussion of this
very important, if not central, issue, Naess to my mind carries the Pyrrhonic tradition well beyond the writings of Sextus. Because the point is of crucial importance to the critical
evaluation of Naess's Pyrrhonism, I shall devote much of my
discussion in this chapter to it.

Since, as I think I have shown in the items I have just listed,
Naess does advance the Pyrrhonic case well beyond the limits
reached in classical times, and since he himself describes his
book as primarily a commentary on the Pyrrhonism of Sextus, we can fairly conclude that he is attempting to accomplish a dual purpose in *Scepticism:* to clarify and defend
ancient Pyrrhonism and to state and defend his own contemporary version of Pyrrhonism. He is, thus, a latter-day Sextus.[4]

Although Naess does not himself distinguish sharply between these two aims, I think the language he uses in his book supports the distinction I have drawn. His agreement with such an interpretation is revealed best by his use of two terms, "sceptic" and "metasceptic." In many passages throughout his book Naess refers to himself as a "sympathetic metasceptic." From the contexts in which he uses this term one can glean that the role he is assuming, which he describes by that expression, is one of an observer or commentator, who, although he does defend skepticism, nevertheless need not identify himself (except in sympathy) with it. (Nor, of course, does it preclude him from doing so; he can, like Sextus, be both skeptic and metaskeptic.) Very near the end of his book, for example, Naess writes:

> The arguments I have offered both in this and the previous chapters are designed to give support to the Pyrrhonian sceptic. The discussion as a whole is an attempt, on the part of a sympathetic metasceptic, to defend the Pyrrhonist against various undeserved objections.[5]

But at the same time that he adopts the role of sympathetic commentator or metaskeptic, Naess also puts on the mantle of skepticism, describing and defending Pyrrhonism as a point of view and way of life that he himself adopts. That he is not limiting himself just to the metaskeptical task of explicating Sextus and defending him from undeserved objections but is taking his own stand in favor of the refined and modernized version of Pyrrhonism he elaborates in his book, so permeates the text that it is difficult to single out a passage that would specifically exemplify his own skeptical commitment. Nevertheless, the following passages (which occur in an extended discussion covering several pages) may serve as an example of Naess's explicit personal adoption of a twentieth-century version of the Pyrrhonian view regarding knowledge:

> ..in what follows I shall argue for the decision to abstain from trying to *use the distinction* between knowing and

not-knowing in three, in part overlapping, kinds of situations. This amounts to a rejection of any Yes or No answers to the question "Can knowledge be reached?" [I.e., it amounts to the Pyrrhonian suspension of judgment.]

First, though we *affirm*, for instance, the principle of contradiction, we nevertheless delimit the scope of the distinction in such a way that it does not make sense to state that the principle furnishes an instance of knowledge or of lack of knowledge. . . .

Then, secondly, there is the situation of scientific research. The rules or principles of research methodology are such that at no point is the evidence for a proposition (if there is evidence for it at all) such that it cannot be increased. . . . As long as this development is kept in mind, there is no occasion, except in popularizations, for using the knowledge and truth terminology. . . .

The third kind of situation in which the use of the terms "know," "knowing," "knowledge," etc. are not to be recommended can . . . be described as the kind of situation in which a definiteness of intention in epistemic matters is required [e.g., in philosophical discourse] that goes beyond that of everyday situations. . . .

That under certain conditions a set of distinctions implied by knowledge expressions cannot be usefully applied is sufficient basis for a recommendation that the corresponding affirmations "I know" and "I do not know" be withheld where these conditions obtain. Under these conditions, then, it is reasonable to withhold judgment.[6]

My purpose in quoting these somewhat lengthy passages is not to scrutinize Naess's modernized form of Pyrrhonic skepticism in detail but only to give evidence that he considers himself to be more than just a metaskeptic, defending Pyrrhonism from the outside, that he does indeed identify himself with that form of skepticism, and that he views the arguments he develops in his book as supporting the skeptical stand that he takes. Furthermore, since our interest here is in Pyrrhonism in its contemporary formulation or, in other words, in Naess's version of the skeptical view, I shall, when I come to a critical evaluation of the arguments he presents, assume that he is, even in those passages in which he adopts the metaskeptical stance in defense of Sextus, arguing in favor of a point of view he himself embraces.

2   The Road to Skepticism

The hallmark of Pyrrhonism, which sets it apart from other forms of epistemological skepticism, is the Pyrrhonists' suspension of judgment. Unlike other proponents of skepticism (e.g., the Academic skeptics), who defend the view that knowledge is impossible, the Pyrrhonists take no stand on this central issue whatsoever. They neither affirm nor deny the possibility of knowledge but reserve their judgment on the question. By refusing to commit themselves to an outright assertion of the skeptical denial of knowledge, Naess maintains, they succeed in avoiding what I have termed in chapter i the standard argument against skepticism; namely, that the skeptic who claims that we know nothing by that very fact commits himself to a knowledge claim, hence contradicts himself. (The question might, however, be raised: Do not the Pyrrhonists, by refusing to commit themselves on this issue, rule themselves out of the debate regarding skepticism altogether? I shall return to this point later in the chapter.)

But the Pyrrhonists do not limit themselves to suspending judgment on the skeptical thesis itself; as total or epistemological skeptics they suspend their judgment on *all* issues, refusing to take a stand of any kind in any field of "articulated cognition or discursive thinking."[7] Or to put this in another way, whatever mental activities they may engage in, Pyrrhonists never commit themselves to a belief in the truth of any proposition. Although the assertions they make (both verbally and in writing) may appear on the surface to resemble ordinary propositions, which they are claiming to be true, such an appearance is deceiving; rather these "propositions" must be construed in a different, nonpropositional way. "...the sceptic of the pure Pyrrhonist community ventures *no proposition whatsoever* that includes a truth or probability claim."[8] The exact nature of the nonpropositional account that the Pyrrhonists, according to Naess, give of their thought, speech, and writing is an issue of great importance to their view and must be examined carefully; I shall take the matter up in the next section. However, I should like here to pursue another implication of the Pyrrhonic disavowal of propositions. If they never, in what they write or say, make any truth claims, we may well ask: Why do they pretend to be philosophers at all? Have they not ruled themselves out of the philosophical arena from the very outset? Naess's answer, with minor qualifications, is that they have.

> Certainly the sceptic does not and cannot *participate* in the philosophical debate. . . . As to whether scepticism counts as philosophy, if we accept as a necessary condition for anything to be philosophy that it must contain at least one proposition, or at least one doctrine, claimed to be true or probable, then scepticism is *not a philosophy.*[9]

Naess, however, sees no more difficulty in the Pyrrhonists' disavowal of philosophy than in their disavowal of propositions. Whatever our judgment on the latter issue may turn out to be, I think we can agree with him on the former, at least to the point of saying that our final decision to accept or reject Pyrrhonic skepticism will not rest on any conclusion we reach about whether the Pyrrhonists should or should not be classified as "philosophers." For it is not the term that is important, but the argument.

Nevertheless, if we accept Naess's thesis that Pyrrhonism is not a philosophy (in the ordinary academic sense of the term), we are left with the question: What, then, is it? Naess's most often-repeated answer to this query is that it is a way of life. On several occasions he refers to "the way of the sceptic,"[10] and in his first chapter he writes, "Indeed, it might be said that Sextus Empiricus's great contribution to thought was his indication of scepticism as a way of life, a way in which the embrace of doctrine is systematically avoided."[11] Yet we are not born Pyrrhonic skeptics. On the contrary, "the way of scepticism" is a goal whose attainment can come only through time and as a result of effort. Naess, following Sextus, lists seven stages along the road to "mature" Pyrrhonic skepticism. These are as follows:[12]

1. Gifted people, faced both with "contradictions" in things and with the opposing views of philosophers, become undecided and frustrated, so set out to find the truth in order to restore their peace of mind.

2. Those who pursue their investigations systematically eventually become philosophers themselves. As philosophers they claim either that they have discovered truth, so become Dogmatists; or that no truth can be found, so become Academicians (or Academic skeptics); or neither that they have found any truth nor that truth cannot be found, so become skeptics (or Pyrrhonists). The last, however, persist in their search.

3. The Pyrrhonist, in his search for truth, finds that the arguments that can be given for every doctrine or proposition he encounters are counterbalanced by the arguments that can be given against it.

4. As a result of his inability to find any propositions whose truth (or falsity) is supported by a preponderant weight of argument, the maturing Pyrrhonist gradually develops a deeply entrenched bent of mind, the suspension of judgment. Rather than affirming either the truth or falsity of any doctrine, he holds the possibilities open. His suspension of judgment becomes for him a state of mental rest or repose. He is now a mature Pyrrhonic skeptic.

5. Without any anticipation of this result he discovers that his suspension of judgment (mental rest) leads to or is accompanied by just that peace of mind which he had originally hoped to find through his search for truth.

6. Having attained skeptical maturity, the Pyrrhonist follows the ordinary rules of his society—its laws, traditions, and customs.

7. The mature Pyrrhonic skeptic remains a seeker. He does not claim (like the Academic skeptic) to know that truth cannot be found. Rather he leaves all questions of knowledge open. But he has abandoned his original aim of gaining peace of mind through the discovery of truth, because he has achieved that peace in another way, through the suspension of judgment.

Naess gives us the following summary portrait of those gifted people who (like Sextus) have completed the pilgrimage that leads finally to the peace of mind of mature Pyrrhonic skepticism:

> The mature sceptic is a philosopher who...makes no philosophical assertions. The most adequate exposition of the philosophy of the mature sceptic is to give an account or narrative of his life in the way Sextus does. However, since Sextus the metasceptic is the same person as Sextus the sceptic, he explicitly denies that he claims the (objective) truth of any of the statements of the narrative. Not that the sceptic cannot allow himself to *say* anything, and must inhibit any tendency to do so. If he feels like it he may express what is in his mind, and sometimes this will result in long narratives. His ways of verbal announcement are many, but they do not include assertion of truth.... In short, although the sceptical philosophy is verbally articulated in a most careful way, among the many ways of using language there is one that the sceptic studiously avoids: the assertive.[13]

3   The "Philosophy" of the Mature Pyrrhonic Skeptic

A careful reading of the quotation with which I have concluded the last section is almost bound to give rise to questions, for there is an obvious air of paradox about what

Naess says in it. How, for example, are we to understand his assertion that the Pyrrhonic skeptic studiously avoids making assertions? Has he not himself derived his understanding of Pyrrhonism from a reading of the works of Sextus? And do these works not consist of assertions, including among them many that we should ordinarily label philosophical assertions?

Naess is well aware of the paradoxical appearance of what he has said. Following the passage I have quoted above he turns immediately to the task of explaining and defending the stance of the mature Pyrrhonist. He begins by writing:

> Sextus, then, is not a philosopher with doctrines. He will not admit to having any definite opinion as to the truth or falsity of any proposition. But in that case how are his own utterances...to be interpreted? What uses of language are they?[14]

In answer to his own question Naess advances one of the most important, and original, theses of Pyrrhonic skepticism, as he interprets it. It must be admitted from the outset that the Pyrrhonist, if he is to communicate his way of life to others and, more particularly, if he is to evaluate the arguments, pro and con, which can be offered concerning any doctrine in order to arrive at the decision that they balance each other and therefore that he should suspend his judgment about it, must formulate his views in a manner that conveys the impression that he is enunciating propositions. Since, however, he has disavowed propositions, such an impression must be deceptive, for his propositions cannot be propositions. The problem for him, thus, is to explain just what they are. Naess makes a determined effort to do so; however, because the explanation he attempts to give is extremely difficult to articulate, it is easy to question the success of his endeavor. To understand and appreciate what he is trying to do, we must, I believe, read his discussion of this issue with considerable sympathy, withholding criticisms until we have clearly before us Naess's interpretation of what the Pyrrhonists mean by propositions.

Put in general terms, Naess's claim is that the Pyrrhonists' propositions, rather than being real propositions (i.e., assertions capable of truth or falsity), are instead *announcements*.[15] But what is an announcement? In order to clarify this notion, Naess offers a whole list of what he calls "sceptical phrases,"[16] whose purpose is to elucidate the meaning of the general term, announcement. These skeptical phrases include: "uttering," "acquiescing in," "putting forward," "saying something indicative of our state of mind," "talking loosely," "giving a message," etc. Taken as they stand, these alternative phrases (to replace "asserting a proposition") are not particularly illuminating or helpful. In addition, they suffer from a more serious shortcoming, as far as Pyrrhonism is concerned, for, as we ordinarily understand the phrases offered, it is hard to see how a person engaged in the kind of discourse they appear to describe could do so consistently and intelligibly without making a fatal commitment to something he believed to be true. Rather than attempting an analysis of all the phrases, I shall simply concentrate on one, pointing out the problem that I see in it. Consider "giving a message." "Message" implies an intelligible statement; one doesn't—unless, perhaps, one is Western Union—transmit gibberish. It also implies the transmission of some specific content (what the message is composed of) from a source to an audience or a receiver. But the messenger, if he is accurately to be described as transmitting a message, must at least commit himself to the truth that the content he passes on is the same content that he has received. Otherwise he would not be *transmitting* a message.

I think most of Naess's skeptical phrases suffer from the same deficiency. Unless they are understood in a quite unusual way, they all seem either to assert or imply some belief about what is true or false on the part of the person using them. Hence they could not be employed by a Pyrrhonist, who suspends his judgment about everything. However, he has produced one skeptical phrase that, if interpreted with care, can avoid the trap of entanglement with propositional meaning and truth commitment. The phrase in question is "verbal gestures."[17] I shall spend a good bit of time analyzing this concept, first showing that it can reasonably be understood in a way that makes it compatible with the Pyrrhonists' disavowal of propositions, and then going on to evaluate its implications for their philosophy. Using this phrase, then, we can say that the assertions made by Pyrrhonists, although they may often look like propositions, are really only verbal gestures. The key term that must be clearly understood is *gesture*. In its normal meaning a gesture is some bodily movement; as such it is neither true nor false. In a parallel fashion, a Pyrrhonist's verbalized propositions (i.e., assertions) are also gestures—and, as such, neither true nor false—but instead of being made with the arms, hands, or feet, etc., they are made with the voice. But this analogy between bodily gestures in general and verbal gestures, as an interpretation of the Pyrrhonists' discourse, must be used with care because there are dangers in it. Suppose I am standing at a country crossroads and a stranger approaches and asks, "Which is the road to Riverside?" I might respond to him by saying, "It is the road that goes north." But I might equally well respond nonverbally, simply by making the physical gesture of pointing to the road heading north. But suppose in this instance I am mistaken; that the road to Riverside is really the one going south. In such a situation I think we should have to say not only that my statement (in the first illustration) is false but that my gesture of pointing (in the second illustration) is equally false. In other words, it is not enough to equate verbalizations with bodily gestures to render them incapable of truth or falsity, because these attributes can be applied to at least some of the physical gestures we make. We must, therefore, refine our analysis of gestures further.

This can be done, I think, by referring to an example that was popular among the ancient skeptics and is reiterated by Naess. I mentioned it in chapter ii, quoting Timon to the effect that "I do not assert that honey really is sweet, but that it appears sweet I grant."[18] In my analysis of that quotation I pointed out that the admission Timon makes that honey *appears* sweet was interpreted in two different ways by ancient skeptics: (a) The ordinary interpretation that the words seem to imply; namely, that, in saying honey appears sweet, the skeptic is claiming knowledge of appearances or phenomena but not of reality as it is in itself, or (b) a quite different interpretation to the effect that, when the skeptic says "Honey appears sweet" he is not making any claim about appearance at all. Rather the words he uses are equivalent to something like "Honey—m-m-m-m." It is the second of these interpretations that Naess insists on, as the correct rendition of the import of all "assertions" made by Pyrrhonists. His analysis of the "Honey is sweet" example takes the following form:

> ...when the sceptic says "sweet," "this is sweet," or "honey, sweet," and so on, just as he does not intend to assert that honey as such, as the object perceived by him and others, *is* sweet, in the sense of having that property by nature, so neither does he intend to stress that what he speaks about is a sense-impression of sweetness, as opposed to an object causing or conditioning the sense-impression.
> The best interpretation seems to me to represent the sceptic as having a definiteness of intention no greater than that which we have in daily life when saying, for example, "honey, mm, yes, sweet."[19]

To put Naess's interpretation into the terminology of verbal gestures, he is arguing that an expression like "Honey is sweet," when used by a Pyrrhonist, is not to be understood as "Honey *appears* (tastes) sweet to me" (for this could be true or false) but rather as a verbalization of a direct feeling-response to the honey. It is thus well translated, I think, as "Honey—m-m-m-m" (or in Naess's equivalent "honey, mm, yes, sweet"). The crucial point that cannot be overemphasized is that if the words or sounds are to be understood as verbal gestures that allow the speaker using them to avoid making any commitment to the assertion of a proposition, they must be construed to convey nothing that could be true or false. That is, we must conceive of them as being the verbal equivalent of some physical act, say, the gesture of dipping one's finger into the honey jar and then into one's mouth, a gesture which, unlike my gesture of pointing to the road going north, is (ordinarily) incapable of being true or false. Only through an interpretation of this kind, an interpretation facilitated by Naess's felicitous phrase "verbal gestures," to which the attributes of truth and falsity are clearly inappropriate, can the Pyrrhonist both permit himself to speak and write and not commit himself to making any assertions, or accepting the truth of any propositions.

Such is Naess's portrait of the mature Pyrrhonic skeptic. Always suspending judgment on every issue, he achieves peace of mind. Although he may (like both Sextus and Naess) write voluminously on philosophical topics, he never participates in philosophical discussion, for he never makes any assertions, never formulates any propositions that can be true or false. Rather he limits himself strictly to the utterance or written transcription of verbal gestures. Whether this is a plausible or even possible portrait of any human being (let alone Sextus or Naess) is a matter which must be considered with care. However, rather than taking up that issue directly, I shall turn first to a related problem, one raised by Naess himself; namely, the question: Is it psychologically possible for a person to maintain his suspension of judgment about all matters, never affirming or denying anything? Naess devotes Chapter II of *Scepticism* to this question; I shall follow him in his discussion of it.

4   Can a Pyrrhonist Believe?

The most difficult question concerning the psychological possibility of Pyrrhonism, Naess believes, is this: How can a person even carry on the everyday activities of life, let alone write treatises on philosophy, if he suspends his judgment on every issue? Must he not, on the contrary, have *some* beliefs if he is to function at all? As Naess sees the problem:

> It is objected to scepticism that by persistently withholding judgment the sceptic is flying in the face of his own experience and practice.... To act at all, it might be said, involves some belief or other; and no matter how diffidently one behaves one cannot act consciously without implicitly accepting the truth, at least temporarily, of some propositions.[20]

In order to come to grips with this problem we have first to clarify some distinctions that Naess is aware of but sometimes blurs in his discussion. These turn on what one means by the notion of "activity." For the purposes of our understanding and evaluation of Pyrrhonism, we can distinguish between activity in which thought (whether this be verbally articulated or not) is an ingredient and that in which it is not. Suppose a sleepwalker, in a deep and dreamless sleep, should perform some physical act. I doubt that anyone would maintain seriously that at the time he was acting he had to be committed to some belief. For the problem that concerns Naess to arise, we must, as he himself points out, be acting *consciously*. Only actions performed under such circumstances seem to require beliefs. But the notion of conscious action is still not adequate to explain the conception of activity with which we are concerned. This can be shown by referring to an example that Naess gives[21] in which a dog, excited by the smell of a fox, sets out in hot pursuit. Would we want to say that even though the dog and fox are both conscious, they believe any propositions to be true? Fortunately, we do not have to answer this question since we are concerned, not with the possibility of animal, but of human skepticism. Nevertheless, the example makes a point. The question of whether belief is a requirement for human activity to occur involves a more sophisticated level of activity than that which is *merely* conscious. I have used the term *thought* to characterize activity at this level and have indicated that in normal circumstances—excluding, for example, the sleep-walker who is also a sleeptalker—any human activity that involves articulation, whether verbal or written, would qualify as *thoughtful activity*. (This is, it should be emphasized, a sufficient, but not a necessary characteristic of thoughtful activity; for we can and constantly do engage in such activity without overtly articulating our thoughts.) I shall not attempt to offer any further, more precise definition of the notion of thoughtful activity here. As we shall see, it is not necessary for the purposes of the discussion to do so because Naess himself is prepared to defend the case that a human being can be active in a way that conforms to my description of thought-ful activity (in contrast to the simply conscious activity we have attributed to animals) and still remain in suspension of judgment about everything.

To support his contention that we can engage in thoughtful activity even though we do not commit ourselves to any beliefs, Naess argues, we must distinguish two different conceptions of what it means to believe. He formulates the alternatives in the following way:

> ...the question of whether [the Pyrrhonist] can believe or not may only turn on what one chooses to mean by "belief." It is clear, for example, that if to believe something he must accept unreservedly some proposition as true or probable, the sceptic cannot believe. If, on the other hand, beliefs are understood more broadly in terms of *behaviour* which may in principle be dissociated from commitment to the truth or probability of propositions, the sceptic can be a believer.[22]

The first alternative that Naess lists, in which belief implies acceptance of the truth (or probable truth) of a proposition, is obviously the standard type of belief, and, as Naess points out, is a kind of activity in which the Pyrrhonist, who must always suspend his judgment, cannot indulge. It need not concern us further at the moment. The second, however, by describing belief as a form of *behavior* in which no commitments to truth or probability are made, seems to be a possibility open to Pyrrhonists. So we need to consider it carefully, to see how successfully it can actually function as a substitute for beliefs involving a truth commitment, both in the affairs of an individual's everyday life and in his activities as a philosophical advocate of Pyrrhonism. Let us begin by looking further into this notion, to see in more detail how Naess describes this alternate form of Pyrrhonic "belief." He writes:

> Sextus . . . distinguishes between affirming the truth of what one says and merely acquiescing in the appearances. By making provision for the possibility of a kind of verbal assent to appearances Sextus would allow that the sceptic may convey in words what *appears* to him, but in a way that does not amount to an assertion in the sense in which to assert something is positively to take a stand, as we have said, on one side or other of a contradiction. . . . Thus, if something feels cold to me and I say "It feels cold," I may be doing no more than publicizing the appearance; ideally my words are then simple effects of my states of perception, unprocessed by interpretation and conceptualization (including any conceptualization to the effect that this is all they are). I may say "It seems cold" and yet perfectly consistently neither affirm nor deny the *proposition* "It seems cold."[23]

I think that the notion of belief that Naess is trying to articulate in this passage is made most clear by his concluding sentence. When the Pyrrhonist says "It seems cold," he does not mean what we ordinarily take a person to mean; namely, that he is stating something that he believes to be true—that it seems cold. Rather, he is "publicizing the appearance"; his words are "simple effects of his states of perception." In themselves these explanations of what the Pyrrhonist means when he says "It seems cold" are, unfortunately, obscure. However, they can be clarified by an appeal to a concept we analyzed earlier, that of verbal gestures. Thus, when the Pyrrhonist says "It seems cold," he is to be understood in the same manner as when he says "Honey tastes sweet"; that is "Honey, mm, yes, sweet," which must on the Pyrrhonic view be understood as a verbal gesture, the linguistic equivalent of dipping his finger into the honey jar. (To use Naess's terminology in the passage quoted on p. 98, his utterance must be interpreted as a bit of verbal behavior.) In the same way, when the Pyrrhonist says "It seems cold," he must be understood to mean something like "The weather, brrrr, yes, cold," which in turn must be interpreted as consisting of a verbal gesture, in this instance some kind of linguistic shiver. And, as I think we may well agree, both the act of dipping one's finger into a honey jar or of shivering, even if they are done in a surrogate verbal way, are acts that can be performed without involving the person who performs them in a commitment to the truth of any proposition (i.e., without involving him in an ordinary belief).

A problem begins to take shape, however, as one reflects on this interpretation of Pyrrhonic beliefs. Supposing that we could, with some plausibility, interpret such simple assertions as "It seems cold" and "Honey tastes sweet" as verbal gestures, conveying no commitments as to what is true on the part of the speaker, can such an explanation maintain its plausibility when used to interpret the more complex statements we make every day of our lives? Naess believes that it can. In support of his view he offers an explanation of an assertion of average, everyday complexity, attempting to interpret what appears to be an ordinary belief statement in such a way that the verbalizations which result involve no truth commitments whatsoever. His example and explanation are as follows:

> Similarly with utterances like "I wouldn't walk on the floor unless I thought it would hold me"; it may be quite consistent to regard these utterances as appropriate to the occasion and yet deny that the act of walking on the floor either implied or compelled acceptance of the *proposition that* the floor was able to support one's weight.

A sceptic, according to the kind of distinction Sextus indicates, may acquiesce, at the time or retrospectively, in his normal and unimpeded entry into the room; he might even publicize it in the form of a running commentary, saying things like "Now I'm walking over the floor, a few creaks there, but everything seems all right. There I've made it!" But in using these words he is only conveying his impression of what happens; he is no more stating that a series of propositions are true than, when he recalls the events later on, he is entertaining propositions to the effect *that* such events occurred.[24]

5 Verbal Gestures and Everyday "Beliefs"

I think the time has come to turn from exposition to criticism; we now have Naess's statement and defense of Pyrrhonic skepticism before us in sufficient scope and detail to enable us to ask what seems to me to be the most important initial question the theory raises: Is it believable?

I shall concentrate my doubts first on the credibility of Naess's view that everyday discourse can be satisfactorily interpreted in a way that permits its users to avoid making a commitment, either directly or by implication, to any belief about what is true or false. As a basis on which to argue the issue I shall use the example that Naess himself provides and that I have quoted just above. According to Naess, the act of

101

a person who says "I wouldn't walk on the floor unless it would hold me" and then proceeds to walk across the floor (uttering a running commentary as he does so) neither implies nor compels his acceptance of the proposition that the floor will hold his weight, because the verbalization of this activity can be interpreted in such a way that nothing said either constitutes or implies his acceptance of the truth of any proposition. Two different questions can, I think, be raised about Naess's thesis: (1) Do the later verbalizations he offers "Now I'm walking over the floor..." (which are clearly meant to be understood in a nonpropositional way), succeed in capturing the full meaning of the original utterance they are held to explain? (2) Can these verbalizations themselves plausibly be interpreted as verbal gestures that neither assert nor imply any belief about the truth of any proposition on the part of the person who utters them? I shall limit my discussion in what follows to the second of these questions.

So that we may have them before us, the utterances to be examined—presumed to be made by a person as he is walking across a floor—are 'Now I'm walking over the floor, a few creaks there, but everything seems all right. There, I've made it."[25] According to Naess, no beliefs need be asserted or implied by the person uttering these words in the circumstances pictured. He is simply making verbal gestures.[26] Such an explanation is, I think, totally unacceptable. Against Naess I would argue that, on any intelligible interpretation of them, these utterances must be understood to imply that the person responsible for them accepts the truth of—i.e., *believes*, in the standard sense of that term—a whole host of propositions. Some of these follow.

1. The word "now": The person believes it to be true that he is speaking *at the time* that he is walking over the floor, not at some other time.

2. The word "I'm": The person believes it to be true that *he himself* is walking over the floor, not that someone else is.

3. The word "walking": The person believes it to be true

that he is *walking* over the floor, not that he is running, skipping, crawling, etcetera, over it.

4. The word "over": The person believes it to be true that he is walking *over* the floor, not through it, under it, etcetera.

5. The word "floor": The person believes it to be true that it is a *floor* he is walking over, not the ground, or a latticework, etcetera.

6. The word "few": The person believes it to be true that the number of creaks he hears can be described as a *few*, not as just one, or a great many, etcetera.

7. The word "creaks": The person believes it to be true that (a) he is *hearing sounds*, not walking in an atmosphere of silence and that (b) the sounds he hears have the characteristics of *creaks*, not those of snaps, whistles, thuds, etcetera.

8. The word "there": The person believes it to be true that the creaks are occurring in a *certain specific area* of the floor, not that they are occurring in a different area, all over the floor, etcetera.

I could go on to enumerate several more beliefs clearly implied in the utterances articulated by the speaker Naess has described. But I think that it is unnecessary to do so. I have made my point.

Let us, however, look at the picture from Naess's side for a moment. The utterances made by the person walking across the floor involve him in no beliefs about what is true at all; instead they amount to no more than verbal gestures. To say "Now I'm walking over the floor..." is analogous in its meaning to saying "Honey is sweet" or "It seems cold," which in turn are equivalent in their meanings to dipping one's finger into the honey jar or shivering. What then, we might well ask, is the gesture to which the statement "Now I'm walking over the floor" is equivalent in meaning? Although Naess does not address himself to the question, it is clear, given his previous interpretations, what his answer would be; namely, the gesture of walking over the floor—perhaps, in this case, with a firm ("confident") stride. The verbaliza-

tions I have analyzed in detail above must, for him, be equivalent to this physical act in the same way that "Honey tastes
sweet" is equivalent to dipping one's finger into the honey jar
and then into one's mouth. But the activity of walking over
the floor is one that an animal—the fox or dog—can do
equally well. So let us suppose a highly trained dog (or perhaps a parrot), which has been taught to bark (squawk) out
sounds that mimic human speech were to walk over the floor,
uttering (at its master's signal) the sounds "Naù Īm wòki ŋ
ōvər thə flōər." Would we be willing to grant that there is no
difference in meaning between its activity and that of the
human being walking over the floor saying "Now, I'm walking over the floor"—that just as the dog can reasonably be
held not to be committing itself to a belief in the truth of any
proposition, so, too, can the human?

It is painfully obvious that Naess, in his interpretation of
this ordinary example of everyday, verbalized thoughtful
activity—the kind of activity that all of us engage in regu-
larly—has gone seriously astray. The explanation he gives is
one of which only a philosopher, driven by the demands of a
theory, could be capable. If all human activity were reduced
to the level Naess describes, the life we live could no longer
be properly described as distinctively human. Or, to put the
matter in another way, it may be true that a dog or fox (or
perhaps some lower form of animal life) could walk across
the creaky floor suspending its judgment all the way, but that
would be because the animal had no judgment to suspend.
But a human being, presumably living at a higher level than
animals, is able either to commit himself to some belief or to
suspend his judgment. And in the situation described, as in
most thoughtful activities of everyday life, he is clearly doing
the former. To sum up my criticism of Naess's analysis of
everyday thoughtful activity, we have found that he offers
the explanation of it consistent with his view that the complete suspension of judgment is psychologically possible. He
does this by attempting to identify our linguistic utterances

(and our thought processes) with verbal gestures, physical acts incapable of being true or false. In doing so, however, he reduces human practical activities to the level of animal behavior. Furthermore, his attempt to accomplish the reduction turns out, as our examination of the case he offers demonstrates, to be totally unconvincing.

If we conclude, as I think we must, that it *is* a psychological impossibility for human beings both to act as humans do every day and at the same time to suspend their judgment about all matters, we might ask: What led Naess and the ancient Pyrrhonists (if Naess's interpretation of them is correct) to embrace the opposite view? Two explanations can be offered. First, they were, as I have already noted, driven by the requirements of a theory. Not only did they believe that the only logically viable form of skepticism was one resting on a refusal to commit themselves to the truth of any proposition but also they believed they saw in the total suspension of judgment a way of life that would have the beneficial effect of peace of mind. So such suspension became for them a goal to be sought on moral as well as epistemological grounds. Finally, if this ideal way of life is to be attained, it must be a possible human option, for if it is a way of life that we are psychologically unable to lead, its worth as an ideal to be striven for evaporates. The second reason that could lead a philosopher to find in the suspension of judgment a goal to be sought lies in the recognition—which we must all, I think, agree to have some merit—that humans in general have a strong tendency to rush to judgment. Most people, even philosophers, are prone to intellectual rashness. We believe too readily. As an antidote to our credulity, the admonition to suspend judgment is far from gratuitous. But this admonition must be applied in a balanced and judicious way. Though it is true that we should suspend our judgment on some issues—and detailed reasons can in each case be given why we should —it does not follow that we should suspend our judgment on all matters. This Naess and his Pyrrhonic predecessors, in

105

their rashness to compensate for the rashness to which we are all susceptible, unfortunately have failed to appreciate.

6 Verbal Gestures and Philosophical "Beliefs"

However impossible the Pyrrhonist finds putting his skeptical ideal into practice in the affairs of everyday life, it may still remain an option that is open to him as a philosopher. That is to say, although he cannot remain in suspension of judgment about whether he is walking over a floor, he may still be able to refuse, as a philosopher, to commit himself to a belief in any proposition. At least Naess clearly claims such a possibility. To repeat some remarks he makes on this subject: ". . . the sceptic of the pure Pyrrhonist community ventures *no proposition whatsoever* that includes a truth or probability claim." "The mature sceptic is a philosopher who . . . makes no philosophical assertions." ". . . although the sceptical philosophy is verbally articulated in a most careful way, among the many ways of using language there is one that the sceptic studiously avoids: the assertive." Since Naess's *Scepticism* is (with the exception of Sextus's *Outlines of Pyrrhonism*) the fullest articulation of the Pyrrhonic philosophy extant, we should expect it to fulfill the conditions of that philosophy in a preeminent way. Does it succeed in doing so? To seek an answer to this question I have run through the pages of *Scepticism* to see if it may contain some counterexamples to Naess's claim concerning the Pyrrhonic philosophers' abstention from propositional commitment. I first looked for propositions in which Naess has asserted (either directly or by clear implication) that he knew (or could know) something to be true. I found the following:

> "The close connection between twentieth-century empiricism and Sextus's Pyrrhonism is obvious."
> "It is true that the mature sceptic tends to influence the

dogmatist in the direction of scepticism . . ."
"All through this discussion I have presumed that we are dealing with questions in relation to which the quest for evidence is relevant. In such cases I know of no other basis except evidence for establishing truth and (true) knowledge."
"Indeed, before raising such a question the sceptic would want to know what the assumptions were . . ."
"It is true that in some cases membership of a religious community may depend on acceptance of this special kind."
". . . ultimately the question of the psychological and social possibility of scepticism has to be attacked from our knowledge of the human beings of today."
"Now, we know that people after a profound religious or political conversion tend to be very inaccurate in their descriptions of their own life before that happening."
"From experiments in social and physical perception we know that value-judgments clearly and significantly influence perception."[27]

For a Pyrrhonist, Naess appears to know far too much. In addition, he seems to suffer frequent lapses from his stance of suspending his judgment by admitting that he believes a number of things to be true, even though he is not positive enough about them to make any outright knowledge claims. I list a few examples from *Scepticism* (assuming that "I think" can reasonably be taken to be synonymous with "I believe").

"There are, it is true, reasons to suspect that Sextus is not altogether accurate in what he says about other sceptics . . ."
"The process or method itself does not imply any assertion with a truth-claim attached, and I think nothing can be said in general here against the sceptic."
"There is reason to believe that St. Augustine was no exception, and in particular that he was not as sceptical as he says he was."
"When, for whatever reason, people go into the details

107

of the evidence, considering one piece at a time, I think most of them, whether they are philosophically sophisticated or not, tend...to stop using the distinctions between known and not-known and between true and untrue..."

"If there is any kind of implied sceptical bent in this, and I think there is, then it is one that cannot appropriately be formulated in terms of knowing."

"I think we can safely say that sceptical locutions in everyday life are not intended to cover, systematically and in relation to current conceptual frameworks, an assertion 'I do not know anything.'"[28]

If appearances are to be accepted at their face value, then it is obvious that Naess does intend both to claim to know many propositions to be true and to believe others to be so as well. Not only is his doing so in contradiction to his assertion that the Pyrrhonist ventures no proposition whatsoever that includes a truth or probability claim (Can this assertion itself escape from the charge of making such a claim?), but also it violates the thesis that the Pyrrhonist, when engaged in philosophical issues, suspends his judgment altogether. Nevertheless, it is possible that appearances may in this case be deceiving. At least Naess offers an explanation of the Pyrrhonist's activity as a philosopher that would, if satisfactory, allow him to make assertions like those we have discovered in *Scepticism*, without committing himself to any truth claims. The account is a variation on his theme (which we have already examined) that utterances made by Pyrrhonists which appear to be assertions are really only verbal gestures. Discussing the "philosophical" activity of the Pyrrhonist, Naess writes:

> Certainly the sceptic does not and cannot *participate* in the philosophical debate.... When the sceptic *throws an argument* into a philosophical debate, and a philosopher finds it worth consideration, the sceptic may support it or fight it with a set of arguments.[29]

One may at the outset find it difficult to understand what Naess is attempting to convey by these statements and why he asserts them. But if we recollect (a) that he is precluded from allowing the Pyrrhonist to assert any propositions and (b) his notion of verbal gestures, we can, I believe, reconstruct his thought easily enough. Ordinary philosophers, when they engage in debate, participate by advancing arguments to establish the truth of whatever thesis they are defending; but the Pyrrhonist, who cannot participate in this way, has recourse to another expedient—he stands outside the debate and *throws* arguments in. In another formulation Naess writes: "Although he throws arguments into the discussion, [the sceptic] takes no part in it."[30] Just as the ordinary person with a sweet tooth may either dip his finger into the honey jar or perform this gesture in verbal terms, so, apparently, the philosopher may perform the gesture of throwing an argument at his opponents, either physically or verbally. In neither case does he assert any proposition that could be true or false.

The problem for the critic here, even a sympathetic one, is to find any similarity between Naess's description of the Pyrrhonist's philosophical behavior and what he and writers like Sextus actually do. The spectacle Naess invites us to picture is graphic enough: A group of philosophers seated around a table debating an issue, with the Pyrrhonist standing somewhere at the side occasionally throwing an argument at them. To make some intellectual sense of this picture, I think we need to concentrate on the two notions "to argue" and "to throw an argument." Concerning the latter, unless we are to assume that the Pyrrhonist writes his argument down on a piece of paper which he then simply wads up and hurls at the others, we must interpret him as verbalizing his point. But if we understand his activity in this more plausible way—and surely *Scepticism* is not meant to be a missile hurled in a street brawl but a philosophical treatise to be read and pondered—we must, I believe, conclude that even though Naess

109

can use the book only as a device for throwing arguments at others, he cannot with any plausibility whatsoever maintain that the book, in being used this way, is a vehicle that does nothing more than transmit his verbal gestures. For obviously, whether he can consistently admit it or not, Naess repeatedly occupies himself in the book with *arguing*, in the old-fashioned, straightforward philosphical way. To claim that he does not participate in the philosophical debate is factually false, and patently so. In substantiation of this point I invite the reader to examine *Scepticism* for himself. Naess's attempt to reduce the verbal activity of Pyrrhonists, himself included, in their capacity as philosophers, to verbal gestures incapable of being true or false, by contending that Pyrrhonists do not argue but just throw arguments proves to be as complete a failure as his attempt to reduce their verbal activity, in their capacity as plain men, to a similar kind of non-propositional, verbal-physical behavior.

But perhaps I have been too severe on Naess here. Was it fair of me to scan his book to discover a dozen or so passages in which he claimed to know, or at least to believe, some propositions to be true? Would it not be more charitable to allow him at least a few lapses from his otherwise unblemished stance of suspension of judgment? By implication at least, Naess appears to hold that some lapses on the part of the Pyrrhonist should reasonably be overlooked:

> ...the sceptic may, under special circumstances, find something to be undeniably true, indubitable, absolutely certain. He does not then *suddenly* cease to be a mature, consistent sceptic. Only if the convictions persist does he leave the brotherhood of sceptics.[31]

Again, in another context, he speaks of a Pyrrhonist's claim to know something as an "inadvertence," which the Pyrrhonist can retract.[32] Such a defense seems reasonable. If the Pyrrhonist were to lapse into positive assertion only very occasionally and then retract when he recognized his inadvertent slip, we should, as sympathetic critics, be willing to blink an eye. The problem becomes difficult only when we ask: Just how many such lapses can the Pyrrhonist reasonably be allowed? And has Naess gone beyond his limit?

As we have seen, the Pyrrhonist makes no assertions; he neither utters nor writes propositions that can be either true or false. As a result he does not and cannot enter into philosophical debate, so must content himself with verbal gestures, with throwing arguments rather than with arguing. Remembering these things, let us turn again to *Scepticism*. The book is just over 150 pages in length. Each of these pages is (largely) covered with declarative sentences, by a conservative estimate ten to a page. So we can say that *Scepticism* probably contains well over 1500 declarative sentences. How many propositions (or assertions) does it contain? According to Naess, it must (overlooking lapses) contain none. Is this really believable? Could any reasonable, fair-minded, honest observer read through what Naess has written and agree with the thesis that there are no propositions intended in all those sentences? Of course, we could all be mistaken. Naess could be systematically deceiving his readers, camouflaging his philosophical verbal gestures as assertions. Since I am not myself prepared to believe that, I find I have no recourse but to conclude that Naess has inadvertently lapsed from his suspension of judgment. Indeed his entire book *Scepticism* must be judged an inadvertence.

But suppose that, for argument's sake, we conceded that in *Scepticism* Naess was not arguing but only throwing arguments. What then? Since nothing he writes can constitute a proposition, none of it can be either true or false. We are left, it seems, with only one alternative, that his writing is cognitively meaningless. And that, of course, is what it must be if it consists solely of verbal gestures. The appropriate conclusion to draw at this point is, I think, that if *Scepticism* were to be interpreted in this way—a way, incidentally, that I cannot believe Naess, regardless of what he says, would be willing to accept—then he should be left to his meaningless gestures while philosophers go about their legitimate work, for he would have nothing to say to us.

To sum up this section, we have been led to a conclusion parallel to the one we reached in §5. It is not possible, we found there, for a Pyrrhonist, constantly suspending his judgment about all things, to carry on the everyday activities necessary for him to lead a human life. It is no more possible, we find here, for him to carry on the activities necessary for him to lead the life of a philosopher.

7 Pyrrhonism and Skepticism

Sextus and, particularly, Naess draw a sharp distinction between Academic and Pyrrhonic skepticism, the distinguishing feature of the former being its thesis that knowledge is impossible, and of the latter the suspension of judgment on all issues. Because the Academics took a stand on the question of whether knowledge is possible, the Pyrrhonists have repudiated them, charging them to be no more than (negative) "dogmatists," hence not skeptics at all. In this section I should like to examine this disagreement in some detail, to see if the Pyrrhonists are justified in their claim to be the only *true* skeptics.

In the last two sections I have argued the case that it is both psychologically and epistemologically impossible for a human being to carry on the activities either of ordinary living or of philosophy under the banner of Pyrrhonic skepticism. But let us put these arguments aside for the moment. Let us assume, on the contrary, that one can attain the goal of becoming a mature Pyrrhonic skeptic, can rest in a state of suspended judgment about all things. What follows from this supposition? An individual in such a state would make no knowledge claims, would utter no assertions or propositions.

If he did talk or write he would be engaging only in verbal gestures. What does this fact imply? Specifically, what do the existence and activities of such an individual have to do with either the existence or possibility of knowledge? On our present assumption, it would still be true that the world is filled with other people who do not suspend their judgment but who claim to know many things. Do these other people in fact know these things? Can they know anything at all? Both of these questions still remain open. In other words, the issue of whether knowledge exists or is possible remains as unresolved after a mature Pyrrhonist appears on the scene as it did before. The fact that *he* suspends his judgment on all things is logically irrelevant to the answers to these questions. Furthermore, since he cannot assert any propositions, nothing he says can be relevant to them either, for a cognitively meaningless verbal gesture can provide no argument, either pro or con, about any question of truth or falsity. The only interest such a Pyrrhonist could have for the rest of us would be psychological or sociological. We might like to know how he got to be that way. But of course he could not tell us.

The point I have been making can be put in another way: If it is to have any relevancy to the problem of the existence of knowledge, skepticism must be a *theory*. To say, as Naess does, that it is only a way of life simply will not do. So are chicken farming or mountain climbing ways of life. But we do not attempt to draw any conclusions about the existence or possibility of knowledge from the fact that some people earn their living by selling eggs. However they may refer to themselves—as skeptics, cognitivists, or something quite different—epistemologists since at least the fifth century B.C. have been concerned with the issue of whether we can or cannot know anything. Whatever other values it may have, the suspension of judgment cannot conceivably contribute anything to the resolution of this issue. Both it and the Pyrrhonism of which it is a manifestation are necessarily irrelevant to this perennial philosophical problem. So, Sextus and Naess to the contrary, the only form of skepticism of interest to epistemologists concerned about the problem of knowledge is Academic skepticism, which is relevant because it states a theory, that nothing can be known. Hence its proponents attempt to engage in the philosophical debate, rather than sit, like the Pyrrhonists, impotently on the sidelines.

Yet I think we must pursue the issue of the relevance of Pyrrhonism to the problem of knowledge further. So far in this section I have referred to the central questions at issue as being those of whether anyone knows or can know anything. Let us, therefore, push the supposition we have just been following a great deal further than we have, by postulating a situation (whether realizable in fact or not) in which not just a few individuals embrace Pyrrhonism but rather one in which everybody does. The entire population rests in the suspension of judgment.[33] What then? Assuming that such a society could exist, I think we should be forced to concede that no one in it could be said to know anything. If we understand the concept of knowledge in such a way that for one to know, he must assert (or assent to) the truth of some proposition, then, if everyone were to suspend his judgment on all matters, knowledge would cease to exist. Certainly such a state of affairs is imaginable. It also seems to be conceivable, for it does not involve any apparent contradiction. In fact I think we can reasonably assume that such a condition prevailed on earth for eons in the past, before man—or, perhaps better, any of the higher animals—appeared on the scene. And in the course of future evolution a similar state of affairs may at some time again prevail.

But what has all this to do with the question of whether knowledge exists? The problem that concerns epistemologists surely is: Does anyone know anything *now*? And I think we can safely say that, whatever the course of future evolution might bring, human beings who are living today do accept certain things to be true. (I am not, of course, implying that we know anything but only that any attempt to bolster the

Pyrrhonic case to the contrary by the assumption that everyone is in suspension of judgment is mistaken, because the supposition itself is factually false.) This line of inquiry leads us to another question: Who is the Pyrrhonist? Can he identify himself to us? Sextus in his time claimed to be one; Naess in the twentieth century considers himself to be one. But has Naess (or Sextus either) really achieved the condition of mature Pyrrhonism? Does he rest in suspension of judgment, asserting no propositions? Certainly he could not have done so when he wrote *Scepticism;* otherwise he could not have written it. If at some other time in his life he has achieved this state, he could not have recognized at that time that he had achieved it, for to do so he would have had to lapse from the state and make judgments—e.g., that he is in a certain state of mind, that this state exhibits certain attributes, that it differs from other states, etc. To recognize that one is in a state of suspension of judgment is, thus, incompatible with being in such a state. So the mature Pyrrhonist can never identify himself as such; he cannot even realize that he is a mature Pyrrhonist.

Who, then, is the Pyrrhonic *skeptic?* If he is a Pyrrhonist, as Sextus and Naess claim to be, he is precluded by his suspension of judgment from rendering any verdict about the possible existence of knowledge at all. And if he is a skeptic, who does address himself to this question, he cannot be a Pyrrhonist, for in order even to consider the issue, let alone take a stand on it, he must exercise his judgment. Pyrrhonism, rather than being the only true skepticism, thus, is no skepticism at all. The two stances are incompatible with each other.

8   Pyrrhonism—Epistemology or Morality?

The conclusion I have just reached leads me to a further one, with which I think the original Pyrrhonist, Pyrrho himself, at least, would agree—that Pyrrhonism is not an epistemological theory at all. Rather it is a morality, an ideal of the good life for man. That no one knows anything because everyone is in a state of suspension of judgment is clearly false, if it is held to describe the actual state of affairs. The thesis, based on similar grounds, that no one can know anything is even more obviously false, because, even if it were to happen sometime in the future that everyone did suspend his judgment, the possibility would remain that someone could break this suspension. Or, to put the point in another way, the fact that individuals do now make judgments presupposes the logical possibility of their doing so. Therefore, the view that no one can or ever could know anything (that knowledge is impossible) cannot be supported by the argument that we all might sometime rest in a state of suspension of judgment. But in a wider sense, Pyrrhonism just cannot be taken seriously as an answer to the epistemological problem of knowledge. As we have seen in the last several sections, in order even to articulate the view, Naess is driven to the expedient of employing fanciful and farfetched metaphors—verbal gestures, throwing arguments, etcetera—which disintegrate when subjected to critical examination. The reason for his failure is that he is attempting to say what, for him, is unsayable. For anyone caught in such a trap, no better advice can be offered than that of Wittgenstein: "Whereof one cannot speak, thereof one must be silent."

If, however, we look at Pyrrhonism as a moral rather than an epistemological movement, we see a quite different and, at least prima facie, more convincing picture, for we are now offered a goal or ideal, which is peace of mind. If we go on to assume, as the Pyrrhonists do, that the prevalent human quest for answers to questions—the perennial search for truth—leads to mental agitation and even intellectual anguish, then we may be willing to accept their advice to suspend our judgment about all things. For only by doing this can we attain the ultimate goal of peace of mind.

It would be out of place in a study of skepticism as an epistemological theory to devote much space to Pyrrhonism as a moral doctrine. So, to conclude this chapter, I shall merely make a few brief remarks about the ideal goal of Pyrrhonists and the route they take to gain it. In the first place, I see problems in the road that Naess has mapped out for the aspirant to mature Pyrrhonism to follow.[34] For one thing, it is not clear to me how such a map (or program) with its various progressive stages can be provided. Specifically, the move from stage 3 to stage 4, which is mature Pyrrhonism, seems to be one for which no logic or rationale can be offered. At the third stage the individual discovers that the pro arguments for every doctrine he examines are counterbalanced by its contra arguments. Now a person finding himself in this situation—and, I wonder, how many of us *really* do—may develop a bent of mind in which he suspends his judgment about all things (stage 4). But, if he does so, it is a matter of personal psychology, not of logic, for there is no logical compulsion operating on him to make this move. I think that what the Pyrrhonist should say is simply (a) that it is psychologically possible for him to make the step and (b) that it is morally desirable that he do so. Supposing that one can and does reach a state (stage 4) in which he suspends his judgment about all things, a second problem arises. This state is held by the Pyrrhonists to be a necessary condition for the attainment of the final, ideal human condition, peace of mind. But, as Naess points out, the Pyrrhonist cannot claim that there is any necessary connection between these two states. On the contrary, he writes: "To his surprise [the mature Pyrrhonist] eventually finds that *epoché* leads to, or is accompanied by, just that peace of mind (*ataraxia*) which he set out to achieve by finding truth."[35] The analysis Naess offers cannot, however, be correct. If the individual really is in a state of suspension of judgment he cannot *find* that he is enjoying peace of mind as well, for the possibility of his making such a discovery presupposes his forming at least the judgment that he is

117

indeed enjoying peace of mind. To find out that his suspension of judgment has brought him peace of mind, he must therefore abandon his suspension of judgment. (Would this abandonment, in turn, destroy his peace of mind? Naess doesn't say.) My point is not that an individual cannot arrive at peace of mind through the suspension of judgment but only that he cannot know (find out) that he has so arrived. Furthermore, having gained peace of mind, he can enjoy it but can never know that he is enjoying it.

These comments lead me to my final remark regarding Pyrrhonism as an ideal way of life. Is the peace of mind it holds forth as a goal to be sought one that any of us would care to pursue? Because it is dependent for its realization and existence on our suspension of judgment about all matters, the Pyrrhonists' peace of mind is a goal purchased at the expense of living a level of life comparable to that of a sleep-walker or of someone sunk in a coma, a level that is presumably surpassed by the more intelligent animals. Not only would a life like this signal the death of the intellect but also it would make it impossible for us to engage in any of the practical activities we consider to be distinctively human. Some of us may at moments of deep despair feel a desire to sink to such a subhuman level of existence, but I would like to believe that such moments are rare occurrences in the lives of any of us.

V Skepticism by Definition

In his book *Ignorance: A Case for Scepticism*,[1] Peter Unger defends a form of skepticism more radical than anything that has appeared in the Western tradition, with the possible exception of the views of a few obscure classical Greeks. Indeed, his skepticism is so extreme that it is difficult to offer any consistent, or even meaningful, account of it in its entirety, let alone to evaluate it critically.[2] The many problems that face anyone trying to cope with the text of *Ignorance*, problems that will become increasingly apparent as this chapter progresses, have led me to adopt certain special procedures that will, I hope, help me deal with the worst of the difficulties, while at the same time being fair to Unger. Specifically, I shall adopt the following procedures: I shall take the statements Unger makes and the arguments he offers both literally and seriously, as I believe he means them to be taken (with a few obvious exceptions); I shall, to the extent that it is possible to do so, base my evaluations of his views on logical considerations; and I shall attempt to find, if not a clear, at least an intelligible meaning in whatever he says, although in some cases this may require that I offer my own interpretation of his intended meaning or even construct some meaning of my own for his remarks, and in a few instances admit defeat in my endeavor.

Of the three contemporary skeptics I am studying in this book, Unger is not only the most radical by far, he is also the most original, complex, and baffling. His originality will soon become apparent; of the main arguments for skepticism he offers, to the best of my knowledge not one has been presented before (at least in the form that he gives it) by any other skeptical writer. Unlike other skeptics, who have often been content with providing one argument in support of their skepticism, Unger offers four. Since these are related to each other in quite complicated ways, the structure of his case for skepticism is considerably more complex than the others we have considered. Finally, Unger's writing is baffling, mainly because it is so hard to understand what he is trying to say. Part of the difficulty results from the extreme nature of his skepticism, but much is due to other causes, the main one being his loose way of arguing. In particular, he often fails to define with sufficient care key concepts in his argument, sometimes using these in ambiguous and inconsistent ways, with resulting confusion. Also, some of his arguments are quite truncated so it becomes necessary for the commentator to do a good deal of reconstruction in order to state his case in a form that is clear and coherent enough to permit analysis and criticism. Lastly, he is less concerned with the requirements of logic than philosophers usually are, and as I feel I must be in this evaluation of his views. Because of these difficulties, it will be necessary for me to devote considerable space, particularly in the early part of the chapter, to the task of clarifying Unger's concepts and putting his arguments in a form that will allow us to evaluate them. If anywhere in the course of this chapter I misinterpret Unger's meaning, I offer my apologies. I believe I have succeeded in understanding most of what he says in *Ignorance*, but I confess that a few passages, even after numerous readings, still remain opaque to me.

1 Preliminary Statement of Unger's Case for Skepticism

Unger defends two forms of skepticism in *Ignorance*. The

first, which he calls *scepticism about knowledge* (i.e., epistemological skepticism as we have understood it), occupies his attention primarily in Chapters I through III and VII. The second, which he calls *scepticism about rationality*, occupies Chapters IV through VI. Unger uses the term, *ignorance*, to express his skepticism about knowledge. Concerning our state of ignorance he writes as follows:

> ...I will say that a being is *ignorant* as to whether something is so if and only if the being does *not know* that it is so and also does *not know* that it is not so; that is, just in the case the being does not know whether or not the thing is so. And I will say that the sceptical conclusion we now seek to yield may be put like this: Everybody is always *ignorant of everything....* And, intending to establish our conclusion as a necessary truth, I will say, finally, that this argument means to show that ignorance is necessary, or inevitable, as well as universal, or complete, or total.[3]

Unger sums up his case for skepticism about rationality in the following words: "...all people are irrational *simpliciter.*"[4] Elaborating this conclusion in somewhat greater detail he writes: "...no one can ever be reasonable in anything, not even in the least degree, and...no one can ever be justified either."[5]

These quotations make it clear not only that Unger is defending two forms of skepticism in *Ignorance* but also that the second is more extreme than the first. His first claim is that we are ignorant, in that we can know nothing, but his second goes on to claim that we are irrational, because we cannot even reasonably believe anything. In making his second claim, Unger goes much further than do most skeptics in the tradition, who limit their skepticism to the issue of knowledge and often hold, in opposition to Unger, that, although we can know nothing, we can still have reasonable beliefs. Although I might examine both of Unger's skeptical claims in this chapter, I shall not attempt to do so but shall limit my attention to the first. My reasons for so limiting myself are three: (1) To examine both would require a great deal more space than I have here; (2) my concern in this book is only with skepticism about knowledge so that skepticism about rationality, although obviously important, is not directly relevant to my purpose; and (3) as Unger himself points out, skepticism about knowledge (i.e., ignorance) entails skepticism about rationality,[6] hence, if it should prove that he does not succeed in making his case for the former, his reasons for holding the latter would disappear, so we would be relieved of the necessity for examining the arguments he gives to support it.

As I have said, Unger offers four arguments in *Ignorance* to support skepticism about knowledge, or epistemological skepticism. Only the first two of these are given an explicit logical formulation. The last two are presented discursively over several pages in the text but never formally stated, so I shall give my own reconstructions of them when I come to consider them. The remainder of chapter v will be devoted to a presentation, analysis, and critical examination of these four arguments. I shall devote considerable space to the first because it contains the most important concept in Unger's case for skepticism, a concept that, as we shall see shortly, is far from clear, hence requires lengthy explication. Even so, I shall not be able to examine this argument, or any of the others, in *all* of its details; *Ignorance* is simply too large and complex a book to discuss completely in a single chapter. I shall, instead, concentrate on the crucial points in each of Unger's arguments, disregarding most of the amplifications and consequences of these arguments, which much of the text of *Ignorance* is devoted to, even though many of them are both interesting and illuminating. For purposes of identification I shall give names to Unger's four arguments as follows: (1) the Argument from the Necessity of Certainty, (2) the Normative Argument from Certainty, (3) the Argument from the Necessity of Clarity, and (4) the Argument from the Impossibility of Truth.

2 *Personal and Impersonal Certainty*

Unger's first and most important argument for skepticism about knowledge, *the Argument from the Necessity of Certainty*, appears in Chapter II of *Ignorance*. He states it in the following way:

(1) In the case of every human being, there is at most hardly anything of which he is certain.

(2) As a matter of necessity, in the case of every human being, the person knows something to be so only if he is certain of it. . . .

(3) In the case of every human being, there is at most hardly anything which the person knows to be so.[7]

Since the argument is logically valid, to determine its cogency we must decide whether its premises are true. This will be my aim in the next six sections. I shall examine each premise in turn, asking first, Is it true, as Unger claims in his major premise, that no one is certain of anything?[8] and second, Is certainty, as he claims in his minor premise, a necessary condition of knowledge?

Turning to Unger's major premise, we immediately run into difficulty. Before we can assess its truth we must understand what it means. The problem of meaning, unfortunately, is acute, for it is almost impossible to determine what Unger means by the term *certain*, which is obviously its central concept. His explanation of this crucial term is quite confused; in fact he offers at least three discernibly different conceptions of its meaning. Of these he recognizes two but then (mistakenly) claims them to be identical. So one of my main tasks in evaluating his first argument for skepticism must be that of clarification. We must be clear just what Unger means by the notion of "certainty." With this note in mind let us turn to the major premise of Unger's argument.

To lay the groundwork for his argument, Unger begins by distinguishing two general classes of terms, which he calls *absolute* and *relative* terms respectively. "Certainty," he then

123

argues, falls within the class of absolute terms.[9] A character-istic of an absolute term like *certain* (in contrast to a relative term like *confident*) is that if the term is descriptively applica-ble to any state of affairs, then it cannot (logically) be more applicable to some other state of affairs. To explain this point, Unger makes use of an analogy, distinguishing be-tween the relative term *bumpy* and the absolute term *flat*. We can truly say of a given surface A that it is bumpy, even though we can say of another surface B that it is bumpier than A. But we cannot truly say of a surface A that it is flat and also say of another surface B that it is flatter than A. For to say that surface B is flatter than A is to imply that A is not flat at all. So Unger concludes:

> . . . as a matter of logical necessity, if a surface is flat at a certain time, then there never is any surface which is flat-ter than it is at that time. . . . Or in other words, if it is logically possible that there be a surface which is flatter than a given one, then that given surface is not really a flat one.[10]

Unger believes "certainty" to be analogous to "flatness" in that it is an absolute term. He writes:

> As a matter of logical necessity, if someone is certain of something then there never is anything of which he or anyone else is more certain. . . . Thus, if it is logically possible that there be something of which any person might be more certain than he now is of a given thing, then he is not actually certain of that given thing.[11]

According to Unger it is the absolute nature of the term *cer-tain* that precludes us from saying of anyone that he is ever certain of anything. Therefore, since, in order to know some-thing, one must be certain of it, Unger is able to draw the con-clusion of his first argument for skepticism—that there is nothing anyone knows to be so.

Although certainty is analogous to flatness in being an

absolute term, Unger recognizes, it is more complex than the latter. Before we can understand its meaning, therefore, we need to elucidate its complexities. Unger distinguishes two "ideas" of certainty, which he labels, respectively, the "impersonal idea of certainty" and the "personal idea of certainty."[12] The difference between these two ideas of certainty is not a difference in their meanings but only in what Unger calls their "contexts." The *impersonal* idea of certainty is used in contexts of which the paradigm example is expressed in the statement "It is certain that it is raining." The *personal* idea of certainty is used in contexts illustrated by the statement "He is certain that it is raining." Summarizing his distinction between the two, Unger concludes: "Though there are these two important sorts of context, I think that 'certain' must mean the same in both."[13]

Before going any further I think we must examine carefully Unger's contention that the impersonal idea of certainty and the personal idea of certainty do not differ from each other in their meanings but only in the contexts of their use. In this he seems to be mistaken for the following reasons: If the term in question had a single meaning, then any proposition that it entailed when it was used in one context would be entailed by it when it was used in the other context. But this is not so. The proposition "It is certain that it is raining" entails the proposition "It is raining," for the proposition "It is certain that it is raining and it is not raining" is self-contradictory. Conversely the proposition "He is certain that it is raining" does not entail the proposition "It is raining," for the proposition "He is certain that it is raining and it is not raining" is self-consistent. Unger would, I think, accept my first contention, but he might reject my second. Yet I have good grounds, taken from *Ignorance* itself, for this second contention. To see what these are we must explore further what Unger means by certain when the term appears in a personal context. Essentially his analysis makes the idea of personal certainty equivalent to what is ordinarily referred to as "psychological certainty." As he puts it:

"He is certain that p" means, within the bounds of nuance, "*In his mind*, it is not at all doubtful that p," or "*In his mind*, there is no doubt at all but that p." Where a man is certain of something, then, concerning that thing, all doubt is absent in that man's mind.[14]

Elsewhere he identifies the personal idea of certainty with someone's *feeling* of certainty.[15] Given this elaboration of what Unger means by the personal idea of certainty, I think we can recognize that I was correct in claiming that for him the proposition "He is certain that it is raining and it is not raining" is self-consistent; for this proposition can be stated more fully by saying "He has a feeling in his mind regarding the weather of such a nature that any doubt that it is raining is removed from his consciousness, and it is not raining." That this proposition is self-consistent is obvious, for no logical contradiction exists between attributing a state of consciousness to an individual's mind and attributing a different condition to the weather. It follows, therefore, that, Unger to the contrary, certain does *not* mean the same thing in impersonal contexts that it does in personal contexts.

I have taken the trouble to distinguish these two different meanings of certainty for Unger, not simply for their own sake, but because the concept of certainty is crucial to his first argument for skepticism. So let us turn directly to our main issue, by asking the question: Can Unger employ *either* of these concepts of certainty successfully to support the major premise of this argument—that there is nothing that is certain—and, therefore, certainty being a necessary condition of knowledge, nothing that anyone can know to be so? I begin with the first, the impersonal idea of certainty. I have already noted that the proposition "It is certain that it is raining" entails the proposition "It is raining." To this I now add that the entailment is reciprocal; the proposition "It is raining" entails the proposition "It is certain that it is raining." For the proposition "It is raining and it is not certain that it is raining" (i.e., it may not be raining) is self-contradictory. To generalize, the existence of any fact entails the certainty of that fact (e.g., the fact that the sun is shining entails the certainty that the sun is shining, etc.). Since there is an indefinite number of facts (like "It is raining" or "It is not raining"; "The sun is shining" or "The sun is not shining"), there must be an indefinite number of certainties of the impersonal type. Therefore, Unger cannot appeal to the nonexistence of such certainties to support his skeptical conclusion.[16]

3 "Contingent" Personal Certainty

Having eliminated Unger's impersonal idea of certainty from further consideration, let us turn to his personal idea of certainty, to see if it can be used in defense of his skepticism. Our first task is to clarify the meaning of this idea of certainty, a task that is complicated by the fact that Unger offers two distinct conceptions of personal certainty in *Ignorance*.[17] The first of these we have already been introduced to briefly, under the rubric of psychological certainty. However, in order to have it directly before us, let us look at this conception of personal certainty again. Unger writes (to repeat):

> "He is certain that *p*," means, within the bounds of nuance, "*In his mind*, it is not at all doubtful that *p*," or "*In his minds*, there is no doubt at all but that *p*." Where a man is certain of something, then, concerning that thing, all doubt is absent in that man's mind.

This account of personal certainty raises a question of interpretation, which needs to be resolved. When Unger states that certainty about anything requires the absence of all doubt in a man's mind about that thing, does he mean the permanent absence of doubt or the absence of doubt at a given, specific time? That the two are different is obvious; one may have no doubt that it is raining at a given time

127

(because he is standing outside in a downpour) but come later to doubt that it is (because he has gone inside and no longer can see or feel the rain). Everything that Unger says, both in the passage I have quoted and in the context from which the passage has been taken, strongly indicates that he holds certainty to be a mental state that one may possess about something at a given time but not possess about it at another time. In the passage quoted, the verbs are all in the present tense. For example, in the last sentence he writes: "Where a man is certain of something, then, concerning that thing, all doubt *is* [italics mine] absent in that man's mind." Again, his illustration "He is certain that it is raining" reinforces the same conclusion; for, as I have just noted, the fact that at some specific time one has no doubt that it is raining does not imply that he never has any such doubt. So I think it is reasonable to conclude that in the definition of personal certainty now under consideration, Unger holds certainty to be a time-dependent concept. If a given person X is considering p and finds, *at that time*, that he is so convinced that p that he is completely free of doubt about its truth, then one can say that X is certain that p. As a result, one can be certain that p at time t_1 but not be certain that p at time t_2. The fact that one loses one's certainty—that doubts do creep into one's mind—at time t_2 does not vitiate the fact that one was certain at time t_1.

This conclusion leads us to a second and more important point. If personal certainty is something we may possess about a given matter at one time and not at another, we can conclude that the concept of certainty being employed by Unger is what I shall label a "contingent" concept. Let me explain. On Unger's analysis, the question of whether a given person is certain that p turns on whether, as a matter of fact, he has no doubt in his mind about p when he contemplates it. And this is a contingent fact, for he may have no doubt, but then again he may have doubt. Whether he does or does not have doubt can depend, as we have already seen, on temporal considerations. But it can depend on other things as well. I may be certain that it is raining (because I am outside) but my friend may simultaneously not be certain that it is (because he is inside). Or I may be certain that a column of numbers totals a given sum (because I have computed them on an adding machine) but I may have doubts that the same numbers equal that sum (because I have attempted to add them in my head). Or I may be certain of any number of things, because I am temperamentally the type who accepts most of what he reads as "the gospel truth," or alternatively, I may be certain of nothing, because my mind has been perverted by the study of philosophy and I doubt everything. To sum up, the answer to the question of whether any given person's mind is in a state of certainty (i.e., free of doubt) about something can depend on a whole host of contingent factors. Furthermore, a person's mind can change; he can be certain of something at one time but not certain of it at another. Hence the proposition "A is certain that p at time t_1 and A is not certain that p at time t_2" is perfectly self-consistent.

I have dwelt at some length on what Unger means by the notion I have labeled the contingent conception of certainty, because I shall later have to compare it with his final view of certainty.[18] But it is time now to turn to the central issue: How is contingent personal certainty related to skepticism? More directly, can Unger successfully argue that, because contingent certainty is a necessary condition of knowledge, no one knows anything, because no one is ever contingently certain of anything? Or, to concentrate on the specific issue before us, can Unger defend the view that the major premise of his Argument from the Necessity of Certainty is true, if he means by certainty contingent certainty? I think not. Rather than its being true that no one is ever contingently certain of anything, I believe the opposite can be established—that many people are contingently certain of many things. For example, on many occasions I have been *utterly convinced* (i.e., there was simply no doubt whatsoever in my mind) that I was suffering a splitting headache, or that it was raining or that I had added two numbers correctly, etc. If someone were to ask me, "Are you certain that you are suffering a splitting headache?" I could honestly reply, "I have no doubt in my mind at all that I am suffering a splitting headache." On any such occasion, we should have to say that I am indeed certain that I am suffering a splitting headache—if certainty is defined in the contingent way that Unger defines it on page 64 of *Ignorance* (in the passage I have twice reproduced above). I conclude, therefore, that Unger's notion of contingent certainty fails to support the major premise of his first argument for skepticism.

4 *"Logical" Personal Certainty*

This leaves us with Unger's third, and final, conception of certainty, which he develops in §4 of Chapter II and formulates explicitly on page 67 of *Ignorance*. As I have already noted, he does not distinguish this conception from the notion of certainty that I have just discussed under the label of contingent personal certainty, even though it is, as we shall soon see, quite different from it. So we might ask: Why did Unger fail to distinguish between these two notions of certainty? Also, which of the two should be considered his definitive notion of certainty? I have been unable to find anything in *Ignorance* which would provide an answer to the first question; as for the second, I think it is fair to infer that the notion of certainty to which I shall now turn does constitute Unger's definitive conception of the term for the following reasons: It *is* the last one he states; he devotes more space and argument to it than to the others; and, most important by far, it is the only one of the three notions of certainty he offers that succeeds in supporting the major premise of his first argument for skepticism.

So let us turn to Unger's final conception of certainty. He offers it at the end of a long discussion designed to show that "certain" is an absolute term, in the same sense that the term "flat" is.[19] As he puts it:

> It is at least somewhat doubtful, then, that "flat" ever applies to actual physical objects, or to their surfaces. And the thought must strike us that if "flat" has no such application, this must be due in part to the fact that "flat" is an absolute term. We may then do well to be a bit doubtful about the applicability of any other given absolute term and, in particular, about the applicability of the term "certain." As in the case of "flat," our paraphrase highlights the absolute character of "certain": As a matter of logical necessity, if someone is certain of something then there never is anything of which he or anyone else is more certain. . . . Thus, if it is logically possible that there be something of which any person might be more certain than he now is of a given thing, then he is not actually certain of that given thing.[20]

We can formulate the conception of certainty that Unger gives us in the last two sentences of the quotation above in the following way: X is certain that p iff there is never a q (i.e., something other than p) of which it is logically possible that he (or anyone else) might be more certain. For purposes of identification I shall label this conception the "logical" notion of personal certainty.[21] Having contended that it represents a new conception of the nature of certainty presented by Unger—one that must be distinguished from the conception I have labeled contingent certainty, which he coalesces with it—I should justify my claim that the two differ from each other before proceeding further, for they appear to be, if not identical, at least closely related to each other. Specifically, it might be argued that contingent certainty entails logical certainty. According to the notion of contingent certainty, X is certain that p iff all doubt concerning p is absent in X's mind. If any given p satisfied this condition, it would seem to follow that it must also satisfy the condition that it is logically impossible that there be a q of which X is more certain than he is of that p. For if *all* doubt is absent from X's mind about p, then for X to be more certain of q than of p, his mind would have to be in some condition regarding q even more extreme than the total absence of doubt. But it would appear to be logically impossible that any such condition should exist, for there can be no absence of doubt more extreme than the total absence of doubt.

I do not find this argument compelling. When Unger speaks of someone as being contingently certain of something, he refers to the state of the person's mind at some given time. For example, X is contingently certain that p at time t_1 because at time t_1 X's mind is free of doubt regarding p. So let us suppose a person whose mind at a given time t_1 is absolutely free of doubt that p for the simple reason that, because he hasn't slept for thirty-six hours, he is in a state of semi-somnolence. He doesn't doubt that p because he lacks the mental energy to engage in the activity of doubting. Let us suppose, however, that p is the sort of proposition about which the person, were he in his normal mentally alert condition, would raise doubts, a proposition that he would find more dubious than many others he might contemplate. I do not think that Unger would describe this person's mental condition at time t_1, even though it was doubt free regarding p, to be such that it would be logically impossible for the person ever to be more certain of some other proposition than he was of p. Or, to give another example, suppose X's mind to be functioning with full efficiency and to be doubt free concerning p at time t_1, hence that X is contingently certain that p. But suppose that the same conditions hold regarding q at time t_2, and that time t_2 represents a relatively long period of time and time t_1 a very brief time period. In such a case I doubt that Unger would claim that X is logically certain of p, admitting, rather, that he is more certain of q. For such reasons I think he would agree that the mental state of a person could satisfy the condition that would allow us to say that he was contingently certain that p but would not satisfy the condition that would allow us to say that he was logically certain that p.

That Unger, despite his apparent belief that he is talking about only one notion of certainty, would nevertheless make the kind of distinction between contingent and logical certainty that I have just described is borne out by the line of argument he pursues immediately after he offers his definition of what I have called logical certainty. In his words:

> What, then, about something of which people commonly do feel absolutely certain; say, of the existence of automobiles?
>
> Is it reasonable for us now actually to believe that many people are *certain* that there are automobiles? If it is, then it is now reasonable for us to believe as well that for each of them it is not possible for there to be anything of which he or anyone else might be more certain than he now is of there being automobiles. In particular, we must then believe of these people that it is impossible for anyone ever to be more certain of his own existence than all of them now are of the existence of automobiles. While these people *might* all actually be as certain of the automobiles as this, just as each of them presumably feels himself to be, I think it somewhat rash for us actually to believe that they *are* all so certain.[22]

Interpreting this passage in the light of his previous arguments, we can say that Unger is making the following points: One can possess certainty that automobiles exist, in the contingent sense of certainty (i.e., "feel" absolutely certain that they exist), yet not possess certainty of their existence in the logical sense of certainty (i.e., "be" absolutely certain that they exist), for possession of a feeling of certainty about automobiles is not incompatible with the logical possibility of one's coming to be more certain of the existence of something else. The distinction Unger makes which allows him to maintain this position is that between *feeling* certain and *being* certain. If we grant Unger this distinction, it is fair to conclude, I think, that his definitive notion of certainty is what he here calls being certain (as opposed to feeling certain) and that it is defined as I have (following him) defined the notion of logical certainty; namely, X is certain that *p* iff there is never a *q* of which it is logically possible that he or anyone else might be more certain. Furthermore, this notion of certainty is not entailed by the notion I have labeled contingent certainty, because one can *feel* certain that *p* (be without doubt that *p*) and yet not *be* certain that *p*.

Having made a distinction of crucial importance to his first argument for skepticism—between feeling certain and being certain—Unger leaves us with a problem. Nowhere does he give us any further information about what it means to *be* certain (as opposed to *feel* certain). Nowhere does he specify the conditions that must be satisfied before we can say of any *p* that X *is* certain of it. (The response that *p* must satisfy the condition of being such that it is logically impossible that X ever be more certain of any *q* than he is of *p* will not help us here, because, unless we have some independent criterion of certainty, we can never decide whether, concerning any *q*, X is indeed more certain of it than he is of *p*.) What, then, can Unger mean by the locution "X *is* certain that *p*" (as contrasted with "X *feels* certain that *p*")? Since we know, from the distinction he made earlier, that he is concerned with personal rather than impersonal certainty, we can say at least that *being* certain means *being in some kind of mental or psychological state*. But what kind? How would Unger characterize the psychological state of being certain? How might we go about recognizing this state, either in ourselves or in someone else? Negatively, we can say that he does not mean by it simply "being in a state in which one is completely without doubt" about something, because that is the state I have labeled contingent certainty and, I think reasonably, have equated with the state of feeling certain, which Unger holds to be different from being certain. But if the psychological state of being certain is different from the state of being without doubt about something, what kind of state can it be? Answers to the questions I have raised are urgently needed, for the state of *being certain* is of central importance to Unger's argument; hence his failure to give this information represents a serious gap in his theory. Presumably, this state would possess the characteristics of the state I have called contingent certainty, for the person who *is* certain of something undoubtedly *feels* certain of it. But that is not enough, for one can *feel* certain of something yet not *be* certain of it. What other additional characteristics the psychological state or "attitude"[23] of being certain possesses, Unger nowhere discusses. Hence it would seem to follow that should one ever achieve the state of being certain of something, he would be unable to recognize—at least by examining his state of mind —that he had done so.

Although we do not really know what Unger means when he talks about "being certain" of something—in the sense of knowing the characteristics of this psychological state, particularly those that distinguish it from the state of "feeling certain"—we can say that for anyone X to be certain that *p*, it is logically impossible that he (or anyone else) ever be more certain that *q* (something other than *p*). Does this requirement yield a conception of certainty capable of supporting the truth of the major premise of Unger's first argument for skepticism; namely, that there is nothing of which we are certain? Or is it, like his earlier notions of certainty, compatible with the thesis that we can know many things?

In attempting to answer these questions, I shall offer two similar but slightly different analyses. I am not sure which of the two is preferable; however, I do not think that we have to make a choice between them, because both lead substantively to the same conclusion, as far as the issue of skepticism is concerned. To introduce the two analyses, I shall return to the concept "flat," which, according to Unger, is analogous to "certain" in that both are absolute terms. The two share yet another common feature; they are both empirical concepts. With flatness, this is evident; to answer the question "Is surface A flat?" we must examine it empirically—look at it, feel it, etc. Although the empirical nature of certainty is not so evident, from what Unger says about it, I think we can conclude that, to answer the question "Is X certain that p?," we should have to conduct some kind of empirical investigation of X's consciousness, or perhaps, of his behavior.

Because flatness is an empirical concept, and remembering that no surface can be flat if it is logically possible that there be a surface that is flatter than it, we can conclude regarding *any* surface A either that (1) it is logically impossible that it be flat or that (2) it is logically impossible for us legitimately to claim it to be flat. (1) is clearly the stronger, and (2) the weaker interpretation. In support of (1) it could be argued that, no matter how even and smooth A is, nevertheless it is a physical surface, hence cannot be *totally* flat; therefore it is always logically possible that there be some other surface B that is flatter than it. In support of (2) it could be argued that, because we must reach our conclusion regarding the question of whether A is flat by means of empirical investigation, we cannot legitimately conclude that it is flat—i.e., that it is logically impossible that we should ever discover some other surface flatter than it, for our judgment regarding its flatness could always be blunted by the weakness of our sensory organs or the limitations of our measuring instruments. Given an improvement in either of these it is quite possible that we should discover another surface that comes closer than A to realizing the ideal of total flatness. It seems to me that the stronger thesis asserted in interpretation (1), though probably defensible, is at least open to counterattack but that the weaker thesis of interpretation (2) is unexceptionable. So we can conclude that, if flatness is an empirical concept and is defined in such a way that no surface is flat if it is logically possible that there be a surface flatter than it, we can never legitimately claim of any surface A that it is flat.

The same dual analysis can be made of the notion of certainty. We can say, very strongly, concerning *any* proposition p, (1) that it is logically impossible that X is certain of it or, less strongly, (2) that it is logically impossible for us legitimately to claim that X is certain of it. Our reasoning in each case would be analogous to that just offered regarding flatness. (1) No matter what the condition of X's consciousness concerning p, it is always logically possible that the condition of his consciousness concerning q should be such that it more nearly satisfies the defining characteristics of being a state of certainty than does the condition of his consciousness concerning p; therefore it is logically impossible that he be certain of p. (2) No matter what our empirically justified conclusions may be about the condition of X's consciousness concerning p, it is always logically possible that we shall discover that the condition of his consciousness regarding q is such that it more nearly satisfies the defining characteristics of being a state of certainty than does the condition of his consciousness concerning p; therefore it is logically impossible for us legitimately to claim that he is certain of p. Since, for Unger, certainty is a necessary condition of knowledge, we can conclude that, according to interpretation (1), it is logically impossible that anyone should know anything and that, according to interpretation (2), it is logically impossible that we should ever legitimately claim that anyone knows anything. Both of these conclusions are skeptical, the first without any qualification, and the second in the sense that it holds it to be logically impossible that we should ever identify any proposition p and legitimately assert of this proposition that it is something known. And if we can never identify any proposition as constituting something that someone knows, we have no grounds on which to base a claim that knowledge exists.

Unger's apparently definitive view regarding the nature of certainty—the view that I have labeled logical personal certainty—thus clearly seems to establish the truth of the major premise of his Argument from the Necessity of Certainty. If

137

the analysis of the nature of certainty as an "absolute" term which this view gives is correct, we must conclude either (1) that no one can be certain of any proposition p or (2) that no one can legitimately claim of any proposition p that he (or anyone else) is certain of it. If, in addition, certainty is a necessary condition of knowledge, it follows that we can never legitimately claim of any proposition p that any person knows it to be so.

Having now completed our examination of the major premise of Unger's first argument for skepticism, we are ready to turn to its minor premise. Is Unger correct, as he claims in that premise, that certainty *is* a necessary condition of knowledge? I shall devote §§5-7 to this question.[24]

5 The Argument from Emphasis

When he writes, in the minor premise of his Argument from the Necessity of Certainty, that, "As a matter of necessity, in the case of every human being, the person knows something to be so only if he is certain of it," Unger is offering a partial definition of knowledge. It is not a complete definition; Unger does not identify certainty with knowledge, believing rather, as we shall see later, that additional conditions must be satisfied before a person can be said to know that something is so. Nevertheless, in defining knowledge at least in part in terms of certainty, Unger is laying his entire argument open to serious risks, for the question of how any concept, particularly one as abstract as "knowledge," should be defined is notoriously difficult and treacherous. An argument based on a definition of such a crucial concept can be defeated by the simple device of showing that the concept in question has been improperly defined. As a result, if Unger's first argument for skepticism is to stand, he must be able to support his claim that one cannot know anything unless he is certain of it with arguments so strong that no reasonable doubt remains regarding the thesis that certainty is indeed a necessary condition of knowledge.

In an attempt to determine whether Unger succeeds in this task, we shall begin by asking: Just what reasons does he offer for defining knowledge in the way he does rather than in some other way? He begins with the claim that his definition, by making certainty necessary to knowledge, simply repeats the traditional conception of knowledge, and cites G. E. Moore's views on the subject in his support.[25] It is worth noting that Moore is the only philosopher whom Unger cites as agreeing with him on this point, a fact that raises questions about the accuracy of his labeling his definition the "traditional" view of knowledge. I think most epistemologists would disagree with him here, holding instead that the traditional view of knowledge, at least in modern philosophy, makes no reference to certainty at all, but, instead, defines knowledge as "justified true belief." In his recent book *Analytical Philosophy of Knowledge*, Arthur Danto refers to this definition as the "Standard analysis" of knowledge.[26] In this I think he is perfectly correct. So we must be aware that Unger is offering us a definition of knowledge which would not be widely accepted, hence that his defense of it as the correct definition must be doubly strong. Furthermore, Moore himself, even though he may have accepted Unger's definition, was not a skeptic but believed that we are able to attain certainty, hence gain knowledge of many things. Had he concluded, as Unger does, that certainty is a state of mind which we can never legitimately claim to possess about anything, I have little doubt that Moore would have abandoned the view that certainty is necessary to knowledge. In any case, however, the question of whether or not Unger's conception of knowledge is accepted by Moore or anyone else is minimally relevant to the issue of whether it is a definition that we must all adopt. To resolve that issue we should begin by considering the *substantive* arguments Unger offers in support of his view.

Surprisingly, considering the great importance of the definition to his case for skepticism, Unger offers only one argument in its defense. Although he elaborates it in a variety of ways and discusses it at length, using several illustrations in its support, the argument itself is quite brief. He writes:

> . . . while we might feel nothing contradictory, at first, in saying "He knows that it is raining, but he isn't certain of it," we should feel differently about our saying "He really *knows* that it is raining, but he isn't certain of it." And, if anything, this feeling of contradiction is only enhanced when we further emphasize, "He really *knows* that it is raining, but he *isn't* absolutely *certain* of it." Thus it is proper to suppose that what we said at first is actually inconsistent, and so, that knowing does require being certain [27]

Although this argument may seem reasonably clear at first glance, further consideration of it raises questions not only regarding its cogency but its methodology as well. To understand what Unger is about, we must try to analyze in some detail what he attempts to do in the argument. In describing this argument, he writes that he makes use of what he calls his "Principle of Emphasis";[28] that is my reason for labeling it "the Argument from Emphasis." Unger's intent in the argument is apparent; he hopes to establish that the proposition "He knows that it is raining, but he isn't certain of it" is self-contradictory. From this he can then conclude that certainty is a necessary condition of knowledge. His application of emphasis to the critical terms is meant to enhance our awareness of the self-contradictory nature of the proposition in question. (To appreciate Unger's procedure in the argument nost fully one might well read the passage I have quoted above aloud, with appropriate emphasis.)

I do not know what effect the Argument from Emphasis may have on other readers, but after having read it aloud several times myself (with emphases added), I have come away with two conclusions. (1) It does not have the psychological effect on me that Unger intends, and (2) its methodology raises questions in my mind about its cogency. To elaborate: First, I do not respond to the argument in the way Unger clearly expects I should. This may be a result of nothing more than a peculiarity of my own psychology, which others do not share, but I find that if I were asked to read the proposition "He really *knows* that it is raining, but he *isn't* absolutely *certain* of it" and then interpret the message it is meant to convey, my response would be that its use of emphasis is designed to impress on the reader that one can indeed know something *without* being certain of it. With me, thus, Unger's Argument from Emphasis produces just the opposite effect from what he intends.

This unexpected and somewhat unfortunate conclusion leads me to my second question concerning the methodology of the argument. In what sense, if any, does the argument establish the truth of its conclusion? The crucial point that needs to be noted here is that the conclusion in question is the claim that the proposition "He knows that it is raining, but he isn't certain of it" is inconsistent or self-contradictory. In support of this conclusion the argument makes use of emphasis to induce the reader to experience a "feeling of contradiction" when he considers the proposition. Two comments about such a methodology seem appropriate. First, I am not at all sure that I understand what Unger means by a "feeling of contradiction." When I read the proposition aloud, using emphasis in the way recommended by Unger, I admit that it sounds a bit odd to me, but I think this can be explained by the fact that we do not ordinarily talk in that kind of emphatic way about such a topic—unless we are philosophers trying to make a point. In any event, however my feeling may best be characterized when I read the emphasized proposition, I do not find the phrase, feeling of contradiction, to be at all descriptive of it. And at least part of my reason for saying this is that I am far from clear about just what the experience of a feeling of contradiction is like. (Perhaps Unger is different from me, but all I can do here is describe my own reaction to the proposition.) The second comment on methodology I would like to make is that the whole argument is vitiated by a category mistake. The conclusion that Unger has to establish is logical in nature: That a certain proposition is self-contradictory. However, the evidence he appeals to in order to establish this conclusion is psychological in nature. Specifically, he attempts to deduce the logically self-contradictory nature of a proposition from an alleged feeling of contradiction we experience when we contemplate the proposition in a certain way. But certainly such a procedure is patently fallacious, and the entire argument a non sequitur.

Having disposed of the only support Unger offers in defense of the minor premise of his first argument for skepticism, we should consider ourselves free to dismiss both the premise and the argument that rests on it and move on to his second argument for skepticism. However, I am not yet ready to do that. Because the argument, especially its central concept certainty, is so important to Unger's entire case for skepticism and because he clearly believes the argument to be decisive, I think we owe it to him to consider it at greater length. In doing so, the first point of note I would like to make about the argument concerns certain interesting possibilities it raises about the defense of skepticism. As we have seen, Unger defends skepticism by making a specific state of mind, the attitude of certainty, a necessary condition of knowledge, and then goes on to establish that because certainty is an absolute term, we can never legitimately claim of any of our states of mind that they exemplify that particular attitude. He completes his argument by justifying his contention that the attitude of certainty is necessary to knowledge by means of his Argument from Emphasis. I should like to suggest that a parallel—and, I think, equally plausible—case

142

for skepticism can be made through an appeal to states of mind other than certainty. Let me offer an example, with its Ungerian-style argument.

1. In the case of every human being, there is at most hardly anything to which he is *committed*.

2. As a matter of necessity, in the case of every human being, the person knows something to be so only if he is *committed* to it.

3. In the case of every human being, there is at most hardly anything which the person knows to be so.

In support of my major premise, I could argue that "commitment" is an absolute term, therefore that one can be committed to p iff there is never a q to which it is logically possible that he or anyone else might be more committed. Since we can never legitimately claim that any p satisfies this condition, we can never conclude that anyone is committed to anything. In support of the minor premise we can turn to the Argument from Emphasis, holding (to put it briefly) that the proposition "He really *knows* that it is raining, but he *isn't* absolutely *committed* to it" feels contradictory to us, so is inconsistent. Therefore, commitment is a necessary condition of knowledge. Put our two premises together and we get a skeptical conclusion, in exactly the same way Unger did through his use of certainty. Since commitment is a state of mind different from certainty, we can conclude that we have produced a second argument for skepticism, apparently as strong as Unger's original one.

But other states of mind seem equally capable of sustaining a parallel argument for skepticism. I shall not spell these possibilities out in detail but only suggest that Unger's argument could be put to work with such states of mind as "adamant" (about), "convinced" (of), "dedicated" (to), "unquestioning" (about), etcetera, all of which seem to be "absolute" terms in Unger's sense of the word. If I am correct, a large number of arguments parallel to Unger's Argument from the Necessity of Certainty could be offered in support of skepticism.

But I do not want to be misunderstood here. I am *not* bringing forth this apparent wealth of support for Unger's thesis in order to strengthen his case for skepticism. Quite the contrary. My aim is to suggest that, because it seems so easy to reach a skeptical conclusion by the route he follows, we should view the entire undertaking with considerable skepticism. Indeed, my (not quite serious) embellishments of Unger's style of argument might well lend support to a suspicion some readers may already have entertained—that the procedure in question is frivolous. These skeptical thoughts take me back (from my brief digression) to Unger's first argument itself and its minor premise. Is Unger correct in his claim that we can know nothing unless we are certain of it? The Argument from Emphasis, which he offers in support of that claim, is, to put the point conservatively, less than convincing. But we should still look at some counterexamples that can, I think, show us how much his claim violates the conception of knowledge most of us, laymen and philosophers alike, share. In the next section I shall offer a few of these.

6 Is Certainty a Necessary Condition of Knowledge?[29]

If we combine Unger's premise that certainty is a necessary condition of knowledge with his description of certainty as a kind of psychological state (or state of mind), we are forced to conclude that a person could know something (if this were possible at all) *only* when he is thinking about it, when it occupies his consciousness. When he stops thinking about it, for example, when he is thinking about something else, he can no longer know it. Thus, I may be standing in a downpour, certain that it is raining, but lose my knowledge about the state of the weather because the rapid approach of an automobile, skidding directly at me, empties my consciousness of everything except the thought of my imminent danger. Again, the scientist, or mathematician, whom we should ordinarily say to know a number of things, loses all his knowledge when he drifts off into a dreamless sleep and can regain it again only when he awakens. But even then, he can never know more than one, or possibly a few, things at any given time, because he cannot hold more than this before his consciousness simultaneously. (It might be noted in passing that in this respect Unger's conception of knowledge is different from the standard notion, which makes belief rather than certainty necessary for knowledge. Because beliefs, unlike certainties, are not states or conditions of consciousness, an individual does not destroy his beliefs about things, as he does his certainties, when he stops thinking directly about them. Rather, we should say that a person has beliefs and hence can possess knowledge about a wide range of different things all at the same time, even when he is asleep.) Perhaps Unger could meet the objection I have just raised by altering his view somewhat, holding that, although certainty is a psychological state, it is not a state we need to possess about something at every moment we are said to know that thing. Rather it is like belief in this respect. Once we have achieved a state of certainty about a given thing (were that ever possible), we can legitimately claim to know that thing even when we do not have it directly before our consciousness. Although this would mark a change in Unger's notion of certainty, it would seem to be a more plausible position. The question is: How plausible would it be?

A person is a mathematician. After lengthy thought and calculation he solves a problem that has baffled mathematicians for generations. Although he is sure that he has made no mistakes in his deductions, the result he has achieved is so momentous that he cannot entirely expunge from his mind a tiny lingering doubt that his solution may be wrong. Gradually, however, his doubt dissipates and he becomes absolutely certain that his answer is correct. When should we say that the mathematician knew the answer to this problem? When he had solved it? Or only when he was psychologically able to overcome his last doubt to become subjectively certain that he had solved it? Most people other than Unger would, I think, opt for the first answer. Or consider the following: Two logicians, working independently, simultaneously solve in identical ways an outstanding problem in logic. However, the two differ temperamentally, the first being confident, and the second diffident by nature. Because of this psychological difference between them, the first reaches a state of certainty that his solution is correct, but the second can never quite reach a point at which his mind is totally free from doubt. Would we conclude that the first possesses knowledge about logic that the second does not? Hardly.

To conclude my critique of Unger's view I shall offer one more counterexample. Consider the following: An individual publishes a series of brilliant papers in the mathematical journals, demonstrating the truth of a number of propositions that no other mathematician had proved before. The world of mathematicians is dazzled and agrees that he knows more mathematics than any other person alive. Then an eminent engineer steps on to the scene and reveals that he has perpetrated a gigantic hoax. The mathematician in question, although he has done these things and is in every external respect indistinguishable from everyone else, is not human at all but a robot the engineer has constructed. Being without consciousness, it can never be psychologically certain of anything. Should all the mathematicians retract their earlier judgment and now conclude that it doesn't know anything? I think this example is harder to judge than the earlier ones. Some people, at least, might be hesitant to admit that a robot could know anything, on the grounds that only human beings can possess knowledge. However, I doubt that many, except Unger, would deny knowledge to the robot simply because it is incapable of achieving a state of psychological certainty. This example, furthermore, has implications that may apply not just to robots but to humans as well. According to some forms of materialism, no one is conscious. Hence no one can be psychologically certain of anything. If such a materialism is true, must we conclude (as Unger would have to contend) that no one can know anything? Does materialism entail skepticism? Or might we not still have a viable conception of knowledge for which consciousness, hence psychological certainty, is not held to constitute a necessary condition?

The purpose of my counterexamples is, of course, to lead us to reject Unger's definition, to the extent that he makes the psychological state of certainty a necessary condition of knowledge. It must be conceded, however, that, because of the very nature of definition, such counterexamples cannot be *logically* coercive, for anyone is free to define any term in any way he wants. I could, for example, define "knowledge" as "an equilateral right triangle" and then conclude that knowledge is impossible because no right triangle can be equilateral as well. And I could continue (logically) to maintain my definition no matter how many counterexamples were offered against it. No one could dislodge me from my position by logical means alone. All that my critics could do would be to point out that what they mean when they (and almost everyone else) talk about knowledge is quite different from what I mean when I talk about it. Or, perhaps better, they could simply dismiss me as a crank.

The remarks I have just made are in no way meant to imply that Unger's definition of knowledge is absurd. On the contrary, it has some initial plausibility. Nevertheless, I think it both can and ought to be rejected for several reasons. (The same reasons would apply to my own variations on his definition which I suggested in the previous section.) (1) It is not, as he claims it to be, the traditional conception of knowledge. (2) It forces us to conclude, as my counterexamples show, that we should not apply the term *knowledge* to situations in which most of us would find this term appropriate, hence is a faulty definition. (3) It seems to be designed to accomplish Unger's aim of substantiating epistemological skepticism. (4) Other, better definitions of knowledge—definitions that do not lead to skepticism but *do* reflect more accurately what most people mean by the term than his does—are available to us. In the next section I shall address myself briefly to my final reason for rejecting Unger's definition of knowledge.

7 An Alternative Definition of Knowledge

Since my purpose in this book is to examine skepticism, not to develop my own theory of knowledge, I shall not go into great detail in my discussion of the alternative definition of knowledge which I shall propose here. The conception I have in mind is a somewhat modified version of the traditional definition of knowledge; namely, that it is justified true belief. (The main difference between my definition and the traditional one is my omission of "belief"; my reason for omitting belief is to eliminate any reference to a psychological state that might be confused with Unger's state of certainty.) My definition will not be complete but only partial; I shall limit myself to stating the sufficient conditions of knowledge. According to this definition, "X knows that *p* if X can establish that *p*."[30] To offer a specific example: "I know that it is raining if I can establish that it is raining."

I should like to make a few remarks about this partial definition of knowledge. Because the conditions it lays down are held to be sufficient for knowledge yet do not incude the notion of certainty, which Unger claims to be necessary for knowledge, it is incompatible with his definition; beliefs that, according to it, would count as knowledge could not be knowledge for Unger, since his certainty condition can never be satisfied. The two important concepts in my definition are "can" and "establish." To understand the definition adequately, therefore, one must first explicate the criteria governing *can* (establish). Perhaps we could say, briefly, that one *can* establish that *p*, if one has established that *p*, remembers that he has done so and how he has done so, and is able to repeat the process on demand. As far as *establish* is concerned, it is apparent that its inclusion in the definition makes truth a necessary condition of knowledge. I cannot establish that *p* unless it is true that *p*. Of course, problems remain, in particular that of determining how we might go about establishing the truth of any *p*. But these are problems not of the definition of knowledge but rather of its acquisition. To resolve them would lead us beyond definition into a theory of knowledge.[31]

To conclude our argument, let us return to the central issue before us. We are faced with two alternative partial definitions of knowledge—Unger's, which makes the psychological state of certainty, a state that we can never legitimately claim to achieve, a necessary condition of our knowing anything, and mine, which makes no reference to our psychological states at all. Furthermore, if we accept my definition (or one like it), we can neatly avoid Unger's skeptical conclusion, which is a consequence of his own definition. Which should we accept? I have already given reasons in my counter-examples for rejecting Unger's definition, and I see no important objections that can be raised against my definition, remembering, of course, that it offers us sufficient (rather than necessary) conditions of knowledge. If someone can establish that *p*, I should claim, we should all agree that he *knows* that *p*. What more is required of him? That he should be in some peculiar psychological state that Unger never even succeeds in describing? Speaking for myself, I should say that, to the extent that I am concerned about what I know and can know, I would find my concerns about any specific proposition laid to rest once I realized that I had established the proposition to be true. That I should still continue to doubt my knowing it is a supposition I find not worth entertaining. And the further supposition that I should continue to doubt my knowing it because I have not achieved some kind of state of psychological certainty about it I find equally not worth entertaining. My possession, or nonpossession of such a psychological state is simply irrelevant to what I know. In this I believe most people would agree with me, as can be seen by the following: Suppose a person has just succeeded in establishing that some *p* is true and Unger accosts him, saying, "You don't know that *p* because your mind is not (because it can't be) in a state of psychological certainty regarding *p*." Is there any good reason why such a person should take Unger seriously?

Since Unger's first argument for skepticism depends for its strength on his own (idiosyncratic) definition of knowledge and loses its force when knowledge is defined in another way, I think we can fairly conclude that the argument has been laid to rest. Granted that anyone can define any term (including knowledge) in any way he wishes and then draw implications from his definition, I believe I have shown in the last three sections that Unger's definition of knowledge—when compared with what most users of the language mean by the term—is simply a misdefinition. In any case other definitions much more consonant with our normal conception of the term can be offered; I have suggested one. Furthermore, definitions like my own do not have the skeptical implications of Unger's definition. For these reasons I conclude that the minor premise of Unger's Argument from the Necessity of Certainty can and ought to be rejected. Its rejection causes the entire argument to collapse.

8 The Normative Argument from Certainty

Unger's second argument for skepticism, which I have called the Normative Argument from Certainty, occupies the first nine sections of Chapter III of *Ignorance*. The argument is stated formally at the beginning of §1, in the following terms:

(1) If someone *knows* something to be so, then it is all right for the person to be absolutely *certain* that it is so. . . .

(2) It is never all right for anyone to be absolutely *certain* that anything is so. . . .

(3) Nobody ever knows that anything is so.[32]

It is obvious, because of its crucial use of the concept of certainty, that Unger's second argument for skepticism is based on his first argument. Since we have already concluded that the state of certainty, rather than being a necessary condition of knowledge, is really irrelevant to the question of what we know, we can say at the outset that Unger's second argument will not add any further support to his case for skepticism. However, rather than dismissing it without examination, I shall take the time to consider it on its own terms, because I think the effort Unger has put into it deserves our showing in detail why it fails.

I shall begin my discussion by turning to the minor premise, which Unger believes to make "the *substantive* claim of the argument."[33] Unger offers one general reason in support of its claim that it is never all right for anyone to be absolutely certain that anything is so; namely, that such a state of mind or attitude is always dogmatic. As he summarizes the point:

> What we have just been arguing for most directly is the idea that the attitude of certainty, this attitude which is always had in being certain, always means that one is (completely) dogmatic in the matter at hand. And, for that reason . . . this attitude is never all right for anyone ever to have.[34]

Although Unger simply assumes in this argument that it is never all right to be dogmatic about any matter, I see no point in questioning that assumption. For I agree with him that dogmatism cannot be justified. Granting this point, however, we still have to ask whether Unger succeeds in supporting his contention that to be certain of anything is always to be dogmatic about that thing. His main line of argument to establish this conclusion (which occupies the bulk of §§4-9) lies in offering examples of situations in which individuals who are certain of something can be shown to be dogmatic. Although some of Unger's illustrations are of interest, any adequate consideration of them would take more space than we have available. In any event I doubt that our results would prove conclusive. Furthermore, as I shall show, the answer to the problem we must resolve cannot be found in any parade of examples. So I shall not attempt a detailed scrutiny of the cases Unger presents, adding, however, that I agree with him at least to the extent of believing that in most situations in which people claim certainty they are being dogmatic. Even though we may not accept Unger's view that certainty is an unattainable state of mind, we must, I think, admit not only that it is difficult to achieve but also that it is never justified unless one knows that of which he claims to be certain.

To grant this much, however, is not to concede that Unger's minor premise is true, because that premise makes a *universal* claim. If, as he holds, the reason why it is *never* all right for anyone to be absolutely certain that anything is so is that such an attitude is *always* dogmatic, we must, if we are to succeed in evaluating the truth of the premise, understand just what he means by "dogmatism." Unfortunately, Unger has little to say on the subject. To explain dogmatism, he writes the following:

> . . . the opposite of scepticism is often called *dogmatism.*
> . . . Given the truth of the first premiss [of the Normative Argument from Certainty], it is for this reason that dogmatism is indeed the alternative to scepticism.[35]

Assuming that Unger means by the "opposite of" and "alternative to" skepticism, the view that we can know things—

that knowledge is possible—we can conclude that he is equating dogmatism with the positive view about knowledge accepted by epistemologists outside the ranks of the skeptics; i.e., with cognitivism. Any theory that makes knowledge claims thus becomes, for him, dogmatic, as does any claim to know anything. But, as Unger correctly recognizes, to assert that a proposition is true is to make a knowledge claim. As he puts it, "If someone asserts, declares, or states that something is so, it follows that he represents himself as *knowing* that it is so."[36] But Unger, in introducing his Normative Argument from Certainty, himself writes: "Each of the two premisses of this new argument is put forward as necessarily true."[37] From this we can conclude that, as Unger understands his own argument, in asserting the minor premise as true he is making a knowledge claim. Such a claim, like all claims to knowledge, must for him be dogmatic. So in making it Unger himself abandons skepticism to join the ranks of the "dogmatists." Of course, the claim is also inconsistent with the conclusion he intends it to support so the Normative Argument from Certainty collapses in self-contradiction.

Although it is hardly necessary to add anything further about Unger's second argument for skepticism, I should like to make one additional comment. The line he pursues in his Normative Argument from Certainty, besides ending in disaster, seems unnecessary. Indeed, given his first argument, one would have expected him to have adopted a quite different tactic in his second argument. If certainty, being an absolute term, describes a state of mind that we can never attain, this conclusion could be used as a reason to justify Unger in holding (as he does in the minor premise of his second argument) that it is never all right for anyone to be absolutely certain that anything is so, for, it could be argued, it cannot be *all right* to be certain of something if it is impossible to *be* certain of anything. Thus, rather than turning to an argument from dogmatism to support his minor premise, Unger could have derived his conclusion in a straightforward deductive way from his first argument. He might, in other words, have reformulated his second argument in some such terms as these:

1. If someone *knows* something to be so, then it is all right for the person to be absolutely *certain* that it is so.
2. Because one *cannot* ever be absolutely *certain* that something is so, it is never all right for anyone to be absolutely *certain* that anything is so.
3. Nobody ever *knows* that anything is so.

I do not know why Unger did not pursue such an apparently natural development of his case for skepticism in his second argument, but I can say that even had he done so, his attempt would still have ended in failure. The reason why it would fail lies in an ambiguity in the major premise. To lay this ambiguity bare it is necessary to expand the premise to read: "If someone knows something to be so, then it is all right for the person to be absolutely certain that it is so, *unless* some other reason can be given why it is not all right for him to be certain that it is so." But, according to Unger, another reason *can* be given: It is not all right to be certain of anything because it is impossible to be so. However, as we have already shown in our examination of Unger's first argument, the impossibility of attaining certainty, hence the impossibility of claiming it to be all right to be certain has nothing to do with our knowing things. Rather, the psychological state of certainty is logically irrelevant to knowledge. So the conclusion that it is never all right to be certain of anything in no way precludes the possibility of our knowing many things.

9 The Argument from the Necessity of Clarity

Unger's third argument for skepticism appears in §§10 through 12 of Chapter III of *Ignorance*. Although he does not state this argument in a formal way (as he does the first two), it is easy to reconstruct. I have labeled it the Argument from the Necessity of Clarity, for reasons that will soon become apparent. My formulation of it is modeled after that of Unger's first argument.

1. In the case of every human being, there is nothing about which he is clear.[38]
2. As a matter of necessity, in the case of every human being, the person knows something to be so only if he is clear about it.[39]
3. In the case of every human being, there is nothing which the person knows to be so.

Just as the notion of certainty provided the basis for Unger's first two arguments for skepticism, so that of clarity is central to his third. Before we can come to grips with the argument, therefore, we must understand what Unger means by clarity. Here, however, we are faced with a problem. I simply find myself unable to explain in any intelligible way what Unger means by the term *clear*, as he uses it in his third argument. All I have to go on is what he says in the text, but I find I can make little or no sense of his language. The problem is not that he fails to say what he means by clear; on the contrary, he is quite explicit on this point. The difficulty lies rather in the fact that I cannot comprehend any relation between his notion of clarity and what I—and, I think, almost everyone else—mean by knowledge.

After contending that clear (like certain) is an absolute term, Unger continues as follows:

I take it that "clear" means the same in each of these sentences:
The water was clear.
His meaning was clear (to her).[40]

Although the term clear tends to be a somewhat vague notion in many of the contexts in which it is ordinarily used, I think its meaning when applied to water—as Unger is applying it in the first of his two examples above—can be specified with considerable precision. When we say that water is clear, we mean that it is free of floating particulate matter (such as mud, sand, industrial wastes, etc.). In ordinary situations we base judgments of this kind on visual evidence. Water in which we can discern objects to a depth of twenty feet we think to be clearer than water in which we can discern objects only to a depth of five feet. Now Unger claims (see his second example) that the conception of clarity, when applied to the notion of "meaning," has the same meaning as it has when applied to water. So we can conclude that for him the meaning of "His meaning was clear" must be "His meaning was free of particulate floating matter." If this is, as I think it is, a fair reading of his statement, we can draw the conclusions that meanings have volume, can be carried in containers, and are probably able to be poured. So we might say, "Look out, your bucket has a leak in it and its meaning is pouring out all over the ground." I confess that I find all of this simply incomprehensible.

But to continue. In his defense of the minor premise of his third argument, Unger explains further what is involved in his view that clarity is both a necessary and a sufficient condition of knowledge, concluding that the two notions—knowledge and clarity—are identical with each other. In his words, "your knowing something is the same thing as that thing's being absolutely clear to you."[41] From the context (and since Unger has said nothing to the contrary), we can reasonably conclude that he means by clear, as he uses it in this statement, the same thing as he meant by it when he was talking of the clarity of meanings; e.g., in his statement (that I quoted above) "His meaning was clear (to her)." So we get the following kind of result: Since "X knows that p" means the same as "P's being absolutely clear to X," we can conclude that "X knows that p" means the same as "P's being absolutely free of floating particulate matter to X." To give an example, if we say, "John knows that it is raining," what we *mean* is "That it is raining [is] absolutely free of floating particulate matter to John." Need I argue that such an analysis is at variance with what all of us mean by knowledge? Or that it is gibberish?

My attack on Unger's third argument for skepticism has concentrated on the unusual—indeed, idiosyncratic—meaning he has given to the notion of clarity. So presumably he could meet this criticism by redefining the notion in a way that does not lead to absurd consequences. But what should the nature of such a new definition be? Unger, naturally, has nothing to say on the subject. Nevertheless, I see no reason that would prevent him from revising his argument by a redefinition of the term. Should he do so, we would have to reexamine the argument. But we could still raise the question: *Can* Unger define the notion of clarity in such a way that his third argument becomes both intelligible and cogent? To answer this question, we must consider a second point that he makes in his elaboration of the third argument, a point independent of the meaning he has given to clarity. Through a consideration of this point we can generate another basis than that of meanings in terms of which we can evaluate the argument. Unger writes:

> . . . our condition [i.e., the clarity condition] implies that the subject is (absolutely) certain of the thing. If that thing [that they left] is (absolutely) *clear* to Mary, then she is absolutely *certain* that they left. It is inconsistent to say "It was *clear* to her that they left, but she *wasn't* certain of it."[42]

In this passage Unger says nothing about the meaning of clarity, although one gets the impression that he is regarding it to be some kind of psychological state, which would, of course, be inconsistent with his original understanding of it, but would be much more like what the rest of us mean by it. But he does say something else of importance about clarity; namely, that it entails certainty. Unless one is certain that something is so he cannot be clear that it is so. Now we have already shown that Unger is mistaken in his view that knowledge entails certainty, concluding, on the contrary, that certainty is not a necessary condition of knowledge. If certainty is necessary to clarity but not necessary to knowledge, it follows that clarity cannot be necessary to knowledge either. So we can reject the minor premise of Unger's Argument from the Necessity of Clarity, thus destroying the argument itself.

To summarize our conclusions about Unger's third argument for skepticism, we can say, first, that it lacks cogency because its minor premise is unacceptable and, second, that it is rendered unintelligible, as an argument concerned with human knowledge, because of the bizarre meaning given to its central concept—clarity. We are left, then, with Unger's fourth, and final, argument in support of skepticism.

10   The Argument from the Impossibility of Truth

Unger never states his final argument for skepticism formally; nevertheless, although it is the most complex of his four arguments, it is fairly easy to reconstruct. I shall formulate it in two syllogisms in which the conclusion of the first, restated, becomes the minor premise of the second.

I. 1. Truth is the property of being in agreement with the whole truth about the world.[43]
    2. There can be no whole truth about the world.[44]
    3. There can be no truth (or truth is impossible).
II. 1. Truth is a necessary condition of knowledge.[45]
    2. Truth is impossible. [Conclusion of first argument]
    3. Knowledge is impossible.

In my examination of the Argument from the Impossibility of Truth, I shall concentrate my attention on the first syllogism. The second need not be examined directly, because its two premises consist of the statement that truth is a necessary condition of knowledge, a thesis in which we have from the beginning concurred, and the conclusion of the first syllogism. If we succeed in establishing that the first syllogism is not cogent, we can reject its conclusion, hence the minor premise of the second syllogism, and along with it the final conclusion, which is the thesis of skepticism.

Turning then to the first syllogism, let us begin with its major premise. Unger claims that the premise—"Truth is the property of being in agreement with the whole truth about the world"—*defines* truth. One's immediate reaction, I think, is that it is an unusual definition; certainly it differs from most definitions that have been offered in the tradition. To say this, of course, is not to condemn it out of hand; as we have seen earlier (in the cases of "certainty" and "clarity"), it is always possible to give different definitions of the same term. However, unless one is to be arbitrary, he should have reasons for offering whatever definition he does of any term. Unger recognizes this, defending his definition (in part) on the grounds of its simplicity.[46] Here I would take issue with him; rather than being simple, his definition, compared with others, is complex. To offer an obvious alternative definition that is more simple than his: Truth is the property of being in agreement with the world. To give an example, we can say "That is true" means "That is in agreement with the world."[47]

But its complexity is only a minor objection to Unger's definition of truth; a much more serious one remains. The purpose of a definition is to explicate the meaning of the word it defines. The definiens, therefore, should be more easily understood than the definiendum. On this count Unger's definition fails, for two reasons: (1) The phrase "the property of being in agreement with the whole truth about the world" is less, not more, easy to comprehend than the word *truth*, and (2) the definiens contains the definiendum (i.e., "truth") in it, therefore, in order to complete his definition of "truth" Unger must include a definition of that word as it appears in the definiens. Since it is the same word as the definiendum, its definition must also be the same. Hence, to complete his definition of truth Unger must say, "Truth is the property of being in agreement with the whole property of being in agreement with the whole truth about the world." But this definition, too, is incomplete because it contains the definiendum in the definiens. To overcome this deficiency Unger would have to offer the following definition: "Truth is the property of being in agreement with the whole property of being in agreement with the whole property of being in agreement with the whole truth about the world." But this definition is deficient in exactly the same way as the previous ones, with the result that truth still remains undefined. Nor can it be defined in Unger's terms, for the regress generated is clearly vicious. So we can reject the major premise of Unger's argument, because it offers us an unacceptable (because necessarily incomplete) definition of truth. Without the major premise of its first syllogism, Unger cannot succeed in making his fourth argument for skepticism.

Unger might dispute my conclusion, on the grounds that he is using truth in a different way in the definiens than in the definiendum, arguing that we must not pull the word *truth* out of its context in the definiens but rather must consider the entire phrase "the whole truth about the world." However, this will not help him, because if the concept "truth" must be defined, so must the concept "the whole truth about the world" (since it includes the undefined concept truth within it). How would Unger define "the whole truth about the world"? If he followed the original formulation of his definition of truth, he would have to begin as follows: " 'The whole truth about the world' is the property of being in agreement with . . ." But then how should he complete his definition? What could the whole truth about the world be in agreement with? I would suggest that the proper object of that agreement is, as the phrase itself indicates, the whole world. This would yield the definition "The whole truth about the world is the property of being in agreement with the whole world." We could then define the notion of a particular (as opposed to a universal) truth as the property of being in agreement with some part of the whole world. But this is simply the alternative definition of truth I offered above. So we can conclude that Unger's argument is based on an indefensible conception of truth and that if we are to come to grips with the difficult issues of truth and knowledge with any hope of resolving these successfully, we must abandon it in favor of some other notion. For this purpose, I know of no better definition than the standard one I have suggested.

The main weight of Unger's fourth argument, however, rests on the minor premise of its first syllogism, which reads: "There can be no whole truth about the world." So I shall consider this premise at some length. For purposes of our discussion, I shall assume that the major premise, although it cannot be accepted as a *definition* of truth, can still be construed as a true statement about individual truths; all such truths are in agreement with the whole truth about the world. (What I have just said, I might add, would be compatible with the standard definition of truth I have offered.)

The minor premise itself appears on the surface to be quite dubious or, at best, controversial. Why, we might ask, can't there be any whole truth about the world? It would seem, on the contrary, that if there is a world, there is a whole truth about it. Such a thesis is, I think, considerably more plausible than Unger's minor premise. Of course, it does not follow from the existence of such a whole truth about the world that any finite being *knows* what this whole truth is. As Unger himself remarks, to know the whole truth about the world would require omniscience.[48] But that is not to deny the existence of such a truth, capable of being known by a possible omniscient being. Before he can win acceptance for his minor premise, it seems to me, Unger has a formidable job to accomplish. He must present arguments capable of establishing that his own implausible denial that there can be a whole truth about the world is correct and that the more plausible view that there is such a truth therefore mistaken.

Unger would not agree with what I have just said. In a discussion of the whole truth about the world, after pointing out its importance to his argument for skepticism, he goes on to claim that his denial of its possible existence is *uncontroversial*, writing as follows:

> The central entity in our account of truth is the whole truth about the world.... I find it almost incredible that there should actually exist or obtain...our central entity, the whole truth about the world. Indeed, I am quite ...confident that there really is no such thing, nothing such at all. And it follows from this, of which I am thus confident, that there really isn't anything either which is any part of that first, that is, there really is nothing which is any part of the truth. The consequences for us of this rather simple and uncontroversial idea now look to be remarkable. As this non-existence is, I suppose, strictly necessary, these remarkable consequences will also hold of the strictest necessity.[49]

Presumably because he is so confident that his thesis that there can be no whole truth about the world is simple and uncontroversial, Unger does not find it necessary to provide any arguments in its support in the text of *Ignorance*. Rather, he relegates the issue to a footnote, where, instead of offering an argument, he writes: "I provide no argument for thinking that there is no such entity as the whole truth about the world, that no such thing really exists or obtains."[50]

As on other occasions I find myself once again bewildered by the nature of Unger's thinking. I simply do not comprehend the basis for his confidence in his thesis regarding the necessary nonexistence of the whole truth about the world. Is this claim *really* so uncontroversial that he need offer no argument in its defense? Why does he find it "almost incredible" that such a truth should exist? At the very least, some discussion of this crucial point in his fourth argument would seem pertinent, if not demanded. So, to fill in the gap left by Unger's missing argument, I shall offer some thoughts of my own on the subject here. Let us turn our attention directly to the minor premise, which reads: "There can be no whole truth about the world." Is this premise true (as Unger maintains) or is it false (as I am inclined to believe), and how can we decide? Before we address these questions, perhaps we should determine what kind of a truth it is, if it is true. (Of course, if it is false its denial "There can be a whole truth about the world" or "The whole truth about the world is possible" is true.)[51]

According to the classification Unger has given, two possibilities need to be considered. The minor premise may be either (1) the whole truth about the world or (2) a particular truth. Can the minor premise be (1) the whole truth about the world? If so, what it states is false, because the premise, in being the whole truth about the world, entails that the whole truth about the world exists. Therefore, if we assume it to be the whole truth about the world we can conclude that the statement "The whole truth about the world is possible" is true a fortiori. And this statement, combined with the major premise of Unger's argument ("Truth is the property of being in agreement with the whole truth about the world"), entails the conclusion "Truth is possible." If, however, we consider the minor premise to be an attempted statement of the whole truth about the world which, however, fails, so is false, we can conclude that its denial "The whole truth about the world is possible" is true. This premise, combined with the major premise, also entails the conclusion "Truth is possible." Thus, whether we consider the minor premise, as an assumed statement of the whole truth about the world, to be true or to be false, we find that the implications of such an assumption, when combined with the major premise, entail the conclusion "Truth is possible."

But what if we assume the minor premise to be, not the whole truth about the world, but (2) a particular truth—a part of the whole truth about the world? On this assumption, if the premise is false, once again its denial "The whole truth about the world is possible" is true, from which the conclusion "Truth is possible" then follows. If, however, the premise is true, it furnishes an instance of a particular truth. But then it is logically inconsistent with the conclusion of the syllogism that states that truth is impossible. If we consider the minor premise to be true, we must reject the conclusion as false. And, as we have just seen, if we consider this premise to be false, the conclusion is also false. If the minor premise is viewed as a particular truth, then, whether it be true or false, it entails the truth of the conclusion "Truth is possible."

The minor premise, if it is true, must either be the whole truth about the world or a part of that truth, for no other possibilities exist. Having canvassed its implications as both, in each instance assuming it to be true and then to be false, we have found that on each assumed interpretation we are logically forced to the conclusion that truth is possible. Furthermore, our canvass has been complete; we have exhausted the possible interpretations. So we can deduce from Unger's argument not only that truth is possible but also that it is necessary. The conclusion that the first syllogism of Unger's Argument from the Impossibility of Truth logically entails, therefore, is: *Truth exists necessarily.*

We can now turn to the second syllogism of Unger's fourth argument for skepticism,[52] which must (on the basis of the preceding argument) be *reformulated* to read as follows:

> II. 1. Truth is a necessary condition of knowledge.
> 2. Truth is possible (because it exists necessarily).
> 3. Knowledge is possible (i.e., not rendered impossible by the impossibility of truth).

I should like to make two brief comments about this conclusion. (1) It establishes that Unger's Argument from the Impossibility of Truth fails as a support for skepticism, because it cannot show that knowledge is impossible, on the grounds that truth is impossible. (2) It does not, however, establish either the existence or the possibility of knowledge, for knowledge has, I think, at least one other necessary condition in addition to truth and it *may* be that this condition cannot be satisfied. Thus, although we have destroyed Unger's final argument for skepticism, we cannot yet claim to have established the positive thesis of the cognitivists that we can and do indeed know things.

11 Consequences of Unger's Conclusion about Truth

Having examined Unger's four arguments for skepticism and found none of them to be cogent, I believe we are entitled to conclude that this latest, and most ambitious, attack on the possibility of human knowledge ends in failure. But I think that more needs to be said about the case Unger makes in *Ignorance* than that it fails to support his skeptical thesis. In this and the concluding section of chapter v I should like to make a few comments on some further consequences of Unger's views about truth and knowledge.

As we have just seen, Unger bases his final argument for skepticism on the thesis that truth is impossible. Nevertheless, during the course of his book he repeatedly makes statements about truth which directly contradict this thesis. Consider, for example, the following:

> ...the full form of our Principle of Identifying Knowledge may be coupled to our thesis of universal ignorance. These two jointly entail that there never is any reason for anyone, to do anything, to believe anything, to want anything, and so on. They establish this as a *necessary truth.*[53]

Since neither necessary nor contingent truths can exist if truth is impossible, Unger simply cannot have it both ways. If we assume that the alternative he accepts is expressed in the passage I have just quoted (and the other similar passages I have referred to in my footnote) and combine this with a position we noted earlier in this chapter which he maintains (and with which I should agree); namely, that "If someone asserts, declares, or states that something is so [i.e., true], it follows that he represents himself as *knowing* that it is so," we must conclude that Unger is *claiming to know* what he asserts to be entailed in the quotation above. But if he knows something to be a necessary truth, Unger cannot call himself a skeptic, for he is really a cognitivist. If, however, we assume that the alternative he would embrace is the one he states last ("Truth is impossible")—an assumption strengthened by the fact that this view forms a premise of his final argument for skepticism as well as the title of the last chapter of *Ignorance*—we are forced to conclude that he did not mean what he said on several occasions earlier in the book when he claimed certain propositions to be true. So we might ask: Then why did he say these things?

Rather than attempting to answer our question, let us instead pursue some implications of Unger's denial of the possibility of truth. If (truth being impossible) none of Unger's assertions in *Ignorance* can be true, then none of the conclusions he reached in his four arguments for skepticism can be true. If none of these conclusions is true, then all of his arguments fail; so Unger apparently is in agreement with my assessment of his case for skepticism. Even further, we seem forced to conclude, if we follow Unger, that *none* of the thousands of propositions that make up the text of *Ignorance* can be true. (In this implication, however, I would not follow him. Although I would concede to him that many of these propositions, particularly those that state and attempt to support his case for skepticism about both knowledge and rationality, are not true, I nevertheless believe that many other propositions in *Ignorance*, some of considerable importance, *are* true.)

At this point in the discussion one might be ready to conclude that Unger believes that everything he writes, since it cannot be true, must be false. That would be a mistake, for, having concluded that nothing can be true, Unger goes on to rule out the possibility of falsity as well:

> . . . nothing can be true and nothing false. This applies as much to the offerings of the present essay as it does to anything else.[54]

Even though we may appreciate the candor of this quotation, we can hardly let it pass unnoted. Ruling out any third alternative, Unger is surely aware that, if he acknowledges the offerings of his book to be neither true nor false, he is inviting his readers to judge them meaningless. So one is led to raise the question: *Is Unger really serious about what he has written in* Ignorance?

Although Unger, understandably enough, never addresses my question directly, he does make some remarks that are relevant to the issue it raises. Immediately following the statements I have just quoted, he goes on to add:

> But even if what I have placed before us is not true, it may well be worth your while to focus on it, to be influenced by it, and even to be guided by it in the construction of some new, better intellectual approach to the world.[55]

I think that these remarks, if they are properly understood, can be accepted. Although it may be difficult "to focus on" and "be influenced by" a book, none of whose propositions is either true or false, I do not myself believe this about *Ignorance*, because I do not accept Unger's statement that nothing he has offered in it is either true or false. On the contrary, if the criticisms I have given of *Ignorance* in this chapter are sound, the book must be judged to be false, as far as its main skeptical theses are concerned. It can, therefore, be worth one's while to focus on it, for we can be influenced by it to the extent of rejecting it and being guided by this rejection toward "some new, better intellectual approach to the world."

12 *Unger's Argument: A Final Twist*

I suspect that the thoughtful reader who has reached this point in my analysis and examination of Unger's case for skepticism may be feeling some misgivings. "Surely," he is muttering to himself by now, "Unger must have something better to say for his skepticism than what has been presented in this chapter. He cannot expect to convince anyone of his views if he bases them on a combination of distorted definitions, bad arguments, and self-contradictions that lead him to accept such outlandish conclusions as those we have found him to embrace in *Ignorance*—that nothing can be true and nothing false, that everyone is irrational *simpliciter*, that snow is white and snow is not white, etcetera."[56] Such misgivings would be well founded, for Unger's case, as I have developed and criticized it to this point, is not complete. Throughout *Ignorance*, usually expressed in a minor key behind the main course of the argument, lies a further complication that Unger brings to the fore for emphasis only at the very end of the book. He does not spend much time on this view, devoting only about a dozen pages of his long book to it. Yet it is clear that he takes it very seriously, for he writes, "I think that hypotheses at least a lot like these [i.e., like the one now to be described] will offer our best bet for a scepticism which may be widely accepted and long maintained."[57] So, before leaving Unger, we must take a look at this final twist that he gives to his argument for skepticism.

Unger begins his case by acknowledging what I have already alluded to—that the conclusions he has reached are hardly ones that most people, including philosophers, will find acceptable.

Going against beliefs or assertions of "common sense," even scepticism about knowledge may be considered a "crazy conclusion," and probably will be by most professional philosophers even at this point. The same goes, only more so, for later conclusions we have reached, especially, perhaps, for the paradoxical contradictions just recently displayed.[58]

But if Unger's arguments lead him to "crazy conclusions," we might well ask, why should we take them seriously? To such a question Unger has a straightforward answer: None of this is his fault; rather the source of the difficulty lies elsewhere:

> . . . I believe that the problems are not of my own making, however disturbing the contradictions I have just exhibited. Rather . . . I believe the problems to originate from quite another source.[59]

What, then, is the source of the problems that led Unger to epistemological skepticism and to all of the contradictions his book exhibits? Again the answer Unger gives is straightforward: the English language. It is the language we use, Unger contends, that makes it impossible for us to know anything. Early in *Ignorance* he writes as follows:

> In order to gain credence for the idea that a quite sweeping sceptical thesis is correct, then, I will look for a basis for that idea in our language, that is, in contemporary English.[60]

Unger's reasons for believing that the language we use is the root cause of our inability to know anything are much too complex to analyze in detail here. Suffice it to say that one of the most important of them is his belief that in English we have defined the concept of knowledge so strictly that no belief we hold can satisfy our definition, hence none can qualify as something we know. To justify this conclusion he then turns (as we have already seen) to the notion of certainty, which he holds to be an unattainable state of mind and by definition a necessary condition of knowledge.

It is hardly necessary at this point to rehearse the reasons we have already given to show that Unger's argument on this issue will not do. It is no feature of the English language which yields Unger's skeptical conclusion, but only his own peculiar definition of the term *knowledge*, which is shared neither by the ordinary user of our language nor by most philosophers. The problem, thus, does not originate with the English language but rather with Unger's misuse of that language. Unger's view that the English language is the cause of skepticism is subject to a criticism of quite another kind as well, for even if his causal analysis were correct, it would not lead to epistemological skepticism (the thesis that knowledge is impossible) but only to *English-language* skepticism. Knowledge would still be possible for anyone speaking or writing in another language than English, for example, French or Chinese.

This last point Unger recognizes. To meet it he proposes his main hypothesis about our language. According to this hypothesis, the reason why English leads to skepticism lies in the fact that it is a descendant of an ancestor language, developed in the remote past, that embodied deficiencies leading to skepticism, and that these deficiencies have been passed on and have ultimately been inherited by our language.

> I often continue to conceive of these things along the following bold, shall we say, anthropological lines. This embodied theory, with its rigid theorems, was the developed view of certain persons who were instrumental in creating an important ancestor, or ancestors, of our language, of English. I place no strict limit on how far back these thinkers go, but I should be surprised if they did not operate, and complete (at least most of) their contribution, a very long time before the Greek thinkers who

are commonly taken to represent "ancient" philosophy. In trying to make sense of things, and in trying at the same time to satisfy certain other deep needs or drives, they developed a theory which in certain respects badly failed in various places, of necessity, to fit the world. While new meanings have sometimes been added, the central meaning of our common words does not differ from theirs, however much pronunciation may differ. While syntax has shifted, deep syntactic relations have been preserved. Accordingly, even if it is without our realizing the fact, their incorrect theory is always on the tips of our tongues. When we make statements we often give expression to it. And, more important, what we state, through analytic connection with the theorems of this theory, always will have entailments which are not true and which fail "to fit the world." Thus, what we state is never true and fails "to fit the world."[61]

Unger's thesis that the ultimate responsibility for our inability either to say anything true or to know anything must be laid at the door of a long-dead ancestor language of English calls for several comments. He describes this hypothesis as "bold"; one can agree with such a characterization, particularly if he recognizes that it is offered as an empirical theory, yet no evidence is provided in *Ignorance*, not even a citation to the findings of any anthropologists, that would lend it factual support.[62] Furthermore, since he states it in English, it cannot, as he implies in the conclusion he derives from it, possibly be true, so one wonders why he takes the trouble to develop it and then try to use it as an explanation of anything. But even if a theory with such dubious credentials were correct, it would not yield epistemological skepticism, for presumably, although we would then be forced to acknowledge that all of us who speak Indo-European languages—English, French, German, etc.—are precluded from knowing anything, those who, like the Chinese, speak a language stemming from another root do not fall under the same

171

interdiction. And one does not have to be born Chinese to learn to speak and write that language; anyone of us can do so and by that process become eligible to know things. Furthermore, if Unger were to broaden his hypothesis to cover all natural languages, we could still avoid skepticism by creating and then communicating in an artificial language.

Although the comments I have made should dispose of what is at best a thesis resting on armchair anthropology, before leaving Unger's "ancestor language" theory I should like to make one additional point, of a different kind, regarding it. This point concerns the conclusion that he derives from it. At the end of the long passage I have just quoted, Unger states that "what we state is never true" (because truth is an impossibility in the English language). In response I shall argue that Unger's conclusion is necessarily false, therefore that its denial ("Some things we state are true") is necessarily true, hence that truth *is* possible in the English language. I begin by noting that Unger's statement (as well as the rest of *Ignorance*) is written in English. Assuming as I do that his statement ("What we state is never true") is false, it follows that its denial ("Some things we state are true"), which is also a statement in the English language, is true. But perhaps my assumption that his statement is false is wrong and Unger is correct. Then his concluding statement is true. But if it is, it becomes a true statement in the English language, hence, by itself being an example of such a thing, entails the truth of the statement "Some things we state are true." Since we have exhausted the possibilities (Unger's concluding statement being either false or true), we can conclude that the English statement "Some things we state are true" is necessarily true. Truth is not only a possibility for speakers of English but a *guaranteed* possibility.

Unger might try to answer the argument I have just offered by launching his attack on the possibility of truth in English in some other language. But he could not succeed for at least two reasons: (1) He would be forced, by the same kind of argument that we have just used, to acknowledge the existence of truth in whatever language he employed, hence could not claim the impossibility of truth as a basis for his epistemological skepticism; and (2) we could always, by hypothesis, formulate Unger's argument in English ourselves, and derive the results we have already reached. So we can say that, as a matter of logical necessity, "Some things we state are true," hence, since this is a true statement in English, that Unger's attack on English and, by implication, on its alleged ancestor language fails. Furthermore, the same results would follow for any other language Unger might try in a similar way to undermine. To the extent that Unger bases his epistemological skepticism on the impossibility of truth, he has no case. Finally, his claim that the reason why we can know nothing rests with deep and ancient deficiencies in our language can be shown equally to end in failure, for this claim and the specific arguments against the possibility of knowledge he has used in *Ignorance*, all being written in English, necessarily require for their cogency a viability of the language that his ancestor language hypothesis denies.

I have not offered this refutation of Unger's argument because I am an apologist for the English, or any other language. None is perfect; rather all suffer from deficiencies. But such an acknowledgment is a world away from Unger's attitude, in which the blame for skepticism is laid at the door of the language we use. This is simply not true. Whatever its shortcomings, English is *not* to blame for the skeptical conclusions about human knowledge and rationality which Unger reaches in *Ignorance*. Rather the responsibility rests with him, being a result more than anything else of his own misuse of our language.

VI   Essays in Skepticism

When I first began to write this book I had no intention to include the present chapter in it. I neither had an argument of my own for skepticism, nor did I think it would be necessary for me to offer one in this study. Instead, I assumed that I would find among the writings of the skeptics (particularly the contemporary ones) as strong a defense of the skeptical view as could be fashioned. Prolonged study of their works has, however, led me to revise my opinion. It is not so much that none of the arguments for skepticism I have considered has proved able to withstand critical examination; that is an eventuality that must be anticipated in respect to almost any philosophical theory. Rather, it is my conviction that the writers themselves have fallen short; that they have failed to make as persuasive a case for skepticism as the possibilities of the situation will permit. So in this chapter I shall attempt to make that case for them; I think I can do better than any skeptic has so far done. If what I have just written sounds presumptuous, that is, perhaps, because it is. Still I would be the first to acknowledge—what will soon become obvious— that if I am able to carry the argument for skepticism beyond the point that the contemporary skeptics have left it, my ability to do so will lie partly in the fact that I shall be launching my efforts from the theoretical shoulders of the writers whose views I have just been criticizing.

But from whose shoulders should I launch my essays into skepticism? The arguments for skepticism which I have reviewed and rejected are all quite different from each other.

Which of them shows most promise of being capable of extension in a way that will bring it to a successful conclusion? Pyrrhonism, whether in its ancient or contemporary formulation, can, I think, be eliminated, for as we have seen, the Pyrrhonists, in adopting the stance of suspension of judgment on all matters, succeed only in eliminating themselves from contention in the conflict between cognitivism and skepticism. Whether or not such a suspension can lead them to their desired end of peace of mind, it can contribute nothing to the resolution of the question of whether knowledge is possible. Turning to Unger's long and complex case for skepticism, I find it hard to make any comments beyond saying that I do not believe any acceptable theory—whether about knowledge or anything else—can be based on bad arguments. So we are left with Lehrer and his elaboration of the Cartesian evil-demon argument. Here I think we have grounds for hope, for the conclusion I reached in chapter iii that Lehrer failed to make his case did not turn on my discovery of any intrinsic weakness in his central argument but rather only of certain mistakes he made in his elaboration of it. Two, in particular, can be singled out: (1) his anthropomorphism and (2) his postulation of a series of higher-order deceivers. Both of these mistakes, it seems to me, can be fairly easily corrected. Freed from them, we may be able to develop a defensible case for skepticism. Let us at least see what can be done.

1   First Essay in Skepticism

Both shortcomings of Lehrer's skeptical hypothesis can be eliminated by the same simple device. Instead of postulating Googols as a race of beings who deceive us (and Googolplexes who deceive them, etc.), let us offer the following hypothesis: There are natural forces in the physical world of such a kind that their impingement on the human organism

175

(or any other organism that might be said to think) is such that our brain processes are distorted to the extent that most of our beliefs, although not necessarily all of them, are slightly in error. Everything we believe, thus, is false, or, if it is true, we are incapable of establishing it to be so. Hence we can know nothing. These natural forces I have postulated are not other beings with high-powered intellects; on the contrary, they are quite mindless. We do not know what they are; they might be characteristics of the air we breathe, or of the food we eat, or even of constituents of our own bodies—our blood or nervous system, etc.

The modified version of Lehrer's skeptical hypothesis which I have just offered—I shall refer to it hereafter as the *revised* skeptical hypothesis—is not meant, as it stands, to be a complete case for skepticism. To make such a case I would need to work out my hypothesis in greater detail. But my object here is limited to correcting the shortcomings of Lehrer's argument. If that can be done successfully, the elaboration of a full defense of skepticism based on my revised skeptical hypothesis would be the next task to be undertaken. Before contemplating such a move, however, we need to ask ourselves whether we have indeed overcome the deficiencies of Lehrer's case and whether, in doing so, we have presented a general line of argument in defense of skepticism which is capable of withstanding critical attack. As far as our first question is concerned, it seems to me that the revision I have offered is successful, for it eliminates by one simple move both of the weaknesses in Lehrer's argument. On the one hand, there is no problem of anthropomorphism—of our having to admit the existence of any type of thinking being, whether referred to as "man," "Googol," "Googolplex," or anything else, who knows something—because human minds are subverted not by the machinations of super-intellects but by unthinking natural forces. And on the other hand, the vicious regress in which Lehrer became trapped is avoided for exactly the same reason; there is no need to postulate ever higher orders of deceivers to subvert the minds of the forces of nature my hypothesis postulates, because these forces have no minds.

So we can conclude that my revised skeptical hypothesis does succeed in avoiding the pitfalls in which Lehrer's original hypothesis became entrapped. That leaves us with the second question we have posed: Can it itself withstand critical attack? Even though it is not vulnerable to the criticisms that destroyed Lehrer's hypothesis, does it not succumb to equally fatal objections? This is a much more difficult question to answer and will require a lengthy discussion. I turn to it next.

2 Evaluation of First Essay in Skepticism

A number of objections can be offered to my revised skeptical hypothesis. What I shall do in this section is to raise several of these, attempting to answer each one in turn and altering my hypothesis, if necessary, in order to do so. My object will be to determine whether any of these objections destroys the hypothesis or whether it can, in some formulation that is still skeptical, withstand all of them.

The first objection that might be raised is that the hypothesis (like Lehrer's Googol hypothesis on which it is based) is simply fanciful. Even if we admit that it is logically possible that our minds might be subverted by natural forces, we have no reason for thinking that this is actually the case. I have offered no evidence on behalf of such an extravagant assumption, and without any evidence to support it, the hypothesis can fairly be dismissed as gratuitous.

This objection can be answered in two different but related ways. In the first place it can be argued that we have no evidence that our minds are being subverted because the nature of the subversion is such that we are not aware of it. If we were aware of the distorting effects the actions of the natural forces had on our minds, we might be able to take steps to compensate for them. It is just because the forces distort our mental processes in a way that leads us to think that these processes are not being distorted that the distortion eludes our recognition and thus succeeds in continuing to cause us to be in error, even when we are convinced that what we believe is true.

But even if we grant that any such distortion, to remain effective, must escape our notice, the objector might reply that he has still been given no reason to think that it does in fact occur. Why should we entertain the hypothesis seriously? This question leads me to the second part of my answer, which will involve me in a brief excursion into autobiography. Many years ago I took a short course in typing, learning the correct "touch" method and undergoing some drill in speed typing. I did not, however, develop a great deal of typing skill. Since that time, I have done a good bit of typing, but only sporadically, so I have not been able to improve or even to maintain my modest skills. As a result, whenever I type I commit a number of errors. I have discovered also that there are correlations between the number of errors I make and certain external variables. For example, I do a worse job of typing if I am working to a deadline, or if I attempt to type early in the morning, or if I am typing philosophical copy, etcetera.

I am not qualified to discuss the detailed causes of mistakes of this sort (surely many scientific studies have been conducted on the subject), but it seems apparent that I am, and, I imagine, everyone else is, prone to similar kinds of error. All of us on occasion make mistakes, not just when we attempt to type but in everything we do. (Consider, for example, how many times the average person makes a mistake when he tries to add a column of numbers.) And although the errors we make are sometimes mainly mechanical and physical in nature—for instance, our fingers hit the wrong keys when we are typing—often they involve us in accepting mistaken beliefs as true. When we add a column of figures, for example, we sometimes believe that the result we obtain is the correct answer, only to obtain a different answer later when we compute the sum on an adding machine. There is no need to pursue further examples; I think it would be acknowledged that all of us are liable to error and that this liability very often results in our believing things that are false. Whatever the causes that lead us into error are and however they may be described in detail, it seems reasonable to conclude that among them are included conditions that might be described as psychological, physiological, and physical. That is to say, these causes are made up of natural forces, which seem to operate on us in such a way that we are led to embrace mistaken beliefs.

One further point must be added about the errors we make. Although we often discover and correct our mistakes, sometimes we do not and they pass unnoticed (perhaps later to be detected by someone else). But if they are never detected, we are never aware that they have been committed. Acknowledging the existence of noted errors in human thought and belief, it would be foolhardy to deny the existence of unnoted errors as well. Granted this much, the hypothesis that natural forces in our environment (including our own bodies) impinge on us not only in the ways that we recognize and attempt to compensate for but also in other ways that we never detect, with the result that most of our beliefs are slightly in error, even if it should not be true, is certainly far from fanciful. On the contrary, for all we now know this may well be happening.

Still, it could be argued, although it may be true that we are not aware of *all* the errors we make, this admission offers scant support for the skeptic. To substantiate his case, he must show that we never succeed either in detecting or in correcting *any* of the errors we make, because the possibility of our doing either of these things presupposes our possession of knowledge. In the first place, to detect an error requires that we identify it as an error; in other words, we must know it to be an error. And in the second place, to correct the error, we must know that the revision we make in our belief is true; otherwise it would not constitute a correction of the error. Now we have good reason, based on evidence, to believe that at least some of the mistakes we make are both detectable and correctable. For example, when I add a column of numbers and then check my computation by re-adding, sometimes I am able not only to correct an error I had made on my first attempt but also, through memory, to recognize the precise point in my original calculation where I had gone astray. Instances such as this are, I think, fairly common occurrences for most people, so need not be multiplied here. We can conclude, as a result, that on two counts we have strong evidence against my revised skeptical hypothesis. Because we can both detect and correct some of the mistakes we make, it cannot be the case that our beliefs are so tainted by forces of whose existence and actions we are not aware that we can never legitimately claim that something we believe is something we know as well.

Nevertheless, as skeptic, I must point out that this cognitivistic reply rests on an assumption: that we do, as we often believe we do, actually detect and correct errors we have made. Can this assumption be justified? To return to my example, although I sometimes believe that I am able to discover and correct an error I have made in addition by recalculating the sum, this is not always true. On occasion, particularly if the computation is involved or I am tired, I may do the same sum three or four times, obtaining a different answer on each occasion. Or I may do this and find that on the third (or fourth) recalculation I obtain the same answer I had gotten originally and had thought to be in error. If we agree that I am describing a situation most of us occasionally, even though not commonly, find ourselves in, I think we must proceed with great caution when we make claims about our ability to detect and correct errors we have made. The situation in which we find ourselves is not so simple as I first pictured it to be.

Granting the difficulties we are liable to encounter when we attempt to determine just what errors we may have made and what constitutes the truth about some particular question (e.g., addition), can we not, however, *sometimes* resolve this issue? Are there not at least some occasions on which we can legitimately claim that a certain answer to a question is true? And if so, are we not justified in concluding that we possess knowledge about the matter in question? To try to resolve this issue let us return to my revised skeptical hypothesis. If we assume that natural forces (of the kind I described earlier) do sometimes cause us to commit errors and that we even commit such errors when we believe we are detecting and correcting other errors we have committed, then may it not be the case that these same natural forces are at work, leading us astray at just those times when we believe most strongly that we are not in error but are apprehending the truth? If this is, as it seems to be, a possibility, then all of our beliefs become suspect. We simply cannot legitimately claim about any one of them that it is true and that we know it to be so.

But here a counterargument seems possible. There *must* be times when we are not in error, for we *cannot* always be in error. The argument in support of this contention is logical: If we are always in error, all of our beliefs are false. But if all of our beliefs are false, then the belief (or theory) that all of our beliefs are false is itself false. And if it is false, then some of our beliefs are true. If, conversely, it is true, it cannot be the case that all of our beliefs are false, for at least one of our beliefs must be true. (Actually more than one must be true because the truth of one entails the truth of others.)

That some of our beliefs must be true I think cannot be denied. But my revised skeptical hypothesis does not deny it. Rather it holds only that most, but not all, of our beliefs are false. So it can escape the counterargument I have just offered. But, it might now be asked, doesn't the concession that some of our beliefs are true itself undercut my revised skeptical hypothesis? Must not the hypothesis, if it is to provide a support for epistemological skepticism, hold that none of our beliefs is true? The answer to this objection lies in the distinction between truth and knowledge. For a person to know something, it is not enough that some belief he holds be true. In addition he must be able to establish its truth. And it is this additional requirement about our beliefs that my hypothesis rules out, for although we believe many things and some of our beliefs are true, we can never isolate a *specific* belief and legitimately claim it to be one of those that is true because it may be a belief that has been distorted by the natural forces the hypothesis postulates. Hence, although we possess true beliefs, none of these constitutes something we can legitimately claim to know.

Still, it might be argued in return, although we must concede that we can never be sure that some particular belief we hold is true, this concession is only partial. Granting that natural forces can distort certain kinds of beliefs (e.g., beliefs based on sense perception or memory), they cannot distort other kinds of beliefs, for certain kinds of beliefs are immune from error. But what kinds are these? This is a question that epistemologists have wrangled over for centuries, with inconclusive results. An obvious candidate for the status of a belief immune from error would be a simple proposition of mathematics, like $2 + 2 = 4$. However, it is a central tenet of my revised skeptical hypothesis that beliefs like these are *not* immune from error, for this hypothesis is an elaboration (via Lehrer) of the Cartesian evil-demon argument, which was formulated by Descartes for the primary purpose of undercutting our knowledge pretensions in the realm of mathematics. If the natural forces I have postulated do subvert our minds, we cannot eliminate certain areas of belief from the compass of their distorting actions, claiming these to be immune from error. Rather, we must offer some grounds for the claim of incorrigibility we make for them. That our attempts to do so could not overcome the objection implicit in my revised skeptical hypothesis has been apparent ever since Descartes's evil demon first appeared on the philosophical scene.

Perhaps, then, we might follow Descartes himself and restrict the realm of incorrigible beliefs to those that we "clearly and distinctly" recognize to be true, claiming that it is impossible we should be misled in regard to such beliefs. If we were to do so, however, we should soon find ourselves enmeshed in problems. In particular, it is doubtful that we could ever formulate an unexceptionable criterion of either clarity or distinctness. Even if we should succeed in conquering that problem, we would be faced with yet another. May it not be possible that the natural forces at work on us operate in such a manner that some (or even all) of the beliefs we clearly and distinctly recognize to be true are nevertheless false and that the clarity and distinctness we experience in respect to those beliefs are themselves a consequence of the distorting actions of the forces at work?

Perhaps we could overcome this difficulty by considering some of the specific beliefs put forward by recent epistemologists as "incorrigible," for example, the belief that I am now experiencing a pain, or as some writers, in order to avoid any possibility of error, sometimes put it "pain-here-now." I shall not spend much time here on this kind of example and the numerous problems it raises, not because these are unimportant, but because they have already been thoroughly canvassed in the literature.[1] The results of the discussions are, I think, decisive against those who claim the incorrigibility of any empirical belief, even one concerned with an immediately experienced simple sensation. Two related objections can be raised against the claim that we can count such beliefs as things we know, on the grounds that they are incorrigible. The first of these is offered by Lehrer and is to the effect that we *can* be in error about even such simple, apparently apparent beliefs. "One might believe one is having a sensation S, a pain for example, because one is having a different sensation, S*, an itch for example, and one has mistaken S* for S, that is one has mistaken an itch for a pain."² The mistake may lie, in other words, in one's direct misrecognition of the sensation he is experiencing. In addition, it can be argued that the reason given for the claim of incorrigibility regarding such beliefs—that they are direct reports of the contents of consciousness (so-called first-person reports), hence cannot be wrong—is mistaken, for these beliefs are not direct reports but are always the result of inferences. For example, when we believe ourselves to be experiencing a pain, in our belief we are categorizing our feeling by placing it within the class "pain." This categorization, which is necessary to our thinking of pains and hence of believing that we are feeling one, is not given to us in sensation. Sensations do not come to us with the label "pain" attached to them. To think pain, it is necessary to perform an inference beyond the "given" of sensation. And our inferences are corrigible.

Viewed from the side of the skeptic, the fatal defect of all attempts to base our claims to know on the alleged incorrigibility of first-person reports of the present contents of consciousness can be summed up in the following way: When it is argued that beliefs of this kind are incorrigible, it cannot be implied that error in such beliefs is a logical impossibility, for the logical possibility of their being wrong always exists. As a consequence, no matter how incorrigible such beliefs may appear to be, the skeptic can still raise the specter of error, a specter that the cognitivist can in no way exorcise. It just *may* be that even at this simple level we are deluded into believing something to be the case which in fact is not the case, our delusion resulting from the actions of natural forces, outside of us and unknown to us, which operate on us to cause our sensations and the inferences we make from them to be distorted.

To justify our knowledge claims the cognitivist must, I

think, find some foundation for them more solid than first-person reports, with their alleged incorrigibility. What he must seek is some guarantee of their truth into which the skeptic cannot insert his wedge of doubt. Once the issue is formulated in these terms, the cognitivist's next move becomes obvious: He must produce beliefs whose truth is logically necessary. Such beliefs would be strictly indubitable, for it would be logically impossible that in believing them we should be mistaken. But are there any such beliefs? One example comes quickly to mind; indeed, we have encountered it before, in chapter iii in our discussion of Lehrer's case for skepticism.[3] This is our belief that we believe something. The argument that such a belief is necessarily true—which Lehrer, I think rightly, accepts—runs as follows: If I believe that I believe something, I cannot be mistaken in my first belief, because to suppose that I am mistaken is to embrace a contradiction to the effect that, even though I believe that I believe something, I still do not believe anything. Granting all this, however, Lehrer (as we found in chapter iii) refuses to concede that such a belief constitutes something we can legitimately claim to know, for the logical impossibility that a belief be in error, although it is a necessary condition the belief must fulfil in order to qualify as something we know, is not in itself a sufficient condition. Something more is needed; namely, we must *know* that the belief is one that (logically) cannot be in error. To repeat Lehrer's own summation of the case about beliefs of this kind:

> For, even if we agree that it is logically impossible for certain contingent beliefs to be mistaken, still it does not follow that we *know* that it is logically impossible for those beliefs to be mistaken, and, hence it does not follow that we know that the beliefs are true. A sceptic may contend that we do not *know* that anything is logically impossible however strongly convinced we may be. And he may conclude that we do not know that those beliefs

are true even where the logical possibility of error is excluded, because we do not know that the logical possibility of error is excluded.[4]

The crux of the skeptic's argument lies in the last two sentences of Lehrer's statement. To put these in the context of my revised skeptical hypothesis, we may well agree that some of our beliefs are logically incorrigible; but we have to recognize that, because of the actions of the natural forces impinging on us, we may well be misled into the conviction that a certain belief we hold is true and necessarily so when in fact it is false. Furthermore, we can *never* detect such spurious beliefs that masquerade as logically necessary truths, separating them from other beliefs that are genuine logically necessary truths, because our minds are so subject to distortion that we are incapable of distinguishing the one from the other beyond any shadow of doubt. As a result, the appeal to logical demonstration is of no more help to the cognitivist in his battle against the skeptic than the appeal to the incorrigibility of first-person reports. If our minds are so liable to distortion that we cannot know that a logically necessary proposiiton is logically necessary, we can never legitimately claim that a demonstration demonstrates.

What then remains for the cognitivist to say? If his appeal to logic has been undercut, to what else can he turn? Before abandoning him to his fate, I think I must attempt to come to his aid at least once more. So let us, on behalf of the cognitivist, try to mount a counterattack. Would it not be in order for him to remind the skeptic that his entire argument supporting the denial of the existence of knowledge itself rests on a hypothesis; namely, that our minds *are* distorted by natural forces to such an extent that we cannot place any confidence in our claims to know anything, including even logically necessary truths? The skeptic's case, the cognitivist might then continue, is only as good as this hypothesis. What reason, he might ask the skeptic, do we have for believing the hypothesis to be true?

Earlier in this section I offered reasons, based on our acknowledged proneness to error in what we believe, for taking my revised skeptical hypothesis seriously. But in that discussion I noted a peculiarity about the kind of error which the hypothesis postulates; namely, that it is unrecognized error. This curious fact about it gives rise to a problem: Does it really exist? More to the point, what reasons can anyone offer for asserting that it exists? If none is forthcoming, perhaps we may consider ourselves free to dismiss the hypothesis as gratuitous. It would appear that from the nature of the case, the skeptic can provide no evidence for the existence of the mental distortion he postulates. Certainly neither Lehrer nor I have attempted to provide any. But is it really necessary that we do so? For our skeptical purposes, is it necessary for us to show that the distortion in question is in fact occurring or only that it *may be* occurring? The latter is, I believe, sufficient, for the cognitivist, to legitimate his claim to know something, must establish that what he believes is true. But if it is possible that his mind is being constantly subverted, then it is possible that none of the reasons he offers in support of his claim to know is in fact cogent. The problem for the cognitivist can be put in this way: Because he makes a claim—that we can know things—he must assume the burden of proof in substantiating his claim. And he cannot successfully shoulder that burden if the possibility remains that every belief he holds, and every reason he gives in support of his beliefs, is in error. As a result, his options are reduced to one. In order to make his case, he must foreclose the possibility that we are always in error in what we believe (or that even though sometimes we are not in error we cannot distinguish when this is so). He must show, in other words, that we (logically) cannot be in error about at least some of our beliefs. Furthermore, he must be able to identify beliefs about which we cannot be in error. To accomplish these results he must establish that natural forces *cannot* subvert our minds about these beliefs in the way required by my revised skeptical hypothesis. If he can do this—but only if he can—he will be justified in concluding that my hypothesis postulates an impossibility so cannot provide the skeptic with an *additional* weapon capable of undercutting his claim to know once he has succeeded in demonstrating the truth of what he believes. Can the cognitivist do this?

To begin to answer the question I have just formulated, let us try to describe the situation in which we are all placed, according to my revised skeptical hypothesis. We believe many things for a variety of reasons, but one of the reasons we can give for believing certain things is that we have demonstrated these things to be logically necessary. So we claim to know them. For this claim to be justified, however, the beliefs in question must be true. Yet they may not be true, because in accepting them as true we may be led astray by the actions of the natural forces. Although we have demonstrated them to be logically necessary they may still be false.

Let us apply these considerations to some proposition p.[5] I have demonstrated p to be logically necessary. Nevertheless, although p may be true, it may also be false. (I may have been led astray in my demonstration by the actions of the natural forces.) If p is true, I can legitimately claim to know p, for it is a true belief, whose truth I have established by logical demonstration. If on the contrary p is false, I cannot legitimately claim to know it. However, if p is false, its denial, $\sim p$, is true. But since p is a proposition that has been demonstrated to be logically necessary, it follows that $\sim p$ is logically self-contradictory (or entails a logical contradiction). Since a logically self-contradictory proposition entails its own denial, $\sim p$ entails p. So, on the assumption that p, which I have demonstrated to be logically necessary, is false, it follows logically that p is true. In other words, it cannot be false. Because it is a proposition I have demonstrated to be logically necessary, *p must* be true and *cannot* be false. The possibility that in accepting it as true, I am the victim of the distorting effects of natural forces is *completely* precluded. So I can safely assert that *p* escapes being a victim of my revised skeptical hypothesis and that I can, therefore, legitimately claim it to be something I know.

If the argument I have just offered is cogent—and, according to the standard criteria of logical demonstration, it is—my revised skeptical hypothesis does not make it impossible for anyone to know anything. If a person can demonstrate a proposition to be logically necessary, then he can claim it as something he knows, because he has established that it cannot be false, hence cannot be one that he mistakenly believes to be true because his mind is being subverted by the natural forces I have postulated. To defend my revised skeptical hypothesis, therefore, I must demolish this counterargument. In attempting to do so, I shall take two different tacks. (1) I shall contend that the counterargument is conditional. It rests for its success on the actual production of a proposition that can be demonstrated to be necessarily true. I (as skeptic) shall therefore challenge myself (as cognitivist) to produce such a proposition. (2) I shall maintain that the counterargument begs the question against the skeptic as well. I have assumed it to be cogent because I have demonstrated its conclusion to be true by an appeal to logical criteria. But if all our minds, mine included, are subverted by natural forces, I cannot put any trust in my logical demonstrations. Nor can anyone else. To consider my conclusion established, therefore, is to assume that in the reasoning I used to reach it, my mind was functioning in a distortion-free manner. But to assume this is to beg the question against my revised skeptical hypothesis. I shall consider each of these skeptical responses in turn.

First, can I meet my own skeptical challenge by actually producing a proposition I know to be true because I can demonstrate that it is logically necessary so must be true? Let me take as an example a proposition that (as a nonphilosopher) I believe to be true and would like to claim as something that I really know to be true: "Some of my beliefs are true." (Again, I shall call this *p*). This proposition might be objected to as a poor example, on the grounds that, as skeptic, I have not denied *p*; for, according to my revised skeptical hypothesis, although most human beliefs are false, some may well be true. In reply to this objection, I should point out that, according to my revised skeptical hypothesis, it may be the case for all we know that every one of our beliefs (rather than merely most of them) is false. After all, if natural forces distort our minds, why might they not do it all the time rather than only most of the time? But, more important, the hypothesis asserts that no one can legitimately claim of any *specific* belief he holds that it is something he knows; for *it* may be false and his mind simply subverted into believing it true. Now *p* is a *specific* belief that I hold; so, if I can demonstrate that *p* is true, I shall have met my skeptical challenge by producing a counterexample to my own revised skeptical hypothesis.

To go about my attempt to demonstrate that *p* is true, hence something I know, I shall begin the argument from the skeptical side. According to my revised skeptical hypothesis, the reason why I cannot know *p* is that natural forces subvert most of my beliefs, including, probably, *p*. And if *p* is among my subverted beliefs, I cannot know *p*, because *p* is false. But here a peculiar point about *p* must be taken into consideration. If only *some* of my beliefs are subverted, *p* is true, because it asserts that some of my beliefs are true (i.e., those that are not subverted).[6] If, then, I can establish that less than all of my beliefs are subverted, I can refute my revised skeptical hypothesis. To establish this, it is necessary to note that if all of my beliefs are subverted, then none of them is true. The proposition "None of my beliefs is true" is the denial of *p*, or ~*p*. I can conclude that *p* is true, then, if I can demonstrate that ~*p* is false. Since my skeptical conclusion—that no one can know anything—rests on the hypothesis that our beliefs are subverted by natural forces, I can refute that conclusion if I can show that these forces cannot subvert all of our beliefs, that is, that the proposition "All of our beliefs are subverted by natural forces" must be false, for if this proposition is false, the proposition "None of our beliefs is true" ($\sim p$) can be concluded to be false as well, because its alleged truth depends on the subversion of our minds. So we can ask: Can natural forces subvert all of our beliefs, so that none of our beliefs is true? As skeptic, I have found myself committed to the proposition (which for purposes of the argument can be viewed as a belief I hold) that no one can know anything because all of our beliefs can be subverted by natural forces. Now, even though I am a skeptic, I still believe something (i.e., what I have just asserted). As a believer (even though also a skeptic) I am as much a victim of natural forces as is anyone else. So I have to ask myself: Considering my belief that natural forces can subvert all human beliefs, is this belief one that is in error because my mind has been subverted or is it not? It would seem that it has to be in error because, like all other beliefs, it is subverted. But if it is in error, it is false, so its denial; namely, "It is not the case that natural forces can subvert all human beliefs" must be true. And if natural forces cannot subvert all human beliefs, it follows that at least some beliefs are true. If, however, I should claim that my belief about the subversion of human beliefs is not itself subverted, it would follow that it is true. If *it* is true, then *p* is true, because *it* itself offers an example of a belief that is true. To sum up, we can conclude that, on the assumption that natural forces subvert all human beliefs, some beliefs are true, and, on the assumption that natural forces do not subvert all human beliefs, some beliefs are true. But these forces must either subvert or not subvert. So in any case we can conclude that some human beliefs are true. We can conclude this because we have demonstrated it to be necessarily true. And if it is necessarily true that some human beliefs are true, then my belief as a skeptic that natural forces can subvert all

191

human beliefs must be false. If my belief as skeptic must be false, my denial of that belief, as cognitivist, must be true. That is, my belief that natural forces cannot subvert all human beliefs must be true. But if this belief (which is one that I as a cognitivist hold) must be true, then we can conclude that p must be true, for if one of my beliefs must be true, it follows necessarily that the proposition "Some of my beliefs are true" (which is p) is true.

But, as skeptic, I think I may see a way out of this predicament. The whole argument I have just offered turns on my making the skeptic himself (myself) one of the victims of natural forces. More specifically, it assumes that my revised skeptical hypothesis itself may be tainted with error. But is this not an allowable assumption? If, as the hypothesis asserts, the minds of all of us are distorted and these distortions may, for all we know, subvert *any* of our beliefs, must we not acknowledge that, in believing that natural forces are at work subverting all of our beliefs, the skeptic may well be in error, because his mind is, in just this case, being distorted by the forces in question? In other words, there seems to be no good reason why my revised skeptical hypothesis might not be revised to read: There are natural forces in the environment at work distorting our minds, but these forces are very selective in their actions. The only belief that gets distorted, so is in error, is the belief that some of us sometimes have that natural forces are at work subverting all human beliefs.

To escape the logical entanglements that I have gone through above, which end in the destruction of my revised skeptical hypothesis, I believe I have only one move left open to me at this stage of the argument. I must insist that my revised skeptical hypothesis itself is exempt from the possibility of error. But this move has the following consequence: If the hypothesis itself is exempt from the possibility of error, then it is demonstrably true. And if it is demonstrably true, I can conclude that p (which its truth entails) is true as well. Hence

I can legitimately claim to know that some of my beliefs are true. Thus I become a knower. And since I have exempted only my revised skeptical hypothesis from the possibility of error, I must conclude that, even though no one else can know anything, I, because I am a skeptic, possess knowledge. But since I am also a human being, my possession of knowledge destroys skepticism in favor of cognitivism. Furthermore, I have no grounds for being so exclusive. If I can accept my revised skeptical hypothesis and thus become a knower, so can anyone else. To demonstrate that he knows something all one need do is to become a Johnsonian skeptic!

From my skeptical point of view, the argument has clearly gotten completely out of hand. I have been trapped in logical contradictions with every move that I have made. Must I, as a result, acknowledge that my revised skeptical hypothesis is untenable? Before doing so let me try one further counter-argument. If we go back through the discussion in which we have been engaged, we shall see that the skeptic has been led into contradiction because he is held to *believe* my revised skeptical hypothesis. By making this assumption we have been able to demonstrate the truth of the proposition that some human beliefs are true and hence that this proposition can count as something we know. Might I not, as skeptic, reject this assumption, arguing, say, that I do not know whether I believe my revised skeptical hypothesis or not, therefore that the question of my beliefs can be disregarded? By making this move perhaps I could undercut the entire cognitivistic case that I have been developing over the last several pages. Let us see if such a move could work.

As skeptic I offer (but *not* as anything I believe) the following proposition: "Most human beliefs are false" (because subverted by natural forces). If this proposition is true, no one can legitimately claim to know anything because whatever belief he claims as knowledge will probably fall into the class of those that are subverted, so will be false and thus incapable of constituting something he knows. (And even if it does not fall into this class, he has no way of showing that it does not.) However, since the proposition I offer is not something I claim to believe myself, the cognitivist cannot employ the self-reference argument against me and force me into a contradiction. Can I not by this device succeed in guarding myself against any cognitivistic counterattack?

Turning to the other side, let me resume the mantle of cognitivist and respond by asking this question: Is the proposition that the skeptic has offered; namely, "Most human beliefs are false," really true? And if it is true, does it not follow that the proposition: "Some human beliefs are true" is true as well? As I ponder these questions I am of mixed mind about them. The first, in particular, perplexes me. Sometimes I feel skeptical about human beliefs and am led to believe that most human beliefs are indeed false. At other times I am more optimistic and believe that many (perhaps even most) human beliefs are true. Now both of these beliefs, which can be more formally stated as the belief (a) "Most human beliefs are false" and the belief (b) "It is not true that most human beliefs are false," are beliefs that the skeptic (whether *he* believes them himself or not) must admit that *I* can have. Having granted, in the statement of his hypothesis, that humans believe things, he cannot preclude me from acknowledging that I believe either (a) or (b), or (a) sometimes and (b) other times. Having argued that I have some belief about the relative truth and falsity of human beliefs, if he claims that I cannot legitimately assert that I believe (a) because my belief that I believe (a) is false, then it follows that I believe (b), and if he claims that I cannot legitimately assert that I believe (b) because my belief that I believe (b) is false, then it follows that I believe (a). Suppose, then, I believe (a) and then change my mind and believe (b). One of these two beliefs *must* be true (and the other false), and I can demonstrate that this is so. Hence I can demonstrate that the proposition "Some human beliefs are true" is true, since either my belief that (a) is true or my belief that (b) is true must be true. But if I can demonstrate that the proposition "Some human beliefs are true" must be true, I am free to believe it and can, furthermore, legitimately claim it as something I know. Therefore skepticism is proved false.

But at this point I might take up the skeptical stance again and object, pointing out that my revised skeptical hypothesis does not deny the truth of the proposition "Some human beliefs are true." This is granted; however it doesn't follow that anyone knows anything because no one can point to a *specific* belief and assert "That belief is true and I know it to be so." Although this reply may have an initial plausibility, it is specious. I *can* point to a specific belief that I hold; namely, my belief that some human beliefs are true, and legitimately claim it to be something I know on the grounds that I have demonstrated its truth. I believe this; I know it to be true; and I can generate further beliefs from it which I know to be true (because they are entailed by it); for example, the belief that some human beliefs are false (since this is entailed by the falsity of the belief that no human beliefs are true which falsity in turn is entailed by the truth of the belief that some human beliefs are true).

I might go on, trying other skeptical stratagems, but to do so would, I am convinced, be a waste of time, for ultimately they would all succumb to logically conclusive refutation. However formulated, my revised skeptical hypothesis (like Lehrer's original hypothesis) can be driven into contradiction. On logical grounds alone, the cognitivistic thesis that knowledge exists always emerges the victor in a contest with skepticism.

But we are still not done with my revised skeptical hypothesis. Every argument we have used to this point rests on logical considerations. It is the weapon of logic which the cognitivist has wielded that has ensured his destruction of my skeptical case. But might we not claim that, in his appeal to logic, the cognitivist is begging the question against my revised skeptical hypothesis? This leads me to the second of my two replies to cognitivism which I noted at the beginning of the argument.[7] The reply (to repeat) is this: The cognitivist has destroyed my revised skeptical hypothesis by the use of logical arguments, but to judge these arguments conclusive, we must assume that our minds are capable of thinking cogently to the point of recognizing and employing such logical devices as entailments, contradictions, etc. But if our minds are, as my hypothesis asserts, subverted, we cannot be sure that what we take to be logical reasoning leading to definitive conclusions is cogent at all. Our thought processes may, on the contrary, be distorted and our reasoning specious. Thus, to assume, as I have done in the discussions we have just been going through, that the logically conclusive arguments I have presented against the skeptic succeed in refuting skepticism is to beg the crucial question against the hypothesis.

Can my revised skeptical hypothesis be defended on these grounds? The hypothesis, it must be remembered, asserts that no one knows anything because our minds are all subverted by natural forces. Two points can be made about this hypothesis: First, it offers an argument, which can be formally stated in the following deductive terms:

Beings whose minds are subverted (by natural forces) know nothing.
We are beings whose minds are subverted.
Therefore, we know nothing.

Second, it implies that cognitivism is false because it asserts that we know things, which is a thesis incompatible with its own conclusion that we know nothing. On the basis of these two points we can conclude that my revised skeptical hypothesis, as an argument for skepticism, makes at least the following two assumptions: (1) that deductive reasoning can be employed to yield arguments that are cogent and (2) that propositions inconsistent with each other cannot both be true. Both of these are assumptions about logic and logical reasoning. Hence in my very attempt to make my case for skepticism through employment of my revised skeptical hypothesis, I beg the question against myself as much, and in the same way, as I have accused my cognitivistic opponent of doing. But if I have to beg the question against myself in order to state my case, I can hardly hold it as a charge against him that he does so as well. Rather, I must admit that in such a situation there is no question to be begged.

Only one move remains open for the skeptic at this point. If he refuses to abide by an argument that refutes his case, on the grounds that its appeal to logic is question-begging, he must go all the way himself and abandon the use of logic altogether. For he cannot attack his opponent for arguing logically and at the same time base his own case on logical criteria; he cannot have his cake and eat it too. So let us suppose the skeptic does take the final step and abandons logic. What then? He is immediately faced with this problem: How can he even articulate his skeptical thesis as a position inconsistent with cognitivism? Suppose the cognitivist says "Someone knows something" and the skeptic replies "No one knows anything." The cognitivist can recognize that these propositions are inconsistent with each other. But can the logic-dropping skeptic? Let us for the sake of argument allow that he can. To substantiate his skepticism, he must further maintain that these two inconsistent theses *cannot* both be true, for if they could both be true, he has failed either to refute the cognitivist or to offer a real alternative to his cognitivism. To make his case for skepticism, as a view regarding knowledge incompatible with cognitivism, a view whose truth renders cognitivism false, he must appeal to the law of noncontradiction. However, there is no way for him to give up this appeal and still articulate a distinctive thesis incompatible with cognitivism. Once he accepts, as he must, the law of noncontradiction, he must accept the consequences that applications of the law bring when they are turned against his theory and the arguments he uses to support it. Because it is impossible for either side to be a side—to articulate let alone defend a theory —without making an appeal to logic and accepting its laws, the skeptic can have no grounds whatsoever for his claim that the cognitivist is begging the question against him when he employs logic to destroy the skeptic's case.

To sum up my first essay in skepticism, I am forced to conclude that my revised skeptical hypothesis is a failure. Although it carries the case for skepticism well beyond the point Lehrer left it with his skeptical hypothesis and, I think, succeeds in avoiding the traps into which that hypothesis fell, it comes to crash on the rocks of logic. It is simply logically untenable and can be shown to be so. Since there is absolutely no escape from logic, its logical refutation entails its destruction.

3 Second Essay in Skepticism

I think the failure of my revised skeptical hypothesis can teach us a lesson from which, as skeptics, we may be able to reap profit. The basic error of my hypothesis—one that is shared by most classical forms of skepticism with the notable exception of Pyrrhonism—is that it attempts to *establish* the skeptical conclusion that knowledge is impossible. In doing so, however, it becomes enmeshed in logical contradictions. The reasons for its self-destruction lie in the nature of the claims it makes. In the first place, in putting forward the theory that knowledge is impossible, the skeptic commits himself to a truth claim; he implies that what the theory states (namely, that no one can know anything) is the case. If he were not to make (or imply) the claim that his theory is true, he could not offer it as an explanation of its subject matter. To say "I advance the theory that knowledge is impossible but I do not claim this theory to be true" is not really to advance any theory about the existence of knowledge at all. But in the second place, he goes further, and it is this additional step he takes which is the direct source of his logical problems. He attempts to offer reasons that establish the truth of his skeptical theory. (A perusal of the first two sections of this chapter will show that this is what I have attempted to do with my revised skeptical hypothesis, particularly by my appeal to "natural forces.") Now a proposition (or belief) which is true and is supported by reasons that establish its truth is an item of knowledge. Hence the theorist who claims that his theory is true and that he can offer reasons that will establish it to be true is committing himself to a knowledge claim; he is implying that he *knows* the theory to be true. And that is precisely what I and most other skeptics have done, with the result, to put it bluntly, that we have claimed (usually implicitly but none the less definitely) to know that knowledge is impossible. Our skepticism has proved too rich for our epistemological blood.

Once we recognize that we are lost as skeptics whenever we argue in a way that involves us in making a knowledge claim, we should strive to be much more self-conscious about our own skeptical stance. It should become obvious to us that a skeptic, if he is to succeed, must be wary rather than bold; for the great danger in skepticism is its seemingly fatal tendency to overreach itself. Warned, is there anything we can do? The apparent direction in which we should move is to mute our skeptical thesis, presenting and defending it in such a way that we are never led to claim, either directly or by implication, that anyone knows anything. This will be the strategy I shall employ in my second essay in skepticism.

So let us try to reformulate the skeptical thesis along more conservative lines. Suppose I were to say: "I believe that no one knows anything. I certainly do not claim or even imply that I know this to be so. I readily recognize that if I were to make such an additional claim it would either render my belief irrational or me a liar, for it is clearly inconsistent to assert both that one knows something and at the same time believes that he knows nothing. So I am not at all dogmatic

199

about my skeptical thesis; rather I advance it tentatively, simply as a hypothesis. Since I do not claim to know that my hypothesis is true, claiming only to believe it to be so, I can escape the logical objections that have plagued traditional types of skepticism."

To distinguish the moderated, tentative view I have just stated from standard or "dogmatic"[8] forms of skepticism, I shall refer to it as "nondogmatic" skepticism. Does it offer a formulation of the skeptical case that is theoretically viable? This is what we must now attempt to determine.[9]

4   Evaluation of Second Essay in Skepticism

Before we begin our examination of my second essay in skepticism, we need to be more clear about just what the nondogmatic skeptic is saying and how his stance differs from that of the dogmatic skeptic, for his claim not to be dogmatic may conceal a problem. To clarify this point we might ask: Why should we label the skeptic who (implicitly) claims to know that knowledge is impossible a dogmatist? To conclude that his dogmatism is a consequence *simply* of his claim to know (i.e., that *anyone* who makes a knowledge claim is a dogmatist) would be question-begging. If one can offer reasons on behalf of a claim to know and these reasons either support or establish the truth of the claim, the charge of dogmatism is illegitimate. But this, of course, the dogmatic skeptic cannot do. So we can conclude that the dogmatic skeptic *is* dogmatic, for two reasons((1) He makes a knowledge claim and (2) this claim is unsupportable; he can provide no reasons on its behalf. Although the first reason alone is not enough to justify the charge of dogmatism, the two reasons together clearly do so.

One difference between dogmatic and nondogmatic skepticism is immediately apparent. The nondogmatic skeptic does not claim to know that knowledge is impossible, hence cannot be charged with dogmatism on the grounds that he makes an unsupported *knowledge* claim. Yet he still might be charged with dogmatism, but for a somewhat different reason. Although he does not claim to know that knowledge is impossible, he believes this to be true. And such a belief claim can be dogmatic. It is so, in the same way that the stronger knowledge claim is dogmatic, *unless* and *until* the believer can provide some reason in its support.[10] In order to resolve the issue of whether nondogmatic skepticism succeeds in its effort to escape dogmatism, therefore, we need to answer the question: Can the nondogmatic skeptic offer any reasons in support of his belief that knowledge is impossible?

Before turning directly to this question, I should like to make a preliminary clarification by couching our problem in a slightly different context. The nondogmatic skeptic tells us he believes knowledge to be impossible. I think we must grant him this belief in the sense that we must admit the human mind's ability to believe anything. No absurdity is so patent that someone, somewhere, at some time has not sincerely believed it to be true. Without begging the question of either the absurdity or the reasonability of the (nondogmatic) skeptic's[11] belief in the impossibility of knowledge, the point that needs to be made is that the *existence* of his belief is irrelevant to the issue we are trying to resolve. What we are concerned with is not the *fact* that the skeptic believes what he does but rather with the question of whether his belief can be given any support. Is it a *reasonable* belief or is it not? If it is reasonable, because it can be supported, nondogmatic skepticism can, I think, be offered as a viable alternative to cognitivism. If it is not reasonable, because it cannot be supported, it is irrational and, for that reason, a dogmatic belief. It is comparable to the fideist's faith. As such it offers no alternative to cognitivism, so can legitimately be rejected.

The skeptic says "I believe that knowledge is impossible." I have just argued that such a belief must be judged irrational, hence dogmatic, unless and until the skeptic can support it by reasons. The requirement I have laid down, although it is one in which we should all acquiesce, seems hardly of a nature to cause the skeptic serious concern. Of course he can give reasons to support his skeptical belief, any number of reasons. Before we attempt to list some of the reasons he might offer, perhaps we should pause a moment to clarify the notion of a reason. An example might help here. Suppose someone were to say "I believe that Bormann is alive." Simply as asserted, such a statement is completely gratuitous. If the person's belief is to be considered reasonable, rather than dogmatic (or an article of faith), he must be able to support it with reasons. Suppose he does so by adding "My reason for believing that Bormann is alive is that his body has never been found." What conditions must the proposition "His body has never been found" satisfy before it can constitute a reason that anyone could give in support of his belief that Bormann is alive? Two, at least, seem necessary. First, what the putative reason asserts must be true. One cannot reasonably say "I believe that Bormann is alive. My belief is reasonable because it is based on the fact that his body has never been found. However, his body has been found." But the truth of the reason is not enough. Another condition must also be met. Let us suppose it to be true that Bormann's body has never been found. However, the person who offers this fact as a reason to support his belief that Bormann is alive has no reason for believing it to be a fact. If someone were to ask him "Why do you believe that Bormann's body has not been found?" he would have to reply "I have no reason for believing it; I just do." Under these conditions the person's belief that Bormann's body has not been found (even though it is true) cannot constitute a *reason* that he can legitimately offer in support of his belief that Bormann is alive. It cannot be a reason because it itself is unreasonable (i.e., he believes it without reason). Hence his original belief that Bormann is alive remains as unreasonable, hence as dogmatic, after he has offered such a "reason" in its support as it was before he did so. To use the claim that his body has never been found as a reason capable of supporting his belief in Bormann's continued existence, he must either know that the claim is true or at the very least be able to provide some reason for believing it to be true. Until one or the other is accomplished, the belief itself (that Bormann's body has not been found), as well as the original belief it was intended to support (that Bormann is alive), remains dogmatic and irrational.

We are now ready to return to the nondogmatic skeptic and the many reasons he might offer in support of his belief that knowledge is impossible. That the putative reasons are many is indisputable. He might, for example, offer one or more of the following: "Many things people claim to know are false." "People claim to know propositions that are logically incompatible with each other." "The human mind is subverted." Etc. Indeed, the nondogmatic skeptic can offer the same reasons for *believing* knowledge to be impossible which the dogmatic skeptic can for claiming to *know* it to be impossible. But, as our example with Bormann illustrates, the crucial question that must be resolved is this: Are the "reasons" he can offer really *reasons?* Only if they are can his belief in the impossibility of knowledge be legitimized as a reasonable belief rather than discarded as an item of irrational faith, dogmatically or fideistically held.

Let us select a "reason" a skeptic might offer to support his belief in the impossibility of knowledge—any will serve our purpose—and examine its credentials as a reason. Suppose the skeptic were to say "I believe that knowledge is impossible because at least some of the things we claim to know are false." For his "reason" to qualify as a reason supporting his belief, it must be true that some knowledge claims are false; he could not use the claim that some of our knowledge claims are false as a reason in support of *any* conclusion if none of our knowledge claims is in fact false. But the truth of his claim about the falsity of some of our knowledge claims is not enough to qualify it as a reason available for the skeptic's use; he must be able to justify his using it. Otherwise it remains dogmatic. If he could say "I *know* that some of our knowledge claims are false," he could then offer the falsity of these claims as a reason supporting his skeptical belief about knowledge. But obviously no skeptic can claim to know that some of our knowledge claims are false, because to claim to know *anything* is to repudiate his skepticism. He would find himself maintaining "I believe I know nothing (knowledge being impossible), but I do know thus and so."

Granting that the skeptic cannot know that some of our knowledge claims are false, he can (consistently with his skepticism) at least believe this to be so. However, he cannot use this belief as a reason supporting his skepticism unless the belief itself is reasonable. He cannot argue: "I believe knowledge to be impossible because some of our knowledge claims are false, but I have no reason to believe that any are false." *Until* he can show his belief in the falsity of some of our knowledge claims to be reasonable, it remains dogmatic and, as such, cannot qualify as a reason supporting anything. So the skeptic, if he is to qualify his belief that some of our knowledge claims are false as a reason offering support for his belief that knowledge is impossible, thus rendering that belief reasonable rather than dogmatic, must offer some reason to support his belief in the existence of human error. But this would not seem to be a difficult task. Suppose he were to say: "I believe that some of our knowledge claims are false because they are disconfirmed by observed evidence." Here, however, we might ask: "Are any knowledge claims ever disconfirmed by observed evidence?" Since the skeptic cannot *know* that any such claims are ever so disconfirmed, his belief that they are is gratuitous and dogmatic, unless he can offer some support for it. Let us suppose that the skeptic recognizes as much and responds as follows: "My reason for believing that some of our knowledge claims are disconfirmed by observed evidence is that scientific journals state that this frequently happens." Once again, however, the skeptic cannot *know* that scientific journals ever do state what he has just asserted. He can only believe that they do, but his belief remains irrational, hence cannot constitute a reason supporting the edifice of belief he rests on it *until* he provides some reason in its support. But any "reason" he might offer will suffer from exactly the same deficiency. It will be a dogmatic (because unsupported) belief *until* he provides reasons in its behalf, at which point the same problem will recur with these "reasons," and so on ad infinitum. Thus, the nondogmatic skeptic finds himself trapped in a regress that is vicious. Because he can never offer a belief that he can show to be reasonable (rather than dogmatic) without going through an infinite series of supporting "reasons," he can never provide any reason to support his original belief in the impossibility of knowledge. Hence that belief remains necessarily dogmatic and can be dismissed as such. As a result, the wary nondogmatic skeptic, who by his caution attempts to avoid the pitfall into which his bolder, dogmatic colleague falls, finds his efforts at escape to be in vain, for he himself turns out to be equally vulnerable to the charge of dogmatism. The only difference between the two is that he is dogmatic in what he believes rather than in what he claims to know.

To sum up, three options can be put forward as putatively available to the skeptic who claims only to believe (rather than to know) that knowledge is impossible, but recognizes that his belief is irrational and dogmatic unless and until he can offer reasons in its support. (1) He can offer a reason and claim that he knows what the reason asserts to be true. If he does know it to be true, then what it asserts successfully qualifies as a reason that can support a belief. But it cannot support his *skeptical* belief; rather it renders that belief false and him irrational if he continues to persist in believing it. (2) He can attempt to make all the "reasons" he offers in support of his belief reasonable, by offering "reasons" in support of these "reasons," then "reasons" in support of these "reasons" for "reasons," then "reasons" in support of these "reasons" for "reasons" for "reasons," until in exhaustion he must admit that he can never establish any "reason" to be a *reason* (i.e., itself reasonable) because he is trapped in a vicious infinite regress. On this option his original belief in the impossibility of knowledge remains forever insupportable, hence dogmatic. (3) He can break the regressive chain at any point by refusing to offer a reason in support of some "reason" he has given. Although such an act frees him from the vicious regress, it leaves him with a "reason" that, because it is unsupported, cannot support anything he has rested on it, including his belief in the impossibility of knowledge. As a result that belief remains unsupported, hence dogmatic.

The nondogmatic skeptic is stymied.

5 Third Essay in Skepticism

Although its shortcomings may not be so immediately apparent, nondogmatic skepticism proves on examination to be no more viable a theory of knowledge than dogmatic skepticism. In both cases the source of trouble lies in the skeptical thesis itself, that knowledge is impossible. Obviously no one can know this to be true, and, as we have just seen in the last section, no one can reasonably believe it to be true either. But if his attempt to advance the skeptical thesis, either in categorical or in hypothetical form, leads the skeptic into logical problems from which he cannot extricate himself, one might well conclude that his only recourse is to abandon skepticism. Thus cognitivism will have won the day. However, I am not yet prepared to concede the case to the cognitivists, for I see one more move the skeptic might make to retrieve himself. This move will be the subject of my third essay in skepticism.

Looking back over my first two essays in skepticism, we can recognize that, although they differ from each other in the strength with which they asserted the skeptical thesis, they do share the common feature of putting forth the view that knowledge is impossible as a *positive* theory. And it is this fact about them which has proved to be their undoing. The lesson we can learn from their example, thus, would seem to be that the skeptic cannot advance his skepticism as a theory. But then, we might well ask, what can he do? I think he has one more option remaining; he can abandon the offensive and move over to the defensive. In doing this he of course acknowledges that in none of its forms can skepticism constitute a viable theory or hypothesis. Therefore he must abandon what I shall term *positive* (or theoretical) skepticism. This the Pyrrhonists early recognized. It was because they did so that they accused the Academic skeptics, who formulated their skeptical theory positively, of being as much "dogmatists" as the cognitivists and attempted to avoid the trap of self-refutation themselves by withholding their judgment on everything. But in so doing they fell into an equally fatal trap by removing themselves from the controversy regarding the existence of knowledge, thus leaving the cognitivists free to make knowledge claims with impunity. If Pyrrhonism were the only skeptical alternative to positive skepticism, I think we should have to conclude that skepticism is intellectually bankrupt. But I believe that one other alternative remains to the skeptic, which the Pyrrhonists failed to see, for between positive skepticism, whether it be of the Academic or the hypothetical variety, and the Pyrrhonic suspension of judgment, I think the skeptic may be able to carve out a third position, which I shall call *negative* skepticism. Let us see how he might go about doing so; as we shall discover, the route he must follow will be a devious one.

The cognitivist, in contending that knowledge exists, is making a truth claim: that the proposition "Knowledge exists" is true. He is also making a knowledge claim: that he knows the proposition to be true, or, at least, that he has reasons for believing it to be true, which entails an implicit knowledge claim about his possession of reasons. In order to qualify as something he knows, the knowledge claim he makes must satisfy the general criteria of knowledge. It must be true and, more especially, he must be able to offer reasons in its support capable of establishing it to be true. If he can offer no reasons in its support, the claim is simply gratuitous, and if the reasons he offers do not establish its truth, he has not succeeded in making his case. In neither event has he been able to justify his thesis that knowledge exists. So we can ask the cognitivist: Can you give us any satisfactory reasons in support of your claim that knowledge exists? If you cannot, we can write your theory off as a failure. In such an event skepticism is triumphant, even though the critic of cognitivism has not revealed himself as a skeptic but has instead carefully refrained from asserting or attempting to defend any positive skeptical hypothesis at all. The cryptoskeptic, in other words, wins the battle by default, for if no one can legitimately claim to know anything, knowledge does not (indeed cannot) exist, even though no skeptic should ever make the positive claim that it does not exist. Such is the form of negative skepticism I shall defend in the remainder of this chapter.

It might be held that the conclusion I have just reached, even if I should succeed in establishing it by an argument, is not strong enough to support the skeptical case. In one sense, of course, this is correct; the conclusion does not support positive skepticism. But that, as we have already decided, is unsupportable. What it does do, however, is to undercut cognitivism. And such a result, besides being all the skeptic can get, is, I think, sufficient to his needs. If we can show that the cognitivist is incapable of justifying his thesis that knowledge exists, we shall have put him in an untenable position. Never being able legitimately to claim to know anything, he must, if he is rational, abandon his quest for knowledge altogether. Theorizing of any kind would, for the cognitivist, become a pointless activity because it could bear no fruits, and he would find himself in serious jeopardy of being forced into the silence of Cratylus. For the cognitivist such consequences must be intolerable. If he is to remain with his cognitivism, he must attempt to find some way of responding to the challenge my negative skepticism lays down. To see how he might do this and at the same time to reveal the force that lies behind this challenge, let us look at the questions I have raised a little more closely.

The cognitivist claims that knowledge exists; thus he claims to know the proposition "Knowledge exists" to be true. But what reasons can he offer in support of this claim? *Any* reasons he offers, to qualify as good (justifying) reasons, must satisfy two conditions: (a) What they assert must be true, and (b) their truth must entail the truth of the conclusion in whose support they are offered. The second condition does not, I think, require much comment. If I offer reasons in support of the conclusion that knowledge exists but these reasons do not entail that conclusion, one can accept the reasons and deny the conclusion. Since, for all the reasons establish, the conclusion may still be false, we cannot use the reasons as our basis for claiming the conclusion to be something we know. The first condition requires longer discussion; for suppose I claim a certain conclusion to be true and offer reasons in its behalf, and the reasons, although they entail the conclusion, are false. Could not the conclusion nevertheless be true? For example, consider the following argument:

> If a person is seventy-six years old, he does not have a father who is living.
> I am seventy-six years old.
> Therefore, I do not have a father who is living.

Although we have to answer our question in the affirmative, we can immediately destroy any force that might be derived from our admission by adding that it is not enough for a conclusion to be true to establish it as something we can legitimately claim to know, for a conclusion "supported" by false reasons may equally well be false as true. For example:

> If a person is seventy-six years old, he does not have a mother who is living.
> I am seventy-six years old.
> Therefore, I do not have a mother who is living.

If the conclusion is false, it clearly cannot constitute something we know even though it is entailed by its premises. And, as we have seen, if the premises that entail it are false, it may equally well be false as true. Hence, such premises cannot provide reasons supporting our claim that we know it to be true.

Having concluded that if we are to offer reasons capable of justifying us in claiming to know something, these reasons must consist of true propositions that entail the conclusion we are claiming as an item of knowledge, our next point is to note that these requirements constitute only necessary and not sufficient conditions that the reasons in question must satisfy. To qualify as good reasons, the reasons must in addition be such that (a) we *know* them to be true and (b) we *know* that they entail the conclusion we derive from them. The justification for this additional requirement is fairly clear. To see its necessity, let us suppose that it has not been fulfilled. We have offered reasons for claiming that knowledge exists; these reasons are in fact true and they do entail the existence of knowledge. However, we do not know that they are true or that they entail the existence of knowledge. Can we, under such circumstances, legitimately claim to know that knowledge exists? Clearly we cannot, for our claim would be gratuitous because we have no justification to offer for it. In order to support that claim it is necessary that we be able to *establish* that the reasons we offer on its behalf are both true and entail it. And to require that we be able to establish either of these things *is* to require that we know them to be true. It follows that in order to justify our cognitivistic claim that knowledge exists, we must employ an argument one of whose necessary presuppositions is that we know something.

That the negative skeptic, who has challenged the cognitivist to offer reasons in support of his claim that knowledge exists, should fail to be satisfied with the results of the analysis we have just completed is understandable, for the cognitivist's attempt to provide such reasons has led him into a circular argument in which, to establish the existence of knowledge, he must presuppose that he knows things. And this circularity inherent in the cognitivist's argument is enough to satisfy the negative skeptic. Although he will not—indeed, cannot—conclude from the failure of the cognitivist to offer an acceptable argument in support of his cognitivism that knowledge therefore does not exist (for then he would transform himself into a positive skeptic to his own undoing), he is justified in coming to the conclusion that the cognitivist has been unsuccessful in his attempt to show that knowledge does exist.[12]

Looking at the results of the argument I have just offered, we might feel inclined to conclude that the opponents have arrived at an impasse, with neither one the victor. But this would not, I think, be correct, for the situation, as I have set it forth as a negative skeptic who has gone on the defensive, forces the cognitivist to assume the offensive. It is he who must bear the burden of proof. He is arguing for the existence of knowledge; the negative skeptic, on the contrary, is arguing for no position of his own at all. So an impasse, in which the cognitivist does not succeed in producing an argument that establishes that knowledge exists, becomes a victory for the skeptic. To one who disputes this, contending that to place the burden of proof on the shoulders of the cognitivist is unfairly to weight the argument against him from the outset, I should reply that this is a burden he must accept. He must, from the very nature of the thesis he wishes to defend, establish a positive conclusion—that knowledge exists. If he cannot successfully do so, he has failed, whether there is any skeptic at hand to point his failure out to him or not. We cannot, as cognitivists, legitimately claim that knowledge exists, unless we can offer an argument that is capable of supporting our claim. And such an argument, if the reasoning I have just offered is sound, is not to be found. So my third essay in skepticism—negative skepticism—by avoiding both the self-contradictions of Academic skepticism and the silent impotence of Pyrrhonism, succeeds in accomplishing the essential aim of the skeptic: to destroy the knowledge pretensions of cognitivistic epistemology.

VII Skepticism, Cognitivism, and the Foundations of Knowledge

1 Who is a Negative Skeptic?

In the last section of chapter vi I made a case for what I have called negative skepticism, arguing that it is the only possible form of skepticism that is viable and that it succeeds in accomplishing the skeptical aim of establishing the cognitivists' inability to offer any support for their claim that knowledge exists. Having reached this conclusion, I find myself in an awkward and uncomfortable situation. As has probably been apparent, I began writing this book from the stance of a cognitivist rather than a skeptic, even a negative one. My commitment to cognitivism has undoubtedly become increasingly obvious as I have proceeded through my criticisms of the various arguments that have been offered in support of skepticism. But now I find my cognitivistic stance to have been undermined by an argument of my own devising. What should I do? As a philosopher and (I hope) a rational being, my only option seems to be to accept the conclusion to which my reasoning has led me and become a negative skeptic. This I shall attempt to do in chapter vii, trying to work out the consequences that such an intellectual reversal must have for me—and for anyone else who adopts negative skepticism.

As I review my argument for negative skepticism, I realize that its revelation of the inability of cognitivism to justify itself did not *create* that inability. If it is intrinsically impossible to provide good reasons in support of the cognitivistic claim that knowledge exists, it always has been and always will be impossible to do so. Recognizing this I am forced to the realization that I have, not just in my philosophizing but in all my intellectual activities throughout my life, been committed to a conviction that could not be supported; namely, that I know things. To abandon this conviction is far from easy to do. The intellectual readjustment that my conclusion in favor of negative skepticism forces me to make is fundamental in nature and far-reaching in scope. I must shift from a mind-set dominated by the cognitivistic assumption that I can justifiably accept some of my beliefs to be true, to one controlled by the negatively skeptical conclusion that I can never give good reasons for anything I believe. Just what is involved in the mental readjustment I must make? Is it a shift that I (or anyone else) can successfully accomplish?

As I ponder these questions I become more and more dismayed by the magnitude of the task I face. I believe so many things—that I am sitting here writing and sipping a cup of coffee, that my chair is hard and the morning too early. Every waking hour of every day I have lived as far back as I can remember has been shot through with such beliefs—mostly trivial, of course—but still beliefs; that is, things I have accepted to be true. And for at least many of these beliefs I have always assumed I could offer good reasons. But now I am asking myself to come to terms with the realization that I cannot offer any reasons capable of supporting any part of this kaleidoscope of belief. How should I react?

The first response that comes to my mind—and, given the situation in which I find myself, it is an obvious response—is that, if I cannot support any of my beliefs, I should set myself for the future to refrain from believing anything. To go about doing this, however, I must give up making any judgments. For any judgment I make—and I mean here *honest* judgment, for the phrase "dishonest judgment" is, I take it, a contradiction in terms—commits me to some belief. When I make the judgment, for example, that the chair I am sitting on is hard, I am committing myself to an acceptance of something I take to be true; I believe that the chair is hard. I cannot judge without at the same time believing. If I am to refrain from believing anything, therefore, I must also refrain from making judgments. So in launching my attempt to give up all my beliefs I find myself setting down the road of the Pyrrhonists, my objective like theirs being to achieve a state of mind in which judgments have no part. Although the line of reasoning that has brought me to this point is different from that of the Pyrrhonists, as is my ultimate goal—for I am not, like them, seeking peace of mind but only the mental readjustment demanded by negative skepticism—nevertheless I seem to be led to join forces with them.

But if my negative skepticism demands that I adopt the Pyrrhonic stance of complete suspension of judgment, I fear that I shall never be able to live up to its requirements, for, as I argued in chapter iv (especially §5), whatever one may desire to do, no one can in fact live the ordinary human life that occupies most of our days without making judgments. The attempt to do so is simply psychologically impossible. On this issue I agree completely with what I take to be Hume's point when he writes: "Nature, by an absolute and uncontroulable necessity has determin'd us to judge as well as to breathe and feel." I don't think the issue is really arguable; in order to engage in any kind of deliberate activity—to accomplish even something as simple as completing the sentence I am now writing—I must make judgments. (I must, for example, judge what words I should best use to convey the thoughts I wish to communicate.) I am making judgments now, I have made them all through my life, and I do not see how I can refrain from continuing to make them in the future.

This is not a matter of choice with me but of necessity; in order to think and to act I must make judgments. And if I must believe in order to judge, then I do not see how I can possibly readjust my mind-set in such a way that I cease to believe anything. To live up to the consequences of negative skepticism seems to require me to accomplish an end that is out of my reach.

Moreover, the problems involved in attempting a general suspension of one's judgment go beyond that raised by the psychological impossibility of accomplishing the task. Supposing that we could overcome the psychological difficulties I have pointed out, we still have to ask ourselves whether we could attain our objective. In the first place, the suspension of judgment requires a deliberate act; one cannot *suspend* his judgment inadvertently. (He might inadvertently—i.e., without deliberate intent—stop making judgments, but this would not be the suspension of judgment.) Second, the suspension of judgment, as a deliberate act, must be exercised not only in a general but also in a specific way. The person who says, "I shall suspend my judgment on all matters," if he is to succeed in fulfilling this resolve, must suspend his judgment on each individual matter that comes before his mind. That is to say, he must refuse to accept as true (i.e., believe) any answer to any issue that presents itself to him. And if he is thinking at all, issues will necessarily present themselves; he will be faced with questions that admit of more than one answer. (For example, should I use this word or that word to convey my thought in the sentence I am writing?) Faced with any such question, the Pyrrhonist, in order to suspend his judgment, will have to judge. He will have to accept it to be true that he has a question to resolve, that the question presents certain kinds of features, that it may have several possible answers, that each of these answers has certain characteristics of its own, that his acceptance of one answer precludes his acceptance of others, etcetera. To suspend his judgment about any particular matter, therefore, he must make judgments about a number of related matters, for to suspend judgment about one matter *is* to make judgments about others. Even to resolve to suspend judgment altogether—to stop thinking—it is necessary to make judgments; e.g., about what is meant and implied by the resolve itself. The program of the Pyrrhonists turns out to be one that we are precluded—not just psychologically but logically as well—from ever successfully carrying out.

However, the line of argument that I have just been following, which has led me to a conclusion that I find myself unable to accept, is based on an assumption with which I started: That because I can give no good reasons for what I believe, I ought to give up believing anything. But this is not the only possible assumption on which I may make the intellectual readjustment I am trying to accomplish; there is at least one other alternative. Recognizing that I can offer no reasons capable of supporting what I believe, I can go on believing anyway. Making such a move would appear to have a decided advantage over trying to follow the Pyrrhonists; it is something that I should at least be psychologically capable of accomplishing, for it requires only that I extend and make general a type of mental set in which I consider myself to have some experience. To put it plainly, I already believe *some* things without any apparent reason. All that I am asking myself to do now is to abandon the effort to give reasons for *any* of my beliefs. Without using the term in a pejorative sense, I am inviting myself to live a life of irrationality.

It is not surprising that I should find myself, as a negative skeptic, seriously contemplating the adoption of irrationalism as a mode of life, for other skeptics have found themselves tracing a similar path. Peter Unger, for example, writes in the following vein: "If nobody ever knows anything to be so, then it follows that it is also true that nobody is ever (even the least bit) reasonable or justified in anything, in particular, in believing anything to be so."[1] John Kekes draws the conclusion linking skepticism to irrationalism in even stronger terms, and although he defends skepticism himself, is under no illusions about its consequences, which he clearly believes to be disastrous.

It might be asked then what difference does it make whether or not a person is an epistemological sceptic? The main difference is that if epistemological scepticism were correct, then any belief would have precisely the same verisimilitude as any other. It would be impossible to criticize, improve upon, or to make more reliable what anybody believes. So science and pseudo-science, history and myth, medicine and quackery, considered judgment and rabid prejudice, would be equally acceptable. Furthermore, rational argument as a method of settling disputes would disappear and those old stand-bys, force and propaganda, would take its place. The difference it would make is that if scepticism were correct and if it were accepted, life would be nasty, brutish, and short.[2]

If Kekes, especially, is right about its consequences, skepticism is far from a palatable doctrine. Indeed, one might wonder why anyone should be led to embrace it. Speaking for myself, I find it—and, more particularly, the irrationalism to which both Unger and Kekes believe it to lead—intellectually repugnant. But that, unfortunately, is beside the point. At the present stage of the argument I seem to be left with no other option than to accept irrationalism along with negative skepticism. Having rejected Pyrrhonism on the grounds that the suspension of judgment it advocates is a logical and psychological impossibility, I can, as I must, continue to believe and to make judgments, but I must do this without reason.

If I follow such a mode of life, never giving or even having any reasons for what I believe, I shall succeed in lapsing into a state in which, although I believe many things, I still know nothing. Whether anyone can know anything or not—and, it should be recollected, the negative skeptic never goes on record as denying the possibility of knowledge but only the possibility of the cognitivists' being able to show that knowledge exists—nevertheless I (or any negative skeptic) who gives up offering reasons for his beliefs gives up, by that act, all pretensions to knowledge, for to affirm that he knows something, one must make a claim; namely, that what he believes is true. Logically, one can say "I *believe* that X is Y but X is not Y," but he cannot say "I *know* that X is Y but X is not Y."[3] When one claims to know that X is Y, he must have as a reason to support that claim at least that X is Y, or that his statement "X is Y" is true. Thus Kekes concludes that for the skeptic "any belief would have the same verisimilitude as any other." Or, to put this point in a slightly different way, to the skeptic who accepts irrationalism as a consequence, the notion of truth becomes irrelevant. He cannot say "I believe such and such because it is true," for to do so would be to offer a reason for his belief thus to violate his irrationality. All there remains for him to say is "I believe such and such." Since, furthermore, truth is a necessary condition of knowledge, to claim to know is to claim that what one believes is true; hence the irrationalistic skeptic's inability to offer its truth as a reason for his believing anything a fortiori precludes him from making any claims to knowledge.

Thus, even though our skepticism is negative, we seem to be left only with beliefs. But these, as Hume said, we *must* have. So let us proceed by examining more closely the nature of the intellectual life we shall find ourselves leading after we have adjusted to believing things without reason. The first question we might raise is this: Will it be necessary for us to curtail our beliefs in any way? The apparent answer is negative; indeed the opposite would seem to be true. If we never have to consider the problem of giving reasons for what we believe, belief, it would seem, should become much more easy. At least many of us, who have been in the habit of withholding our belief on questions until we have gathered sufficient reasons to support an answer to them, would be freed from that kind of intellectual constraint. Without the possibility of providing reasons for any of our beliefs, we can believe whatever we want, with utter abandon. Irrationalism, whatever its dark side may be, seems at least to offer us total intellectual freedom.

Nevertheless, before we embrace the freedom that the irrational life appears to extend to us, we need to be sure that the gift being offered is one that we are really able to accept. To convince ourselves of its acceptability, we must, I think, consider the notion of "unreasoned belief" or "belief without reason" with some care. Just what does this notion mean? To begin the task of clarification, we can say immediately that our concern here is not with our possible reasons for believing, in the sense of those things that have *caused* us to believe. For example, I may believe that I am floating in the air because I have taken some hallucinatory drug; the drug is the cause of my believing but not a reason for my believing. When we talk about irrational or nonreasoned beliefs, the kind of reasons we are concerned with, and find to be lacking, is reasons that contribute to the support of our beliefs in the sense of providing some justification for their truth. So we can pose the following query: If we are to believe irrationally, we must believe without any reasons, in the sense of support or justification, at all. How do we go about doing this? Let us try to adapt our procedure to some simple belief, say, my belief that the chair I am sitting on is hard. Can I believe this without reason? The first thing we need to note is that my belief does not exist in an intellectual vacuum. Rather it is part of a whole system of beliefs I hold. Furthermore, this system of beliefs is of such a nature that I could not believe any given thing unless I believed a number of other things as well. Let me explain, using my example. It is impossible for me to believe that the chair I am sitting on is hard unless I also believe, at the very least, (a) that I am sitting and (b) that the object on which I am sitting is a chair. In accepting the original proposition as true, i.e., in believing it, I must accept the truth of these other propositions as well. Nor is the necessity here merely psychological; rather it is logical. It is logically impossible that I should believe that the chair I am sitting on is hard and not believe that I am sitting. In addition, these required beliefs provide reasons offering support for my original belief. If either one of them is false, that belief must be false as well, for it cannot be true that the chair I am sitting on is hard if either (a) I am not sitting or (b) it is not a chair on which I am sitting.[4]

If we grant that beliefs like the one I have just analyzed cannot be irrational, in the sense that it is not possible for us to hold them without any reasons that offer support for their truth at all, we might nevertheless argue that this is only because they are complex beliefs and therefore that their truth entails the truth of other, simpler beliefs. Once we get down to the level of basic beliefs of the most simple kind, we shall find that the situation has changed, because such beliefs can be held without reason. In response to this point I think it has to be recognized, first, that it acknowledges a very sharp circumscription of the realm of possible irrational beliefs. If a belief as simple as "The chair I am sitting on is hard" cannot be irrational in the sense in which we are discussing, then neither can the vast majority of our everyday beliefs; for most of them are at least as complex as it is. Hence, the offer of a life of irrationality—that it gives us freedom to believe anything we want without reason—turns out to be largely spurious, for it precludes us from believing most of the things we ordinarily believe, and must believe, if we are to carry on any kind of life at all. But in the second place, we do not yet know just how narrowly circumscribed the realm of things we can believe without reason must be. If the belief "The chair I am sitting on is hard" is too complex to be held without reason, to find a possible irrational belief we must move toward greater simplicity. So let us consider the belief "I am sitting on a chair." This belief is clearly more simple than my original belief, yet it entails (a) "I am sitting" and (b) "The object (on which I am sitting) is a chair." If either (a) or (b) were false it would necessarily be false as well, and if I did not believe both (a) and (b)—that is, accept them to be true— I could not believe my proposed belief. So it cannot qualify as an irrational belief. Let us simplify further. We have two beliefs remaining to consider: "I am sitting" and "The object (on which I am sitting) is a chair." For the sake of brevity let us concentrate on the latter. Can I believe without any reason that an object is a chair? Let us try the following experiment: Suppose someone showed us an object that looked like a chair and asked us what it was. We might honestly reply, "It is a chair." But then suppose the person revealed to us that we were suffering from an optical illusion; that what we had taken to be a chair was only a number of separate sticks, with none touching any other, but the whole arranged in such a way, through the clever use of mirrors, that it gave us the visual impression of a chair. If he now asked us, "Do you believe that it is a chair?" we should unhesitatingly answer in the negative. Why? Because (at least) we no longer believe it is a single object. Thus we can conclude that the belief "This object is a chair" entails the belief "This is an object"; hence it is not an irrational belief. So let us move to something even more simple. Take the belief we have just reached: "This is an object." Clearly it is no more irrational than the belief "The object is a chair," for the mirror experiment would destroy it as well. That is, after being shown how the mirrors have led us into the illusion, we should abandon our belief that the separate sticks constituted *any* object, whether chair or anything else. What is the next step toward basic simplicity? Perhaps, "This exists." But do we really have an authentic belief here? As long as "this" is unspecified, to affirm that "this" exists is to affirm nothing definite. Thus, our "belief" that "this" exists is a belief with no specific content at all. It seems dubious, at best, to label it a real belief. Rather, in order to believe, we should have to give some specification to "this," to demarcate it from what it is not. But as soon as we specified it, believing "this thing" or "this object" exists, etcetera, we should find ourselves back in a context in which our belief could be destroyed by a device like the one I offered above based on optical illusion.

The line of argument I have just been pursuing could be carried out in a number of different directions, using different kinds of beliefs and gradually stripping them back to the basic beliefs that provide their necessary support. But however one might trace such believing situations back to their sources of support, I am convinced that he would be led to the following conclusion: Any belief we hold, to constitute a belief, must have some content. It must be complex to the extent that it embodies a judgment in which some predicate is affirmed of a determinate subject. All such beliefs, furthermore, entail other beliefs so that, in order to believe them—to acquiesce in their truth—it is logically necessary that we acquiesce in the truth of the others as well. It follows from this that it is impossible to have a genuine belief that is irrational; i.e., that we hold without *any* reason at all.[5]

To sum up the discussion to this point, my object has been to find some answer to the question: Having realized, because of my argument for negative skepticism in chapter vi, that the cognitivistic case for the existence of knowledge cannot be supported and, hence, that neither I nor anyone else can ever legitimately claim to know anything, how should I respond to this realization? If I cannot provide any rational justification for my beliefs, what should I do? One apparently possible answer is to suspend judgment and stop believing anything. But this we found to be both psychologically and logically impossible. A second apparent alternative is to continue to believe but to do so without reason, to embrace total irrationality. But this we found to be logically impossible. There seem to be no other alternatives. So what *are* we to do?

Rather than trying to answer my question, I shall pose another: Why does the impasse to which I have now come constitute a problem? I think the answer can be found in the title

I have given to this section: "Who is a negative skeptic?" The question assumes that philosophical reasoning is an activity carried on by beings who, because they are human, engage in many other activities as well. Among these activities is that of believing a wide variety of things, some theoretical but most by far practical. In order to believe these things, however, it is necessary for us to make assumptions that are inconsistent with our negative skepticism. Thus, although I can claim to be a negative skeptic, I necessarily belie that claim whenever I step beyond my role as critic of cognitivism and engage in any kind of rational intellectual activity. And the same holds true of everyone else. No one can *really* live the intellectual life of a negative skeptic.

Before deciding finally that no one can be a negative skeptic, however, we must consider some objections to such a conclusion, for it might be argued that it rests on two distinct errors. In the first place, it assumes that negative skepticism leads to certain consequences its adherents must accept. But this is to misunderstand the nature of negative skepticism, by conceiving of it as a theory that has implications. But this it simply is not. The negative skeptic has no theory; he completes his task when he shows that the cognitivist cannot establish his case for the existence of knowledge. What he believes thereafter and the reasons he gives for believing it are independent of his negative skepticism, just as it is irrelevant to them. In addition, to justify the consequences I have attempted to derive from my negative skepticism, I must claim to establish that certain things are true (e.g., that to accept a given proposition as true yet not to accept as true another proposition entailed by it is irrational). But this is to make knowledge claims, and the whole point of my negative skepticism is to undermine knowledge claims. Hence my discussion in this section, rather than illuminating any possible consequences of my negative skepticism, proceeds on an assumption that it has ruled out as illegitimate.

I think the second of these two criticisms is just. A negative skeptic (like myself) is not in any position to pursue the consequences of his negative skepticism. Indeed, it can have no consequences, in the sense that, if it is correct, no one can legitimately claim to know anything about anything, including the "consequences" of negative skepticism. But this leads us to the first point. If negative skepticism has no consequences, then its adherents are free to go on believing anything they wish. As a result, they could be indistinguishable in their beliefs from everyone else. It would seem to mean nothing practically to be a negative skeptic. But, unlike everyone else, they would be in the situation of believing all these things randomly. Bertrand Russell's remark certainly seems to be applicable to such a negative skepticism: "Scepticism, while logically impeccable, is psychologically impossible, and there is an element of frivolous insincerity in any philosophy which pretends to accept it."[6]

It does not follow from this conclusion either that one cannot or should not be a negative skeptic. Yet at the least it is hardly a comfortable position in which to rest. To reach a conclusion whose consequences turn out to be consequences one cannot legitimately draw is bound to leave anyone, and particularly a philosopher, uneasy. Russell has, I believe, put his finger on one awkward and embarrassing aspect of all skepticism: In his attempts to escape contradiction, the skeptic seems driven into insincerity and frivolity. So we may return to the question I raised a moment ago: What are we to do? To recapitulate, the position we have now reached is this: (a) We have concluded that all forms of positive skepticism are untenable; (b) we have argued that the negative skeptic can undermine the knowledge pretensions of cognitivism; but (c) we now find negative skepticism to involve unacceptable consequences of its own. Where do we go from here? I am inclined to think that, at this stage, rather than trying to move forward we should move backward. Specifically, we need to return to the argument I gave in §5 of chapter vi which I there held to constitute a conclusive refutation of cognitivism, for it was this argument that led us into negative skepticism and the subsequent theoretical tangles in which we have become enmeshed in this chapter. Although that final argument against cognitivism appeared to be conclusive, was it really so? On reflection one point concerning it begins to stand out; namely, that its entire objection to cognitivism consisted in showing that the cognitivist can support his claim that knowledge exists only through the use of a *circular argument*.[7] So if the argument of the negative skeptic does destroy cognitivism, it must be because circular arguments are illicit. What then is wrong with them? I never considered this question in chapter vi. Although some philosophers believe their inadequacy to be apparent, because of the impasse into which we have now been driven, we cannot afford to pass over this question without further inquiry. I shall turn to it in §2.

2 Circular Arguments

Perhaps the best way to get clear about what is wrong with circular arguments is to begin with an example of one and then examine it. So let us consider the following dispute between two epistemologists, X and Y, who are arguing the question of the status of knowledge claims based on memory. X maintains that he knows many things about his own past because he remembers them. When Y questions the reliability of X's memory, suggesting that it may not always be accurate and asking him why he places the confidence he does in it, X replies that he knows he remembers these things because he is *certain* of it.[8] To this Y responds by pointing out that X's argument, by assuming that to be certain of anything is to know it, makes certainty a sufficient condition of knowledge. But this is debatable. If certainty is a psychological state, then, if one is in a state of certainty about any matter (e.g., that he remembers a past event), according to X he also possesses knowledge about this matter. But if truth is a necessary condition of knowledge, it would seem that certainty cannot be a sufficient condition of knowledge, for one can be in the psychological state of certainty about something, for example, that he remembers some past event, but still not know that the event occurred, because in fact it did not. Despite his psychological certainty, he is mistaken; his memory has played tricks on him. Furthermore, Y might conclude, this counterexample so undermines the appeal to certainty as a basis for a claim to know that, unless X can offer some additional argument in its support, the notion that certainty is sufficient for knowledge must be abandoned. Ending with a challenge, Y asks X: "You have claimed that certainty is a sufficient condition of knowledge; how do you know this?"

Although there are several different ways in which X might answer this question, from the point of view of our discussion of circular arguments, there is a uniquely appropriate response; namely, "I know that certainty is a sufficient condition of knowledge because I am certain of it." With this answer X undoubtedly offers a reason in support of his claim, but the reason he gives involves him in a circular argument. Formally X's reasoning could be stated as follows:

Whatever I am certain of I know.
I am certain that certainty is a sufficient condition of knowledge.
Therefore, I know that certainty is a sufficient condition of knowledge.

How should Y respond to an argument of this kind—other than to point out that it is circular? Undoubtedly, he would find it unsatisfactory—and in this we should surely agree with him—but in what does its insufficiency lie? Must we reject it *simply* because it is circular? Before we do that we should, I think, realize that the argument itself is valid. There is nothing formally wrong with X's reasoning. Our misgivings with the argument must, therefore, lie at a deeper level. Probing it further, we might point out that the argument, because it is circular, does not support its conclusion, in the crucial sense of providing any *reasons* for our accepting the conclusion to be true, for the "reason" given in the major premise assumes the truth of the conclusion. The conclusion thus is "supported" by an appeal to itself. What is offered to us in the form of an argument is no argument at all.

But even if we grant that X has misled us (and perhaps himself) in offering a circular argument in support of his view, what is so heinous in all that? To answer this question, we must turn to consider the situation from the side of Y. He, it must be remembered, denies that certainty is a sufficient condition of knowledge. Thus the conclusion that X reaches, if it is just, refutes his denial; for, if X knows that certainty is sufficient for knowledge, it must be true that it is sufficient, hence Y's denial of its sufficiency must be false. So X, by using a circular argument, has "refuted" Y, but his refutation cannot be a genuine refutation at all because the "argument" employed to effect it is not a genuine argument. What X has done is to conclude against Y *arbitrarily* (i.e., without reason). Or to put the point in slightly different terms: The question at issue between X and Y is whether or not certainty *is* a sufficient condition of knowledge, X claiming that it is and Y that it is not. To support his claim, X uses an argument that presupposes the truth of his claim, thus resolving the original question in his own favor from the outset. But to do this is to *beg the question* at issue between him and Y. Furthermore, it is against X's question-begging procedure that Y has a legitimate complaint. If X had merely used a circular argument, the only charge that could be laid against him would be that he was deluding himself in supposing that he had provided support for his conclusion. But when he uses such an argument to refute Y's position, he commits an intellectual offence against Y, because he arbitrarily (without reason) concludes Y's view to be false. To sum up, circular reasoning is objectionable and should be rejected not because it is circular but rather because it is question-begging.

If the conclusion I have just reached is correct, what follows? One might say: Nothing at all. Admitting that I have drawn a distinction, that distinction unfortunately has no useful consequences, for all circular arguments are question-begging as well. Hence it is immaterial whether we reject them because of their circularity or because they beg the question.

The point I have just made would be decisive, if it were right. Let us see if it is. Imagine another dispute between epistemologists (this time A and B) on the issue of whether a proposition can or cannot be both true and false, A claiming that it cannot be and B claiming that it can be. To support his view A presents an argument. Without taking the space to elaborate in detail here, we can agree that whatever argument he uses, its premises must satisfy the requirements of the law of noncontradiction, for if they do not satisfy these requirements, *any* conclusion (including the denial of the one A draws) could with equal propriety be derived from them. But an argument which, in order to reach the conclusion that a proposition cannot be both true and false, must use premises that fulfill the requirements of the law of noncontradiction is circular. The law must be presupposed in order to establish a conclusion that states the law. Can B therefore legitimately charge that A, by using such a circular argument, has begged the question at issue between them and thus arbitrarily concluded his (B's) position to be false? To answer this question let us look at the issue from B's side for a moment. To justify his view that a proposition can be both true and false, he must be able to offer some argument in its support. Otherwise, it is simply arbitrary. So the burden of proof shifts to B's shoulders. But obviously he can produce no such argument. For *any* argument that he offers will of necessity presuppose the law of noncontradiction; otherwise it would equally "support" the denial of his view. The crucial point here is not that B is unable to produce any argument to support his case, a deficiency that he might eventually succeed in eliminating, but that it is logically impossible for him to support that case. There can be no argument that leads to a conclusion denying the law of noncontradiction because any argument put forward to yield that conclusion, to be cogent, *must* presuppose the law, hence contradict the conclusion to which it is designed to lead.

For an argument to be question-begging, there must be a question to be begged. In the instance we have been considering, for A to beg the question against B, it is necessary that B have a view that A, by assuming his own position in his argument against B, arbitrarily rules out. But that is exactly what A, in this instance, cannot do. For B, to support his case, must accept A's view to be true.[9] In disagreeing with A, B must, in other words, agree with A. But if B must agree with A, there is no question at issue between them, hence A cannot beg the question against B.

We have here a case in which someone (A) has employed a circular argument against his opponent (B) but has nevertheless not begged the question against him. If a circular argument is objectionable not because it is circular but only because it is question-begging, we can conclude that in this case A has committed no intellectual offense against B. The reason why A, although he has used a circular argument against B, has nevertheless taken no objectionable advantage over him (in a way that he would have done had he begged the question) is that he has not by this device *arbitrarily* ruled B's case out of court, for B's case must itself rest on the acceptance of A's case. So if we should contend that A is arbitrarily ruling against B, we should likewise have to contend that he is arbitrarily ruling against himself. But obviously, in presupposing the truth of his own position, he cannot arbitrarily be ruling against his position. Hence he cannot arbitrarily be ruling against B.

The point I am making can be put in a somewhat different

way. Some propositions, including, for example, the proposition that a proposition cannot be both true and false, can be supported *only* by an argument that is circular. No argument used in their support which does not itself presuppose them to be true can possibly be cogent. Since, however, their truth is a presupposition of *all* argumentation, the fact that they cannot be deduced from premises without circularity becomes innocuous. We must simply recognize that if we believe we are deducing such propositions from premises that do not presuppose their truth, we are deluding ourselves. Although we cannot give them support in this way, that does not matter, for they do not require such support. Because any attempt to deny their truth must (logically) presuppose their truth, we can conclude that their truth is logically necessary. The establishment that the truth of a proposition is logically necessary is the strongest support any proposition can have and therefore all the support any proposition need have. There is nothing better we can possibly ask for or require. Propositions whose truth can be supported *only* by circular arguments, thus, must be regarded as paradigm examples of things we know.

We have now examined two cases of circular arguments. One of them has proved objectionable because it was question-begging as well, but the other has turned out to be innocuous because it begged no questions. With this background in mind we can now turn to the case that directly interests us —the cognitivists' claim that knowledge exists. In the last section of chapter vi we concluded that this claim is one the cognitivist can support only by a circular argument in which he must presuppose the truth of the conclusion he is attempting to establish. But, as we now see, the charge of circularity in itself is not sufficient grounds for rejecting an argument; rather, the argument must beg the question as well. Having reopened the issue we prematurely closed at the end of chapter vi, we must ask ourselves: Granting that the cognitivist must use a circular argument whenever he attempts to establish the conclusion that knowledge exists, must his argument beg the question against the skeptic as well? Is the cognitivist like X in his argument against Y, or is he rather like A in his argument against B?

To resolve this issue the first thing we must do is to determine what question the cognitivist would be begging if his argument for the existence of knowledge were to be question-begging. His argument is circular because, to deduce the conclusion "Knowledge exists," he must presuppose that he knows things. The only opponent against whom he could beg the question, whose theory he could arbitrarily rule out by his circular argument, would thus be someone who defended a thesis that denied his; namely, the proposition "Knowledge does not exist." In other words, the epistemological skeptic. So the issue we must resolve is whether the cognitivist, in using a circular argument to establish the existence of knowledge, begs any question against the skeptic, who denies that knowledge exists.

In chapter vi we examined the structure of any argument that the cognitivist might use to reach his cognitivistic conclusion and found that all such arguments would be circular for two reasons: To support the conclusion that he knows something the cognitivist (1) would have to use premises that he knew to be true and (2) would have to know that the premises he used entailed the conclusion he derived from them. Having already found the cognitivist involved in a circular argument in his attempt to support his case, we must now turn our attention to the argumentation the skeptic would find himself constrained to use in support of his opposed case. Since I have gone through the issue in some detail in my examination of the cognitivistic argument in chapter vi (§5), I shall not repeat myself at length here but only summarize the essential points that emerge. For the skeptic to support his thesis that knowledge does not exist, he must employ an argument whose premises are (1) true and (2) entail the conclusion that knowledge does not exist. But more, he must

(a) know the premises to be true and (b) know that they entail this conclusion. That (a) and (b) are conditions that must be fulfilled follows from the fact that in asserting his conclusion, the skeptic is making a truth claim, to the effect that knowledge does not exist. To justify himself in making such a truth claim, he must know that it is entailed by premises he knows to be true.

We are now in a position to answer our question of whether the cognitivist, in using a circular argument to establish his case, begs any question against the skeptic. The answer is a clear negative, for to support his *own* case, the cognitivist's opponent, the skeptic, is forced to make knowledge claims as well. Since an argument that assumes that knowledge exists could beg the question only against the view that it does not exist, and since both the articulation and defense of the latter view must themselves rest on the assumption that knowledge exists, the cognitivist cannot beg the question against the skeptic. In this debate there is simply no question to be begged. The situation is like the controversy I described between A and B, and not like the one between X and Y.

Before leaving this issue, however, we might look further into the skeptic's argument, as I have just sketched it, for it offers one important contrast to the parallel argument of the cognitivist. Unlike the cognitivist's argument for the existence of knowledge, it is not circular, for the skeptic does not presuppose that he knows *nothing* in order to reach the conclusion that knowledge does not exist. Rather he presupposes the opposite, that he knows *something;* instead of being circular, his argument is self-contradictory. So the skeptic destroys his own case in his very attempt to make it.

Before we can bring our critique of skepticism to an end, we need to be sure that we have shown the skeptical thesis to be completely untenable. Coming to the defense of the skeptics, might we not point out that the argument I have just offered rests on an assumption: That the skeptic must defend his negative thesis about knowledge by offering reasons in its support? Suppose the skeptic rejects that assumption and then contends that his case does not fall into any contradiction. In response to this move, the first thing that must be noted is that the skeptic's thesis now becomes gratuitous. He asserts that knowledge does not exist but then declines to offer any reasons to justify his assertion. How seriously should anyone take a theory for which its proponent offers no supporting reasons, indeed, who cannot do so except on pain of contradicting himself?

But the case against the skeptic can be carried further. When he asserts that knowledge does not exist, the skeptic is, in that act, making a truth claim. He is claiming it to be a fact (the case) that no one knows anything. This much I believe has to be granted; otherwise skepticism would not be a theory at all. Indeed, if the skeptic is not making a truth claim, one might well wonder what he could possibly be doing. In any event it is only on the assumption that he is making a truth claim that he needs to be answered, for if he were not there would be nothing to be answered; *skepticism* (i.e., the theory) would be nonexistent. Can the skeptic possibly be correct in the truth claim he makes? Let us call his skeptical truth claim, "no one knows anything," *S*. Now *S*, considered as a truth claim, must be either true or false. (If it were neither, skepticism would not qualify as a theory requiring an answer.) If *S* is false, its denial—"Someone knows something"—*C*, is true, *C*, of course, being the cognitivist's claim. But what if *S* is true? What follows from the assumption that the skeptic's thesis that no one knows anything is true? Specifically, does the skeptic himself know that no one knows anything or does he not know this? The two alternatives are exhaustive; one must be true and the other false. If we assume that the skeptic knows that no one knows anything, we can immediately deduce *C*, because the skeptic's knowledge that no one knows anything entails that the proposition "Someone knows something" is true. Not only does this alternative establish the cognitivist's case but also it is inconsistent with the skeptical thesis itself. Logically, the skeptic *cannot* know that no one knows anything,[10] for the skeptical thesis that no one knows anything entails the truth of the proposition "The skeptic does not know that no one knows anything." Assuming the truth of the skeptic's thesis *S*, I have just succeeded in establishing the truth of the proposition "The skeptic does not know that no one knows anything."[11] If, as is agreed, knowledge consists in propositions whose truth we can establish, it follows that I can legitimately claim as something I know that the skeptic does not know that no one knows anything. But my knowing this entails the truth of *C*. To sum up, if we assume the skeptic's thesis *S* to be true, either (a) the skeptic himself must know something or (b) I must know something. In either case someone knows something and *C* must be true, hence *S* false. And if *S* is assumed false, *C* is true. Since these alternatives are exhaustive we can conclude that *S* is necessarily false and *C* necessarily true.

Although my argument so far may be conceded to be cogent, certain skeptics, as well as, perhaps, some nonskeptics, would nevertheless deny that it succeeds in demolishing skepticism altogether. Against Academic skepticism, they might agree, it is decisive, but Pyrrhonic skepticism can escape its coils, for I have made a crucial assumption throughout my argument—that skepticism must be a *theory*. Once this is assumed, it is relatively easy for me to show that it becomes enmeshed in contradictions from which it cannot escape. But if the skeptic is careful, as Sextus, for example, is, he can neatly avoid all of the traps I lay for him by the simple device of refusing ever to put his skepticism forward as a theory. As he writes:

> So whenever the Sceptic says "I determine nothing,"
> what he means is "I am now in such a state of mind as
> neither to affirm dogmatically nor deny any of the mat-

ters now in question." And this he says simply by way of announcing undogmatically what appears to himself regarding the matters presented, not making any confident declaration, but just explaining his own state of mind.[12]

Although I have discussed such a *nontheoretical* variety of skepticism before,[13] I think I ought to pause briefly here and digress from my main line of argument to make a few more remarks about it before writing skepticism off finally, for the charge might be made that my arguments beg the question against such a nontheoretical or Pyrrhonic form of skepticism by assuming that skepticism must be a theory, an assumption that Pyrrhonists (like Sextus) reject.

What, then, might such a Pyrrhonist say? Suppose we were having a discussion and I were to claim, "People know things," and he were to respond, "No, nobody knows anything." Clearly I mean by my statement to assert a theory (I would call it a fact) about the existence of knowledge, but the nontheoretical skeptic, although he may appear to be disputing my theory by stating an inconsistent theory about the existence of knowledge, is not really doing this at all. Rather, he is only, as Sextus says, making an announcement; he is "just explaining his own state of mind."

The first thing we can say about our imaginary dialogue is that the two of us are talking at cross purposes. I am referring to one thing, the existence of knowledge, Sextus to another, his state of mind. Thus my remark, although it may appear pertinent to his, is quite irrelevant to what he says. By the same token, however, his remark is equally irrelevant to what I have said. Or, directly to the point, my statement has no relevance to the question of what his state of mind is, and his statement has no relevance to the question of whether anyone knows anything. As far as relevance to that question is concerned he might just as well have said "I am dreaming of castles in Spain." This last point can be generalized. As long as someone like Sextus limits his remarks to an explanation of his own state of mind, *nothing* he says is in any way relevant to the question of whether knowledge exists. Because he offers no theory about the existence of knowledge, the cognitivist need take no heed of what the nontheoretical skeptic says. In disregarding him, the cognitivist does not beg the question against him because he has never entered the debate. So the cognitivist can, with complete impunity, assert his theory that people know things both as an undisputed and as an indisputable fact.[14]

The only kind of skepticism which needs to be taken seriously, as far as the dispute about the existence of knowledge is concerned, is a skepticism that advances a *theory*; i.e., Academic skepticism. But such a skepticism, in any form it may take, we have found to be logically untenable. Every argument we attempt to mount, no matter what its content and purported conclusion, leads to cognitivism because it presupposes cognitivism. Although most epistemologists are probably ready to accept this verdict, some may remain uneasy about the fact that the cognitivistic claim, that knowledge exists, can be supported only by use of a circular argument. I have already tried to mitigate any uneasiness on this score by the distinction I have drawn between circular arguments and question-begging arguments, but I should like to return to the theme for a few additional remarks.

We might begin by asking, What is it about a circular argument that causes us uneasiness? The answer is fairly clear: A circular argument is not an argument. It gives the impression of providing us with reasons supporting a certain conclusion, but these reasons cannot *support* that conclusion because its truth has been presupposed from the outset. In ordinary situations (as typified by my example of the dispute between X and Y) this objection to circular arguments is well taken; but, as we have seen, the real charge being made is not that the arguments are circular but rather that they beg the question against their opposition. However, when we find ourselves in an unusual situation, as in the case of the argument between

A and B, in which the arguments to support *both* sides rest on the same presuppositions, the charge of circularity should lose its sting; for in these situations no question gets begged. One cannot, after all, legitimately accuse an opponent of taking an unfair advantage in a dispute by making a certain presupposition in his argument if one must make the same presupposition oneself.

But more can, I think, be said in defense of circular argumentation. If one recognizes that knowledge exists and remembers that, in order to know anything, one must be able to give reasons that establish its truth, then he can conclude that two alternatives regarding the reasons given in support of any proposition are open: Either (1) these reasons must be supported by other reasons capable of establishing their truth, and the supporting reasons in turn need support from further reasons, and so on ad infinitum or (2) the reasons given (or some set of reasons at some level) must be self-supporting, so need no support from a further set of reasons to establish their truth. And to say that a reason is self-supporting is to imply that any argument given in its "support" will be circular. On alternative (1), we can never legitimately claim to know anything because any knowledge claim we make generates a vicious infinite regress, but on alternative (2) we can know things. Since we have established that we do know things, we must accept alternative (2).

The purpose of the considerations I have just offered is to place circular argumentation (in certain cases) in a perspective different from the one in which we ordinarily view it. The point they intend to make can be formulated in the following way: The truth of some propositions is *self-justifying*. When I say this I do not mean the same thing as saying that the propositions are "self-evident," for I am not arguing that we directly "apprehend" or "intuit" the truth of these propositions. We may or we may not; in any case whether we do or do not is irrelevant to my thesis. Rather, I am arguing a logical point—that the truth of some propositions can be established only by an argument in which their truth is presupposed; i.e., by a circular argument. However, all arguments, including even those that attempt to establish the truth of the denial of these propositions, must presuppose the propositions to be true. Although such propositions can be supported only by an appeal to themselves, since all possible arguments must accept them, we are *justified* in asserting them to be true, for no conceivable grounds exist that can be given to support the contention that they are false. It is this feature of propositions like "A proposition cannot be both true and false" or "Someone knows something" to which I am referring when I call them "self-justifying." Because they are self-justifying, arguments offered in their behalf will necessarily turn out to be circular, but it is their self-justifying character that is epistemologically crucial.

The question with which I began this section "What is wrong with circular arguments?" has been answered. Simply put: nothing. If a circular argument is objectionable—as most are—that is because it is question-begging as well. And it is because it is question-begging rather than because it is circular that it is objectionable. I have gone on to show that an argument used to establish that knowledge exists, although it must be circular, cannot be question-begging, for there is no question to be begged. Therefore the objection to cognitivism I raised in §5 of chapter vi, and labeled negative skepticism, can be dismissed. So I am free to resume the cognitivistic stance with which I launched this study but which I was prepared to abandon in favor of negative skepticism, with all its disastrous consequences, at the beginning of this chapter.

3 Logic and the World

Some propositions (e.g., "Knowledge exists"), I have concluded, are self-justifying. Their truth is not dependent on something other than themselves; rather they are true because they *must be* true. They would be true in all possible worlds; so they cannot be false in any world, including the world that exists.[15] Such propositions must be true because they are logically necessary; their denial involves a contradiction. The case I have made for these propositions thus rests on logical considerations alone. In doing so, however, it may seem to involve an assumption that might conceivably be questioned. Since a proposition, to be true, must faithfully articulate or describe its object (which is a part of the world independent of the proposition itself), my conclusion that a logically necessary proposition must be true *assumes* that the laws of logic apply to the world. That is to say, it assumes that the world abides by these laws, that it is logical rather than alogical.

The contention that I have made an assumption here—in the sense that, in basing my case on logical considerations, I have done something questionable—is one that most epistemologists would certainly dismiss out of hand, for they would agree with me that all arguments *must* be based on logic. Nevertheless, a skeptic by the very nature of the position he is trying to defend must be a peculiar epistemologist. Also, he has been driven by the argument of the last section into a corner from which every route of escape seems blocked. Even though I have destroyed his thesis logically, perhaps he has one chance of escape, by a repudiation of logic. So let us give him that chance; let us see if he can construct a case for the skeptical view that, since the world does not (or may not) exemplify the laws of logic, my demonstration, that "Knowledge exists" is a logically necessary proposition, is consistent with the real or actual nonexistence of knowledge.

Since an alogical world would be one in which the laws of logic could be violated, to consider such a world, perhaps the best device would be to examine the possibility of a world whose nature is not dictated by the requirement of noncontradiction embodied in the most basic of those laws. In this world, a proposition could be both true and false. Is such a world possible?

The world about whose possible existence we are now inquiring would have a nature quite different from that of the world as I have assumed it to be in my argument. But in what specific ways would such a world differ from a logical world? What could we say if we were asked to give some positive characterization of this world? Could we say, for example, that it is infinite? In a world to which the law of noncontradiction does not apply, the adjective *infinite* is not incompatible with the contradictory adjective *finite*, so to characterize our world as infinite is equally to characterize it as finite, which is to affirm nothing whatsoever about its size. Is it eternal? Then it is equally temporal. Etc. It is clear that whatever attempt we might make to give our alogical world any definite attribute whatsoever would lead us into the same dilemma. So it would seem that we are unable to say anything definite about it at all. Rather the only characterization we can make of it is that, being alogical, it is different from the logical world I have been assuming. But this point of difference must be examined further. To suppose a world to be alogical is to suppose that it is not governed by the law of noncontradiction. Since this law is necessary to distinguish different things from each other and to prevent both of two inconsistent properties from characterizing the same subject, a world in which the law of noncontradiction is void, although it possesses the property of being different from a logical world, is still a world to which the inconsistent property of being the same as a logical world equally belongs. Thus we cannot say of an alogical world that it is different from a logical world. Since we cannot distinguish the two worlds, the skeptic has not succeeded in embodying his vision of a world that differs from the world I have been assuming, in the sense that the law of noncontradiction does not apply to it.

Here, however, I think we must pause and allow the skeptic to reply. I believe he would have to concede that the argument I have given establishes that we cannot conceive of a world to which the law of noncontradiction does not apply, our very attempts to do so always thrusting us back into a world in which the law does apply. But he might challenge the conclusions I would draw from this concession; namely, that such a world is inconceivable, that what is inconceivable cannot exist, and therefore that an alogical world is an impossibility. He might contend that to reach these conclusions I have employed an argument in which I am guilty of two non sequiturs. In the first place, I have concluded from the fact that we cannot conceive of an alogical world that such a world is inconceivable. But our inability to conceive of this world may be a reflection only on our limited powers of conception. May it not be true that if we had greater powers, we could conceive of it? Might not Lehrer's Googols, for instance, be able to conceive of it? If they, or any being, could conceive of an alogical world, such a world is obviously conceivable. On what grounds do we make our limited capacities of conception definitive of the nature of things? In the second place, it does not follow that an alogical world, even if it should prove to be inconceivable, cannot exist. To argue in this way is to assume that whatever is inconceivable is impossible. But why should we assume that? May it not be the case that an alogical world exists, even though we cannot describe it, or even talk about it to the extent of distinguishing it from a logical world, because, being alogical, it is inconceivable?

The questions I have just raised on behalf of the skeptic may appear gratuitous. Indeed, it might be wondered why I take the trouble even to consider them. The stock response philosophers have given to such questions—on those rare occasions when they have even raised them—is to brush them off peremptorily; for it is obvious that the skeptic, who uses them to support the view that, since the world may be alogical, the logical demonstration that knowledge exists is compatible with the actual nonexistence of knowledge, in the very process of articulating them must assume the logicality of the world, so contradict himself every time he opens his mouth. I myself believe that this response is both appropriate and decisive, for we must not forget the point that is at issue in our controversy. On the one hand we have the theory about knowledge offered by the cognitivist, which we have found to be logically necessary, and, on the other, the "theory" offered by the skeptic, which we have found to be self-contradictory. Our problem is to decide which of these two incompatible theories we should accept. One might say that under these conditions it would be a mark of insanity were we to opt for skepticism, but this would really miss the point, for the difficulty is much more basic than anything captured by such an epithet. We simply *cannot* accept skepticism and the alogical world it attempts to dangle before us.

Still, looked at from the side of the skeptic, such a response may seem cavalier. At least we should offer him the courtesy of a reply to the charges he has made against our argument, particularly since he is now reduced to his last desperate expedient. So let us consider them a bit further. Is it a non sequitur to conclude that what we cannot conceive of is inconceivable? I think the answer turns on what is meant by conceiving of something and what the reasons are for making us unable to conceive of an alogical world. Here analogies are sometimes brought into play, but they are misleading and dangerous. At one time it was said that Mt. Everest was unclimbable, because no one could climb it. But then it was shown to be climbable when mountaineers reached its summit. Or, coming closer to our problem of conceivability. one sometimes hears that something—a chiliagon, say—is unimaginable, because we cannot imagine it. Yet it is quite possible to conceive of beings with much stronger powers of imagination than ours who could imagine a chiliagon without difficulty. So we cannot legitimately infer from our inability to imagine a chiliagon that it is unimaginable. Such analogies, particularly the one based on imagination, are enticing; but they are misleading because the situations we must compare are in a crucial sense disanalogous. There is no logical contradiction involved in climbing Mt. Everest or in imagining a chiliagon, but there is in attempting to conceive of an alogical world. Because it is logically impossible to conceive of an alogical world, the only being who could be said to conceive of it would be one who is capable of performing an act of conception that it is logically impossible to accomplish. There is and can be no such being.

Turning to the skeptics' second objection, can we justify our conclusion that a world that is logically inconceivable cannot exist? To try to cope with this question, let us for the moment put aside the fact that we cannot conceive of an alogical world and attempt to postulate such a world to see what results we get. A world, we shall say, exists and it is alogical. As we have already seen, we can say nothing about the nature of this world. But presumably we can say that, because it is alogical, the laws of logic do not hold in it. Central among these laws is that of noncontradiction. So we could offer at least the following true proposition about this world: "The law of noncontradiction does not hold." However, the law of noncontradiction stipulates that the same proposition cannot be both true and false. Thus in a world in which the law does not hold, the same proposition can be both true and false. So we can conclude that in this world the truth of the statement "The law of noncontradiction does not hold" does not preclude its falsity. In such a world the proposition is equally as false as it is true. But if the proposition "The law of noncontradiction does not hold" is false in the world we are attempting to postulate, the world is not alogical at all because it does not void the basic law of logic. We have failed in our attempt to postulate an alogical world.

One more argument: If the skeptic is correct in his contention that all logical arguments against his position fail to be coercive because the world is (or may be) alogical, he is claiming the possible existence of such a world. Let us attempt to suppose this possibility actually to be realized. The proposition "An alogical world exists" would then be true. But the proposition would, for obvious reasons, also be false. If the proposition is false, we have not succeeded in actualizing the possibility of such a world. Nor can we ever succeed in doing so. But a possibility that cannot be actualized is an impossibility. So we can conclude that it is impossible that an alogical world could exist. The skeptics' attempt to avoid the cognitivists' demonstration of the necessary existence of knowledge by retreating into a world in which logical demonstrations can be set aside can end only in failure, for there is and can be no theoretical "space" into which the skeptics can move, no world that can possibly exist in which the laws of logic do not hold.

4 A Qualification

The conclusion that we reached earlier, that the cognitivists' thesis "Knowledge exists" is necessarily true, can now be reiterated, not only as logically necessary but as ontologically necessary as well, for what is logically necessary is ontologically necessary. There can be no world in which knowledge does not exist.[16] Yet there is a peculiarity about this truth and its necessity that needs to be pointed out, for it differs in at least one way from certain other necessary truths. Consider the proposition "A proposition cannot be both true and false." This proposition is not only necessarily true but universally true as well. It is an example of what Leibniz describes as an "eternal verity." There are no conceivable circumstances in which it could be false; it always has been true and always will be true. The proposition "Knowledge exists," however, does not seem to be an eternal verity. Rather, its truth seems to have temporal limitations. For knowledge to exist, someone must know something. Unless we assume the eternal existence of a knowing mind—an assumption I cannot defend so am not prepared to make—we must admit the possibility that at some time in the past knowledge did not exist, for the simple reason that no beings capable of knowing existed. Assuming our planet to be the sole abode of intelligent beings, we have strong empirical evidence for the actual existence of such a past time, before the evolution of man (or possibly the higher animals). And we can equally well visualize a possible future time in which all beings capable of knowledge would be eliminated from the universe. Again, knowledge would cease to exist.

Granting these qualifications, what are we to say about the necessary truth of the proposition "Knowledge exists"? We seem to have in it a necessary truth that may be false, that, in fact, was almost surely false at some time in the past. But if a proposition can be false, how can we claim it to be a necessary truth?

Surely we are faced with something odd here. But not unique, for there is a famous parallel example in the literature, whose analysis can help us in resolving the issue we have raised. In the second *Meditation* Descartes demonstrated the necessary truth of the proposition "I exist."[17] But he noted a limitation in that necessity. He recognized that he could establish his necessary existence *only* as long as he thought, for to *think* "I do not exist" is self-contradictory. When he was not thinking, Descartes readily admitted, it was possible that he did not exist. Or, to put the same point in a somewhat different way, although it is self-contradictory for Descartes to think "I, Descartes, do not exist," it is certainly not self-contradictory for me to think "Descartes does not exist." We have, thus, in Descartes's claim that he must exist a proposition that is necessarily true when he asserts it but is not universally true in the sense of being an eternal verity like the law of noncontradiction.

Let us now transfer our analysis of the Cartesian proposition to our own case "Knowledge exists" to see what results we get. We can say that this proposition is necessarily true whenever anyone thinks it, asserts it, or even denies it, because the attempt to deny it, whether in thought or speech, being self-contradictory, entails its truth. But what if neither it nor its denial is ever thought, what if there are no cognitivists in existence to assert it, or skeptics to deny it, or any intelligent beings to think at all? What effect does this lack of thinkers have on the necessary truth of our proposition? Here the analogy with the Cartesian case can be brought into play. Although Descartes alone could demonstrate his own existence, this limitation does not detract from the cogency of his demonstration. If it is self-contradictory for Descartes to think and yet not to exist (or to think of himself as not existing), then logically he must exist whenever he thinks. By analogy, if it is self-contradictory for anyone to think that no one knows anything, then logically such a thought entails that someone must know something. The fact that at some time no one would be thinking (because no thinker was in existence) does not obviate the necessary existence of knowledge once cognitivists and skeptics appear on the world scene.[18]

Nevertheless, the analogy between Descartes's situation and our own is not complete. The case for the necessary existence of Descartes is much more limited than that for the necessary existence of knowledge. Only Descartes could claim that he existed necessarily. Anyone else can doubt his existence.[19] But when we turn to the existence of knowledge, this limitation does not apply, for everyone who considers the question, cognitivist and skeptic alike, must agree that knowledge necessarily exists. We can without contradiction assert that the world has contained no French philosopher named Descartes; we can also without contradiction assert that the world at some time in the past contained no knowers and hence no knowledge; but we cannot without contradiction assert that the world contains no knowers and hence no knowledge at all, for (as we have already shown) we must make knowledge commitments ourselves in our very attempt to formulate such a claim. Knowledge that the proposition "Knowledge necessarily exists" is necessarily true is, unlike that of the proposition "Descartes necessarily exists," something that all of us can share.

To summarize, we seem to have to distinguish at least three varieties of necessary truth. At one extreme are the "eternal verities," for example, the law of noncontradiction. No circumstances can be conceived in which propositions embodying them can be false. On the other side are what might be termed "existential verities," of which Descartes's proposition "I exist" is an example. Although it is necessarily true that Descartes should exist while he is thinking, it is not necessarily true that the world should have contained the thinker, Descartes. In an intermediate position are what might be called "theoretical verities," truths like "Knowledge exists." A world in which knowledge at one time in the past did not exist or at some time in the future will not exist is possible, but a world in which knowledge does not now exist is impossible. As long as the world contains cognitivists or skeptics, who assert theories about the existence of knowledge, knowledge must exist. Hence the skeptics' claim that knowledge does not exist must be false.

5 Is Knowledge that Knowledge Exists Knowledge?

I know that knowledge exists; anyone can know that knowledge exists. But in knowing this what are we knowing? Indeed are we knowing anything at all? In this section I should like to consider an objection to my cognitivistic conclusion of a type that I have not raised before, one that I believe some epistemologists would take very seriously indeed.

The objection I have in mind is directed against the method I have used to demonstrate my case for cognitivism. Basically, that method has been to establish that the proposition "Knowledge exists" is true (hence something I know) because it is logically necessary, its denial involving a contradiction. Now, goes the objection, if we are to possess authentic knowledge, the propositions we claim to know must have some content; they cannot be vacuous. But a proposition whose truth is logically necessary *cannot* have any content; rather it *must* be vacuous. So, although I may have demonstrated that the proposition "Knowledge exists" is necessarily true, I have not succeeded in acquiring any substantive knowledge, for this proposition, being logically necessary, is necessarily empty of content.

That this is a serious objection cannot, I think, be denied. Nevertheless, I believe that a satisfactory answer can be found for it. I shall try to provide such an answer in this section, offering two responses to the objection, one specific and the other general. On the specific side, the question that must be faced is whether the propositions I claim as knowledge because I have demonstrated them to be true, "Knowledge exists" or "Someone knows something" and "I know something," constitute substantive items of knowledge. Now it might be argued that they do not, because they give no information about *what* knowledge exists. To know, one must know *something*, but to know only that one knows something is not yet to know anything at all. Before I can legitimately claim that I know, I must establish the truth of some proposition that constitutes a specific example of the knowledge I have shown to exist. To begin to answer this charge, I should acknowledge that in knowing something, even in knowing that knowledge exists, I do not know a great deal, and certainly not anything specific (other than that knowledge exists). Therefore, to elaborate my cognitivistic epistemology I should go on to establish the truth of many more propositions, thus augmenting my stock of knowledge, to the extent that this is possible. Yet it must be remembered that my purpose in writing this book has not been to augment my stock of knowledge but rather to answer the question: Can I (or anyone else) know anything at all? In accomplishing that purpose, moreover, I have offered a method that one can use in order to augment the stock of things he knows; if he can establish a proposition both to have substantive content and to be logically necessary, he can then legitimately claim it as an item of knowledge. How many and what type of propositions can be shown to constitute things we know by use of this method is, as yet, an unanswered question; but I believe it to be one to which cognitivistic epistemologists should devote more attention than most of them now do. (Of course, this advice is pointless, if the objection I have just raised is cogent, for it holds that *no* such propositions exist.) But, to return to my propositions "Knowledge exists" and "I know something," though I would grant that they contain no specific items of knowledge (beyond themselves), I think it is a mistake to call them vacuous. On the contrary, to be able to make the legitimate claim that one knows something is, in my opinion, extremely important. Speaking for myself, I should say that of the untold number of things I desire to know, it ranks very near the top. Surely, I would like to succeed in establishing the truth or other, more specific propositions, but, in my own mind, to establish that I can and do know something, so need not remain in ignorance, is an accomplishment of no mean dimensions. I decided to write this book because I considered skepticism to be a serious, even if highly unpalatable, option for epistemologists. And as the beginning of this chapter shows, I crossed the line briefly into a form of skepticism. To have been able to reach a definitive resolution of the controversy between cognitivism and skepticism is a goal I believe to be well worth the efforts I have expended. If, on one hand, the contention that the proposition "I know something" is vacuous entails that this goal is empty—and that I have, as a result, accomplished nothing—I reject it. If, on the other hand, the contention is simply the entailed result of the established self-contradictory nature of skepticism, I would respond that it is either misleading (in that it gives the ordinary word *vacuous* a special technical—and innocuous—meaning), or else that it is false.

But, it might be replied, the argument that I have just given misses the point. In response to the charge that propositions like "Knowledge exists" are vacuous, I have claimed them to be important. However, might they not be both? To answer this question, as well as to respond to the objection with which I began the section, I shall now turn to a general argument. Before I can begin, however, I must clarify two crucial notions. The first is the term *tautology*, which has a standard use in technical logic. According to this usage, the denial of any proposition that involves a contradiction is a tautology. Thus the proposition "Knowledge exists" would be a *logical* tautology. If that is *all* that is meant—and if it is agreed that a logical tautology can contain *substantive* content, even of an important nature—I should be willing to accept it as a technical term descriptive of the things I have claimed to know. The second term that needs clarification is *vacuous*. If it is agreed that "vacuous" is synonymous with "tautologous," so that a vacuous proposition can also have *substantive* content, I should not refuse to accept it. Unfortunately, both of these terms—particularly vacuous—have ordinary, nontechnical meanings of a very different kind, being used to refer to statements that are empty, or lacking in content. So understood, a tautology, or vacuous proposition, can contain no information about anything. It is this notion of emptiness or vacuity which I would refuse to apply to the propositions whose truth I have demonstrated, for they cannot be empty, in the sense of telling us nothing about the nature of things, and important, in the sense in which I believe them to be. So, in the argument that follows, I shall be directing my remarks solely against the contention that all logically necessary propositions are tautologous or vacuous, in the sense of being empty of content. In this I do not believe I shall be attacking a straw man, for I think that at least some, and perhaps many, epistemologists do accept the thesis that a logically necessary proposition must be empty.

To turn directly to my argument, my objective is to show that the general case directed against my methodology—to the effect that the propositions I claim as things I know cannot be substantive so cannot give us any information because all logically necessary propositions are vacuous, in the sense of lacking any content—is mistaken. I shall begin by asking a question: Agreeing that some epistemologists would accept this case against my methodology, why should they do so? What reasons can be offered in support of the universal connection that such epistemologists affirm between logically necessary and vacuous propositions? For me the answers to these questions are crucial, because if it is true that all logically necessary propositions are vacuous, my entire case against skepticism is put in jeopardy. If my "knowledge" that knowledge exists is empty, telling me nothing, it is hard to see how I can use it to demolish skepticism, for a vacuous proposition containing no information cannot, it seems apparent, succeed in refuting a philosophical theory. So, to preserve the case I have made against skepticism, I must somehow show that the thesis that all logically necessary propositions are vacuous is false.

It might be argued that I have set myself a task I cannot possibly accomplish, because the reason why all logically necessary propositions are vacuous is that the proposition that embodies it (i.e., "All logically necessary propositions are vacuous") is true by definition, for those who accept it *define* the concept "logically necessary proposition" in such a way that the definition includes "vacuous proposition." Hence the notion of a logically necessary nonvacuous proposition becomes a contradiction in terms. In response I should ask: Why do they define it in this way? Do they or do they not have any reason for so defining it? If they do not, their definition becomes arbitrary or conventional, thus lays no constraint on anyone. Just as they can arbitrarily define logically necessary proposition in such a way that all propositions that satisfy their definition must be vacuous, so I am equally free to define it in such a way that some or even all propositions that satisfy my definition must be nonvacuous. In a contest along these lines both sides are reduced to playing with words and consequently miss the real issue; namely, *Are* all logically necessary propositions vacuous? So we can put aside a solution based on arbitrary definition and turn to the only viable way of seeking a resolution of our issue. To pursue this alternative, we must begin by assuming that those who define logically necessary proposition in such a manner that all propositions satisfying their definition must be vacuous as well do not do so arbitrarily but have reasons for defining it in this way. We do not need to delve in detail here into what these reasons might be because we can say, generally, that they are summed up in a positive answer to the question I asked just above. The definition is justified because all logically necessary propositions *are* also vacuous. This, of course, is a statement of the objection with which I began the section. Since I do not think it to be true, I must try to show why it is false. In order to go about doing so, I think it best to begin by resolving a couple of preliminary problems. We must have a clear conception, first, of the nature of the proposition itself and, second, of the method by which its truth might be established.

When I ask, What is the nature of the proposition "All logically necessary propositions are vacuous"? my question is concerned with seeking an answer to the way in which this proposition should appropriately be classified within the two (exhaustive) categories of vacuous and nonvacuous (or informative). Is the proposition itself vacuous or is it informative? The answer to this question depends on the *meanings* of the concepts which the proposition contains. If the proposition were vacuous, these meanings would either have to be identical with each other or else be related to each other in such a way that the class of logically necessary propositions must fall within that of vacuous propositions. It would, in other words, have to be like propositions such as "All geometrical triangles are three-sided plane figures" or "All geometrical triangles are plane figures." Thus, to claim that a proposition was logically necessary but not vacuous would be like claiming that something was a triangle but did not have three sides (or was not a plane figure). Are the meanings of the concepts with which we are concerned related to each other in this way? First, "logically necessary" proposition: What does it mean to say that a proposition is logically necessary? What information are we giving about a proposition when we call it logically necessary? We are saying, first, that it is true and, second, that its truth can be demonstrated by logical means alone. The information we give about a proposition when we call it logically necessary concerns its truth-value and the manner in which that truth-value is established. Second, "vacuous" proposition: What does it mean? What information are we giving, when we say of a proposition that it is vacuous? This adjective, when used to describe a proposition, is concerned with the contents of the proposition; it tells us that the proposition is empty, or noninformative. If, for example, someone knows the meaning of the concept triangle, we do not add to his information when we tell him that all triangles are three-sided.

Putting our results together, I think we must agree that the proposition "All logically necessary propositions are vacuous" must be judged to be a nonvacuous or informative proposition. It asserts a connection between propositions in terms of characteristics of quite different kinds, the first having to do with their truth-value and the second with their content. The nonvacuous nature of this proposition can also be shown by considering its denial. If the proposition were vacuous, because of a relationship of identity between its subject and predicate, its denial "Some logically necessary propositions are informative" would be a contradiction in terms. It would be comparable to the proposition "Some triangles are not three-sided." But clearly it is not. Although it may be false, its assertion does not involve one in a verbal self-contradiction.

One other reason can be given in support of the view that the proposition with which we are concerned is nonvacuous; namely, that to provide an objection to my cognitivistic conclusion, it must be nonvacuous. If the proposition were vacuous, it would be noninformative, so could tell us nothing about anything. Specifically, it could not give us any information about other propositions so could not tell us that the proposition "I know something" is either informative or vacuous. As a result, we could with perfect consistency accept the proposition that all logically necessary propositions are vacuous and still claim that the proposition "I know something" is *both* logically necessary and informative. But the whole purpose of the objection, based on the thesis that all logically necessary propositions are vacuous, is to show that if my proposition "I know something" is logically necessary, it must be vacuous as well. If the thesis, therefore, is held to be vacuous, the objection collapses. Because of both the meanings of the concepts it is composed of, and the task it is employed to perform, I conclude that the proposition "All logically necessary proposition are vacuous" must be nonvacuous.

I turn now to the second preliminary problem to be resolved concerning this proposition; namely, how might its truth be established? What grounds can those who accept it give for believing it to be true? One possible answer is that it is a generalization. But this explanation runs into at least two difficulties. First, if it is a generalization, it can be falsified by the production of an exception. If a proposition is found that is both logically necessary and informative, the generalization is overthrown. And I have in fact found such a proposition; namely, "Someone knows something." So we can conclude that the proposition we are considering is a generalization that has been falsified.

I am sure that those who hold that all logically necessary propositions are vacuous would deny that I have produced a genuine exception to this dictum. (In any case, if they did not deny this, they would have lost the argument.) So I might ask them: Why is my proposition not an exception? Also, what kind of proposition would they accept as an authentic exception? I think the last question is the crucial one, because of the way in which it would be answered, for I would be told that it is futile to go on searching for exceptions. I should never be able to produce one because it is impossible that there should *be* one. If this is the kind of answer that holders of the thesis under examination would give me, their proposition clearly is no generalization, for generalizations always admit of possible exceptions.

The second difficulty with the view that the proposition in question is a generalization lies in the grounds on which it could rest, if it were a generalization. To justify the generalizations we make, we must have some evidence we can offer in their support. Although secondary forms of evidence are often used (like hearsay or authority), ultimately our evidence must rest on an examination of the objects about which we make our generalizations. For example, the naturalists who made the generalization "All swans are white" did so on the basis of their observation of swans. (And their generalization was overturned when an exception to it was observed.) So we have to ask: Can one accept the truth of the proposition we are examining, as he can that of the generalization about swans, on the basis of observed evidence, of an extensive, empirical examination of propositions? In the first place, those who have accepted the proposition have never conducted such an examination. And in the second place, they could not do so, for no *observation* of logically necessary propositions could ever provide evidence that they are *either* vacuous or informative. Indeed, no observation of propositions could provide evidence that they are logically necessary. The reason is simple: No proposition can be observed; propositions are not observable objects. Although we can observe the sentences in which propositions are embodied and make empirical generalizations about them—that some are written, some are spoken, etc.—we cannot reach conclusions like "All logically necessary propositions are vacuous" through an observation of anything. So this proposition cannot be a generalization based on evidence.

What then is it? On what grounds does it rest? We saw earlier that it cannot be an arbitrary definition. And surely those who believe it do not accept it as an article of faith. Only one viable alternative remains. The proposition must be held to be a logical truth. All logically necessary propositions are vacuous because they *must be* vacuous. It is for this reason that it is futile for anyone to search for an exception. To maintain, however, that the truth of the proposition rests on logical grounds is to imply that the proposition is logically necessary. Thus we have resolved the second preliminary problem I raised about this proposition. Those who accept the proposition "All logically necessary propositions are vacuous" must believe it to be true because they hold it to be logically necessary.

Having completed our consideration of the two preliminary problems that needed to be resolved, we are now ready to turn to our main issue: Is the objection to my cognitivistic conclusion; namely, that the propositions "I know something" or "Knowledge exists" cannot constitute items of knowledge because they are logically necessary and all logically necessary propositions are vacuous, cogent? But we should now be able to see that we do not need to pursue this issue any further, for our preliminary investigation has already resolved it. We have discovered that the proposition on which the objection rests "All logically necessary propositions are vacuous" must *itself* be (a) logically necessary and (b) nonvacuous. It must, that is, be an example of a type of proposition it claims to be logically impossible. It is, thus, self-referentially self-refuting. Because it is, we can conclude that its denial "Some logically necessary propositions are informative (nonvacuous)" is necessarily true. And as we have already by implication shown, this proposition is informative as well. Thus it is an example of a logically necessary informative proposition.

Because I have established that the informative proposition "Some logically necessary propositions are informative" is true, by showing it to be logically necessary, I can legitimately claim it to be something I know. Besides increasing my stock of knowledge, my demonstration of its truth allows me to conclude (a) that the proposition "I know something," even though it is logically necessary, can still be informative, thus a possible authentic item of knowledge, and (b) that its necessary truth is given a second grounding because the proposition "I know that some logically necessary propositions are informative" entails the proposition "I know something." This last proposition is not just possibly but actually informative, as well, because it connects two concepts independent in their meanings—that of "I" (simply a being) and that of a possessor of knowledge. (That I—as a distinct being —should exist without knowing anything would involve no contradiction in terms.) Finally, the proposition, equally informative, "Knowledge exists" is shown to be true, being entailed by the proposition "I know something."

I conclude that my demonstration that knowledge exists is indeed knowledge. By accomplishing the demonstration I have established that I myself know something. Although I may have been in a state of complete ignorance at one time and other beings (including human beings) may presently be in such a state, I am not now myself ignorant. Nor need others be, for they can establish that some informative propositions are true as well as I can. Thus they can legitimately refer to themselves as *knowers*. Having eliminated the final serious objection to my argument, I rest my case for cognitivism.

6 The Range and Limits of Knowledge

My concern in this book has been to resolve the question of whether knowledge exists. I believe that I have succeeded in doing that, so the task I set myself at the beginning has been accomplished. Yet, before I conclude, I should like to make a few brief remarks about a problem that, to my mind, is of comparable importance to the issue of the existence of knowledge. Assuming a positive resolution of that issue, we can then ask ourselves: What is the extent or range of our possible knowledge? Just what and how much can we know? To deal with this question adequately is obviously far beyond the scope of our present project, for it would require at least a book in its own right. Nevertheless, I should like to give a short sketch in these last two sections of what seem to me to be the salient points and problems with which such an inquiry would have to deal.

Although I have not discussed the question of the extent of our possible knowledge directly in my earlier arguments, I have reached conclusions that bear on that issue, notably in the present chapter. I have, that is, offered several examples of things that I know—and that others can know as well. Do these examples offer any clue to the range of our possible knowledge? To pursue this point, perhaps the best way to begin is to recollect the grounds on which I claimed them to be things I know. Looking back we can see that the principal reason I gave for such a claim was that I was able to demonstrate the propositions in question to be logically necessary, their denials involving a contradiction. Furthermore, the propositions were found to be substantive or informative. Making use of these examples we can generate two general criteria of knowledge, saying that X knows that p if X can establish that p is (1) logically necessary and (2) substantive. Thus we can say that I (or anyone else) can include in what I know all those propositions that I can establish to satisfy these conditions. Such *at least* is the range of my possible knowledge.

The conclusion we have just reached presents us with an opportunity and raises a problem we need to resolve. The opportunity is to enlarge the domain of knowledge we have carved out, determining the number and kind of propositions which can fulfill the criteria I have just enumerated. One can recognize that the number of such propositions is indefinite, but their precise nature cannot be discovered prior to an actual investigation. To conduct the kind of investigation necessary is not something for which I have space here; I suggest, nevertheless, that it is an undertaking of great importance to epistemology.

The problem raised by our criteria turns on what we take their exact nature to be. I have stated them in such a way that they offer *sufficient* conditions of knowledge. If we can show that a proposition satisfies these criteria, we can legitimately claim it as something we know. However, we might state the criteria in a way that would make them *necessary* as well as sufficient conditions of knowledge. Thus we might say, X knows that *p* iff X can establish that *p* is (1) logically necessary and (2) substantive. If we make this move, we limit the domain of possible knowledge to those propositions we can show to satisfy the criteria, and to them alone. In doing so, however, we remove from the realm of possible knowledge vast—and, I think, extremely important—areas of human belief. Should we do this or should we, to the contrary, relax the necessary conditions of knowledge in ways (yet to be determined) which will allow us to extend the range of possible knowledge beyond that of substantive propositions we can establish to be logically necessary? And if we decide to do the latter, how far should the criteria we select as necessary for knowledge permit that range to extend?

In the brief remarks that follow I shall limit myself to a discussion of the first of the two questions I have just raised. Let us suppose that we undertake the consideration of defining knowledge in such a way that the conditions necessary and sufficient to qualify a proposition as something we know are to be significantly relaxed beyond those I have already listed in this section. Are there *any* restraints that control the extent to which we can pursue our procedure of relaxation? I think we can agree that one restraining factor must be taken into account; namely, that, whatever other, looser criteria of knowledge we adopt, we must retain as a necessary condition of knowledge that a proposition, to qualify as something we know, be true, for a definition of knowledge that would sanction a proposition like "He knows that it is raining but in fact it is not raining" is simply unacceptable as a rendition of the concept that people, whether philosophers or laymen, have traditionally and almost universally accepted. Implicit in our conception of knowledge is the assumption that knowledge without truth is a contradiction in terms.

If we agree that truth is a necessary condition of knowledge, we must still recognize that it is not a sufficient condition. So our proposed definition must include other necessary conditions to supplement it. Before we cast about for additional conditions to add to our definition, however, we need to be aware that we are already faced with a problem that will control the nature of the conditions that will satisfy our need. As we have already agreed, given any proposition *p*, we can say that if it is to qualify as something we know, *p* must be true. But how are we to determine of any *p* that it *is* true, that it *does* satisfy the truth condition of knowledge? We cannot discover its truth simply by looking at it, or writing it on paper, or repeating it aloud. No proposition wears its truth on its face. (In what I have just said I am, of course, denying that any substantive propositions are "self-evidently" true, in the normal meaning of that term. Although I believe that I can support my denial successfully, I shall not attempt to do so here.[20]) The only method by which we can determine that any proposition satisfies the truth condition of knowledge is to show that it satisfies some other condition, which, through its satisfaction, *guarantees* the proposition to be true. So we are led to some form of the standard definition of knowledge; namely, that knowledge is "justified true belief," which, when unpacked, means "belief justified to be true." Thus, to say of a proposition *p* that it satisfies the justification condition of knowledge is to imply that its truth is justified. The proposition cannot, in other words, satisfy the justification condition without satisfying the truth condition as well; for, to say of a proposition that it is justified but false is to contradict oneself.

To have a conception of knowledge which will determine the range of things we can know, therefore, we need to stipulate some method by which we can justify the truth of propositions.[21] If, furthermore, we wish to enlarge the range of propositions which we can claim as knowledge (beyond those that we can establish to be logically necessary), we must develop a method that will succeed in producing the desired result. That is, our method must be one through whose use we can justify the truth of a wider range of propositions. But what should such a method be? Many answers have been offered to this question, several of which have been accepted as adequate by different philosophers. Nevertheless, I believe that all suffer from a fatal defect. Given any one of these methods it can, I think, be shown (1) that, although some proposition *p* succeeds in fulfilling the conditions that the method claims sufficient to justify *p* as true, nevertheless (2) *p* may be false. But if truth is a necessary condition of knowledge, a proposition *p* that may be false (i.e., one whose truth is not guaranteed by its satisfaction of our justification condition) cannot qualify as something we know. Hence the method in question, because it allows such a result, must be unsatisfactory. To clarify the point I have just been making, let me give a brief illustration. Suppose an epistemologist were to say that we can know many things beyond what we can demonstrate to be logically necessary. The method by which we can know these things is *intuition*. More specifically, we can apprehend by an act of direct intellectual insight that these things are true. To offer an example, we can directly intuit that the proposition "Pleasure alone is intrinsically good" is true. Let us suppose that someone does, as apparently Henry Sidgwick did, intuit this proposition to be true. It does *not* follow from this that the proposition *is* true, for the proposition "Someone intuits the proposition 'Pleasure alone is intrinsically good' to be true, nevertheless that proposition is false" is perfectly self-consistent. The method used to provide a justification for the truth of the proposition does not entail its truth. It may, in fact, be false. Since its truth is a necessary condition of its constituting knowledge and since the only basis on which we can claim it to be true is the justification we offer in its behalf, we must conclude that the proposition fails to qualify as anything we can legitimately claim to know.

The deficiency in the method of intuition, as an example of a way in which we might justify the truth of propositions, is, I believe, not peculiar to this method but is shared by all of the other methods epistemologists have advanced to extend the range of possible knowledge. Since I cannot review all of these methods here, I shall content myself with posing a single question that can be addressed to each, in order to determine its viability as a conception of knowledge. Suppose a proposition p, which satisfies the conditions that the method in question lays down as sufficient to justify its truth: Does p's satisfaction of these conditions entail its truth or does it not? If it does not, the conception of knowledge in question must be rejected.

Accepting truth to be a necessary condition of knowledge, I have been led by the argument embodied in the question I have just asked to conclude that the only propositions we can legitimately claim to know are those for which we can offer a justification that entails their truth. To say of such propositions that they satisfy the conditions of the method used to establish their truth and are nevertheless in fact not true is to contradict oneself. For example, to say that the proposition "I know something" is an item of knowledge because I can establish it to be logically necessary yet it is in fact not true is to assert a self-contradiction, for its logical necessity entails its truth. Because I find this method of justification the only one capable of establishing the truth of propositions, I have been forced to conclude that propositions that fulfill its conditions encompass the range of our possible knowledge. All attempts of which I am aware to broaden our range of knowledge beyond these limits I have found to end in failure. Until I am offered some new method that is capable of surmounting the difficulties I have sketched, I must remain with the view that our knowledge is limited to the domain I have just marked out. However, I do not hold to this position dogmatically. On the contrary, I would welcome a way of showing that the range of our possible knowledge is broader than I now take it to be. I would like to be able to say "I know" much more often, and about many more things, than I now believe I am justified in doing.

7 Belief and Reasonable Belief

I am a cognitivist because I am logically compelled to be a cognitivist. Yet my cognitivism limits the range of what I believe myself justified in claiming to know to propositions I can establish to be logically necessary. So, if I were asked to describe my present view, I should refer to myself as a *logical cognitivist*. But, it might well be urged, my logical cognitivism, even though it is incompatible with total (or epistemological) skepticism, seems to be a species of mitigated skepticism, for it so circumscribes the range of our possible knowledge that the kinds of beliefs that are included within it are vastly smaller in number than those that are not. Most of what we believe is not anything we know or can know.

Although I think this conclusion is correct, I believe that

the charge of mitigated skepticism it seems to imply can be satisfactorily blunted. I should like to conclude by offering a suggestion as to the way in which that charge can be mitigated and then raise some questions about the suggestion itself. In these questions will be embodied what I consider to be the most difficult unresolved problems of epistemology. To begin my discussion, I think we must recognize, as an extremely important epistemological category, the notion of *reasonable* or *rational* belief. Our beliefs can thus be grouped under two main heads: (1) things we know and (2) things we do not know. But the second category can be further subdivided into (a) reasonable beliefs and (b) beliefs that are not reasonable. Although it may not be possible to draw a clear line of demarcation between subcategories (a) and (b) in the case of individual beliefs, nevertheless we should be able to develop criteria that will distinguish the two classes of belief from each other. Having done this, we can then go on to establish that many of the things we believe, covering a wide range of content, fall into the category of reasonable beliefs. So, although our beliefs regarding these things do not satisfy the conditions necessary to qualify them as knowledge, nevertheless they do qualify us as being reasonable in believing them to be true.

The proposal I am pursuing, which makes use of the notion of reasonable belief as a category distinct from knowledge but of great epistemological importance in itself, raises at least two problems that need resolution. The first is this: *Can* we establish the existence of any such category of belief? Earlier in the chapter I discussed briefly the conclusion of both John Kekes and Peter Unger—with which I agree—that skepticism entails irrationality.[22] If we can know nothing, neither can we reasonably believe anything. Assuming that we have succeeded in falsifying the hypothetical clause of the last sentence, does it follow that we can deny the consequent? In other words, can we conclude that, since we do know things, we can also reasonably believe things?[23] Logically, the conclusion does not follow, because our alleged incapability of knowing anything might be only one of several different reasons for our inability to have reasonable beliefs, therefore the demonstration that we are capable of knowing things does not of itself succeed in establishing that we can, as a result, reasonably believe things as well. I think an independent argument is required to establish the notion of reasonable belief as a legitimate epistemological category. Perhaps it can be shown that cognitivism does entail the existence of reasonable beliefs. But I have never seen the required argument worked out, nor can I visualize what form it would take.

The second problem I see concerning the notion of reasonable belief develops out of the first. Suppose we could establish the existence of an authentic category of reasonable belief. We would then need some criterion (or set of criteria) which we could apply to our various beliefs in order to qualify certain of them as falling within this category. What should our criterion be? The problem that arises here is this: If we adopt some specific criterion, we shall find ourselves authenticating certain propositions, or kinds of propositions, as qualifying as reasonable beliefs. But suppose we had adopted a different criterion from the one we in fact chose. Then we could find ourselves authenticating as reasonable, propositions different from, and even inconsistent with, those we would have authenticated under our first criterion. This problem is real. Given the incompatibility of criteria—an incompatibility that is not only logically possible but also has in fact occurred and has given rise to some of the most intractable disputes in the history of thought—which of the alternative possible criteria should we choose? And on what grounds could we justify our choice? Although a vast literature exists on these questions,[24] I know of no solution to the problem which can be considered decisive. Rather, all proposed solutions with which I am acquainted can be shown to be inadequate in some important way. The issue therefore remains one of the great open questions of epistemology.

I know that there are things I know. I believe, but do not now know, that there are other things I reasonably believe. Because many of the things I believe, and believe I am reasonable in believing, are of great importance to me, I should like to be able to say that I know I am reasonable in believing them. I would rather live by reason, even where I cannot have knowledge, than by ungrounded faith. I have the faith that I can do so, but I would prefer to know that I can do so. To gain that knowledge, however, I must resolve the problems I have raised in this final section.

Epilogue

At the beginning of this book I referred to Socrates's young friend Cratylus as an "archetypal skeptic." I did so not only because he is one of the earliest-known skeptics in the history of Western thought but also for the more important reason that he seems to have woven the logic of skepticism into the very fabric of his own life. Driven by his philosophy to the conclusion that he could know nothing and recognizing therefore that any utterance he might make would be an abandonment of his skeptical stance, he accepted the inevitable and lapsed into silence.

In this decision and action Cratylus proved himself to be not only strong-willed but clearheaded as well, for if the possibility of meaningful speech entails the possession of knowledge, the conviction that we can know nothing entails silence. In acting on his conviction in the way he did, Cratylus deserves a commendation to which few of the skeptical writers who have followed since his time can lay claim. The contrast, for example, between him and the twentieth-century skeptic, Peter Unger, is worthy of remark. In his *Ignorance*, Unger, like Cratylus, came to the conclusion that our ignorance enjoins us to be silent, but having done so, he then proceeded to write for another seventy pages. To the often-heard remark that philosophy has made no progress, perhaps the appropriate response is that for this much at least we should be thankful.

Even though we may admire him for having had the courage of his convictions, we must still, I think, judge Cratylus to have been frustrated in his skepticism, for he was, despite (or really because of) his silence, no skeptic at all. (Nor have any of his "skeptical" successors been skeptics.) To see this let us attempt to picture Cratylus as he worked his way through the various arguments that led him down the road toward skepticism. If we do so, we must recognize that as long as he continued to think and to argue, he had not yet attained his skeptical goal. If we then focus on him as he approached that goal, we become increasingly aware of the irresolvable dilemma that confronted him. The goal he had to accomplish was to enunciate his skeptical conclusion that nothing can be known and *then* lapse into silence. But this process he clearly was unable to carry out. For the skeptical dictum that was for him the necessary condition of his lapse into silence was something he could not consistently articulate. The words "Nothing can be known" can be spoken but they are hollow, for the thought they pretend to convey cannot be thought. Skepticism, in its very articulation, necessarily contradicts itself. For this reason it is a paradigm case of a nontheory. Thus Cratylus was forced into silence *before* enunciating the theory that would have rendered him a skeptic and justified him in thereafter remaining silent. And although history has witnessed many epistemologists since his time who have called themselves skeptics, it has produced no real skeptics. Those who have claimed to be skeptics have purported to embrace a theory about knowledge which does not, because it cannot, exist.

If, as I think I have shown, epistemological skepticism, being self-refuting, is incapable of theoretical articulation, what value can it possibly have for philosophy? It seems to me that it can be, and in fact has been, useful in a way that the "skeptics" themselves do not recognize; namely, as a foil to cognitivism, for skepticism, because it is self-contradictory, entails cognitivism. One wishing to establish the thesis of cognitivism, thus, can commence with *theoretical* skepticism and by his use of it transform it into *methodological* skepticism. Such was the procedure employed by Descartes in the *Meditations*, a procedure of which he must be recognized the grand master. By using his imagination and dialectical skills to push the case for skepticism to its uttermost limits in the first *Meditation*, he gained an epistemological platform from which he could launch his argument for cognitivism in the second *Meditation*. If we accept the conclusion that theoretical skepticism itself is a nontheory hence can have no claim on either the allegiance or the attention of epistemologists in its own right, we may nevertheless continue to emulate Descartes and use skepticism methodologically, as a tool in the pursuit of our legitimate cognitivistic goals.

Notes

I Introduction: The Skeptical Stance

1. Aristotle, *Metaphysics*, Γ. 5, 1010a, from *The Works of Aristotle*, ed. W. D. Ross, Vol. VIII, 2d. ed. (Oxford: Clarendon Press, 1928).

2. For example, see Kathleen Freeman, *The Pre-Socratic Philosophers*, 2d. ed. (Oxford: Basil Blackwell, 1949), pp. 284-285.

3. Sextus Empiricus, *Against the Logicians*, trans. R. G. Bury, Loeb Classical Library (Cambridge: Harvard University Press, 1935), II, 35.

4. Sextus reproduces these arguments at some length in his *Against the Logicians*, but scholars tend not to be very impressed with them. Philip Wheelwright, for example, makes the following comment: "The argument supporting the first argument, as presented by Sextus Empiricus in what looks like direct quotation, is unduly long, involved, and conceptually fussy, containing repetitions and quibbles which serve no valid purpose." P. Wheelwright, ed., *The Presocratics* (New York: Odyssey Press, 1966), p. 256.

5. Keith Lehrer, "Why Not Scepticism?" *Philosophical Forum*, II (1971), 283.

6. See John Kekes, "The Case for Scepticism," *Philosophical Quarterly* XXX (1975), 28-39. I have used the term myself, in my "Mitigated Scepticism," *Ratio* 18 (1976), 73-84.

7. I am indebted to Mr. Joseph Bush for first suggesting this term to me. The term *cognitivism* has appeared in recent literature, applied to views that in some respects resemble the position I shall use it to characterize. See, for example, R. Chisholm, *Theory of Knowledge* (Englewood Cliffs: Prentice-Hall, 1966), chap. 4 and I. Levi, *Gambling with Truth* (New York: Alfred A. Knopf, 1967), pp. 12-21. However, I have not seen the term employed to describe the *general* view that holds, against the epistemological skeptics, that knowledge is possible.

8. The word *skepticism* itself, although it has from early times been used to identify the theory that knowledge is impossible, is derived from a Greek verb with quite different connotations. Originally, it meant simply to inquire or to examine closely.

271

9. Cf. Hume's distinction between "antecedent" and "consequent" skepticism, in *Enquiries Concerning the Human Understanding*, §12.

10. I shall, therefore, concern myself in what follows with "logical" or "a priori" skepticism. However, since the proposition "Knowledge is impossible" ("We can know nothing") entails "Knowledge does not exist" ("We know nothing"), I shall use both formulations of the skeptical thesis in the course of my discussion. Likewise, I shall use both formulations of the cognitivistic thesis—"Knowledge exists" ("We do know something") and "Knowledge is possible" ("We can know something").

11. Descartes obviously comes to mind.

12. At least one skeptic (as we shall see later) uses the same type of argument against a conception of knowledge which differs somewhat from the traditional definition.

II Skepticism: The Historical Tradition

1. Richard H. Popkin, *The History of Scepticism from Erasmus to Descartes* (Assen: Van Gorcum, 1960), pp. xii; ibid., p. 42; ibid., p. 38.

2. Some ancient skeptics, like Pyrrho, Arcesilaus, and Carneades, did not write anything and the writings of others like Clitomachus, the pupil of Carneades (who according to Diogenes Laertius was the author of over four hundred treatises), have disappeared, with only a few scattered fragments remaining.

3. The best source in English for the writings of Sextus is Sextus Empiricus, *Outlines of Pyrrhonism, Against the Logicians, Against the Physicists, Against the Ethicists, Against the Professors*, trans. R. G. Bury, Loeb Classical Library, 4 vols. (Cambridge: Harvard University Press, 1933-1949). References to and quotations from Sextus in this book will be from that edition. A one-volume abridged edition of Sextus in English is also available: P. P. Hallie, ed., *Scepticism, Man, & God: Selections from the Major Writings of Sextus Empiricus*, trans. S. G. Etheridge (Middletown: Wesleyan University Press, 1964).

4. A number of scholarly books are available, which deal both historically and critically with the ancient skeptics. For those interested in a clear and concise analytical study of the epistemology of the major figures, I strongly recommend Charlotte Stough's recent book *Greek Skepticism: A Study in Epistemology* (Berkeley and Los Angeles: University of California Press, 1969).

5. Eduard Zeller, *The Stoics, Epicureans and Sceptics*, trans. O. J. Reichel, rev. ed. (London: Longmans, Green, 1880), p. 521.

6. In his introduction to the writings of Sextus, Bury offers a chronological outline of ancient skepticism, dividing it into four periods he character-

izes in the following way: (1) Practical Scepticism (Pyrrho and Timon), (2) Critical Scepticism and probabilism of the New Academy (Arcesilaus and Carneades), (3) Pyrrhonism revived, systematized, and developed dialectically (Aenesidemus and Agrippa), and (4) final development of Empiric Scepticism (Sextus Empiricus). See Sextus Empiricus, *Outlines of Pyrrhonism*, p. xxx.

7. Sextus Empiricus, *Outlines of Pyrrhonism*, p. 139. Later in the same chapter he refers to Arcesilaus as a "dogmatist"; see p. 145.

8. See ibid., pp. 25-93. In his *Against the Logicians*, Sextus attributes the ten Tropes to Aenesidemus; see ibid., p. 183.

9. Stough, *Greek Skepticism*, p. 67.

10. Sextus Empiricus, *Outlines of Pyrrhonism*, p. 47.

11. Ibid., p. 53.

12. Ibid., p. 73.

13. Ibid., p. 83.

14. Ibid., p. 93.

15. Sextus Empiricus, *Against the Logicians*, p. 429. To the question, Why did the skeptics accept the empiricist assumption? the obvious answer could be made that it is—or, at least, has been believed by many philosophers throughout the Western tradition to be—not only a reasonable but the correct view to take concerning the scope of our knowledge. But a more direct, historical answer can be offered as well, based on the fact that much of the impetus to skeptical thought in the ancient world lay in the Stoic philosophy, which the skeptics were intent on refuting. The Stoics accepted the empiricist assumption also, but they contended that because we can empirically apprehend certain images of objects (which they called "cataleptic impressions") with infallibility, we are, through such apprehensions, able to construct theories that provide us with knowledge concerning the ultimate composition and structure of reality. The skeptics flatly rejected this Stoic epistemology and metaphysics. To undercut what they considered to be the totally unwarranted knowledge claims of the Stoics, they began with the same assumption and endeavored by appeal to the Tropes to show that if knowledge must be limited to what we can apprehend through our senses, we can know nothing regarding the nature of an external world, let alone of ultimate reality.

16. Quoted in Stough, *Greek Scepticism*, p. 21. In Sextus we read, "honey appears to us to be sweet (and this we grant, for we perceive sweetness through the senses), but whether it is also sweet in its essence is for us a matter of doubt, since this is not an appearance" Sextus Empiricus, *Outlines of Pyrrhonism*, p. 15.

17. Nevertheless, it should be noted that not all of the ancient skeptics would agree with Timon in his admission that we can know appearances. There are strong indications in the writings of Sextus that at least some

were reluctant to dilute their skepticism even to the point of allowing us this much knowledge. To avoid doing so these skeptics adopted the device of contending that so-called assertions about appearances (e.g., "The honey tastes sweet") are not reports describing the nature of the appearances but simply "expressions" of these appearances. Thus, to use the example given, the statement "The honey tastes sweet," they would claim to convey no more than "Honey—mmmm." Understood as direct expressions (or responses) such statements are neither true nor false hence cannot convey knowledge. This view, which is associated with the Pyrrhonic tradition, merits serious consideration. I shall examine it at length in its modern formulation, in chapter iv.

18. For the purposes of my argument here both the reasons the cognitivist in question might give for his assertion and the strength of these reasons are irrelevant.

19. That the skeptics would agree with this reply to my suggested counterargument is implicit in their argument, for an essential reason why the illustrations presented in the Tropes lead them to conclude that we cannot know reality but only appearances lies in their acceptance of the assumption that reality cannot be inconsistent with itself. In the second Trope, for example, Sextus writes, "But if the same objects affect men differently owing to the differences in the men . . . we shall reasonably be led to suspension of judgment. For while we are, no doubt, able to state what each of the underlying objects appears to be, relatively to each difference, we are incapable of explaining what it is in reality. For we shall have to believe either all men or some. But if we believe all, we shall be attempting the impossible and accepting contradictories" Sextus Empiricus, *Outlines of Pyrrhonism*, p. 53.

20. One might say that the taste (appearance) of honey can have inconsistent characteristics, in that the same honey might taste sweet to you but not to me. However, there is no real inconsistency, even of taste, here, because in talking of the taste of honey to you and the taste of honey to me, we are talking about two different tastes.

21. The self-refuting nature of the empiricist assumption does not depend on the use to which the skeptics put it in their argument, for the claim that the assumption is true, unless it is purely gratuitous, is a claim to knowledge. But this alleged knowledge—that all of our knowledge consists of what we apprehend through our senses—is not apprehended through any of our senses.

22. This reluctance of the Pyrrhonists to commit themselves to a positive statement of the skeptical theory because of its logical consequences is implicit in Sextus's characterization of the Academic skeptics, who were bolder on this matter, as "dogmatists" (see above, p. 273 n. 7).

23. Sextus Empiricus, *Against the Logicians*, p. 489.

24. R. H. Popkin, *The History of Scepticism,* p. 1.

25. As far as I know the evil demon argument is original with Descartes. I have found it neither in earlier writers nor in histories or commentaries devoted to the skeptical tradition before Descartes.

26. This argument is quite short. It occurs at the beginning of §1 of Part IV of Book I of the *Treatise.* See David Hume, *A Treatise of Human Nature,* ed. L. A. Selby-Bigge (Oxford: Clarendon Press, 1888), pp. 180-183.

27. Ibid., pp. 267-268.

28. Ibid., p. 183.

29. His argument for his final position takes up the remainder of §1 and continues in §7, which is the conclusion of Book I of the *Treatise.* See ibid., pp. 183-187 and 263-274.

30. It is probably not necessary to mention at this stage that my interest is not in the scholarly, historical task of determining just what Hume *finally* concluded about the possibility of knowledge but rather in examining critically the arguments he offered in support of epistemological skepticism, without regard to the issue of whether he should or should not be classified in the final analysis as a total skeptic himself.

31. Hume adds a variation to this argument, citing the case of merchants, who increase the probability that the computations of their accountants will be correct by the use of artificially constructed accounting methods. I might note also that, although Hume generally formulates his case in subjective terms, talking about the degree of "confidence" or "assurance" we feel about the truth of our beliefs, his arguments have an objective application as well. If correct, they establish, first, that we can justifiably claim only a probable truth for our beliefs and, secondly, that this claim can be undermined so that we are left unable to offer any legitimate support for them whatsoever. That Hume believes his skeptical conclusion to be both subjectively and objectively cogent is clear from the way in which he formulates it, saying that the result of his argument is "at last a total extinction of *belief* and *evidence.*" Hume, *A Treatise of Human Nature,* p. 183 (italics mine).

32. Ibid., p. 181.

33. Ibid.

34. Ibid., pp. 181-182.

35. Ibid., p. 183.

36. Ibid.

37. Ibid. It might be noted in passing that Hume also rejects the stance taken by the Pyrrhonian skeptics that we should always suspend our judgment, and for the same reason: It is psychologically impossible for us to do so. See p. 184.

38. Ibid., pp. 270-271.

39. Ibid., p. 269.
40. Ibid.
41. Ibid., p. 273. For Hume's full discussion of this "truly" skeptical view see ibid., §7.
42. Ibid., p. 270.
43. Ibid., p. 273.
44. For example, what can Hume be doing but attempting to state a truth, which he is prepared to defend, when he writes "Nature, by an absolute and uncontroulable necessity has determin'd us to judge as well as to breathe and feel" or "Where reason is lively, and mixes itself with some propensity, it ought to be assented to. Where it does not, it never can have any title to operate upon us."
45. Hume, *A Treatise of Human Nature*, p. 268.
46. Ibid.
47. Ibid., p. 181.
48. Ibid., p. 182.
49. Ibid., p. 183.
50. Cf. ibid., pp. 181-182.
51. Ibid., p. 182.
52. "...I have prov'd, that these same principles, when carry'd farther, and apply'd to every new reflex judgment, must, by continually diminishing the original evidence, at last reduce it to nothing, and utterly subvert all belief and opinion" ibid., p. 184.
53. Ibid., p. 181.
54. Ibid., pp. 186-187.
55. See above, p. 42.

III Cartesian Demonology Revived

1. Kai Nielsen apparently disagrees with me. In the first sentence of his book *Scepticism* published in 1973, he writes: "Philosophical scepticism has few defenders nowadays." (London: Macmillan Press, 1973), p. 1. To account for Nielsen's judgment, I think two comments can appropriately be made: (1) He did not consider the writers with whom I shall be concerned here true skeptics (particularly since the most skeptical of their writings had not then been published), and (2) he made the statement before their ideas had had a serious impact on the philosophical scene.
2. See Keith Lehrer, "Why Not Scepticism?" *Philosophical Forum* II (1971), 283-298; Arne Naess, *Scepticism* (London: Routledge & Kegan Paul, 1968); and Peter Unger, *Ignorance: A Case for Scepticism* (Oxford: Clarendon Press, 1975). In addition Unger has published several journal articles supporting skepticism.

Two other skeptical writings, which I shall not discuss in detail but only refer to briefly in this book, should be mentioned: W. W. Rozeboom, "Why I Know So Much More Than You Do," *American Philosophical Quarterly* IV (1967), 281-290 and John Kekes, "The Case for Scepticism," *Philosophical Quarterly* XXV (1975), 28-39. My reason for not devoting space to the views of Rozeboom and Kekes is that, although they are distinctly skeptical, they are presented in a tentative and incomplete rather than a theoretically elaborated way in the articles in question. Also, there is reason to believe, in Kekes's case, that he does not consider himself to be a skeptic.

3. An earlier version of the study of Lehrer's skepticism contained in this chapter was read before a meeting of the American Philosophical Association, Eastern Division, in Washington, D.C., on December 29, 1974, under the title "The Googol Gambit."

4. It should be noted here that Lehrer no longer holds the skeptical position that he defends in "Why Not Scepticism?" In his book *Knowledge* (Oxford: Clarendon Press, 1974), he formulates a positive theory of knowledge which leads him to conclude that we can legitimately claim to know things. In the final chapter of the book he discusses the relationship between his current epistemological views and his earlier skepticism (see especially pp. 236-241).

Although in this chapter I shall engage in a critical discussion of a view Lehrer has since abandoned, I do not think that fact is particularly important, for my concern in this book is with skepticism, not with the writers who have defended it. And Lehrer's argument for skepticism, whatever he may think of it now, is in my opinion among the most ingenious and definitely the most persuasive in the current literature. It is worth a chapter in any book devoted to skepticism.

5. Lehrer, "Why Not Scepticism?" pp. 283-284.

6. Ibid., p. 288.

7. Ibid., p. 289.

8. Ibid., p. 292.

9. Lehrer offered his subsequent interpretation in an unpublished paper read before the American Philosophical Association, Eastern Division, in response to my paper mentioned in note 3 (above).

10. This has to be qualified. The humans whom they would be deceiving could not include the Googolplexes but only those of us, whom we normally think of as humans, who possess intellects of a much more modest capacity than those of the Googols.

11. The reader may find it helpful to return to the skeptical hypothesis as I have reproduced it on pp. 66-67 to pick up the continuity.

12. Although Lehrer does not himself describe the falsity infecting human beliefs in precisely these terms in the skeptical hypothesis, I think

they accurately describe the situation as he pictures it, for he says that our beliefs are subverted by the Googols to the extent that, although they are erroneous, they are still very nearly correct.

13. For example: X believes that he knows a.

X's belief that he knows a is true.

Therefore, X knows a.

14. It is not relevant to my argument to consider human beliefs that are rendered false by causes other than the Googols' deceitful activities.

15. This is taken from the unpublished paper I referred to earlier. (See above n. 9, p. 277.) The "objection" to which Lehrer refers in the last sentence of the quotation was one I had made in my paper "The Googol Gambit." (See above n. 3, p. 277.)

IV Verbal Gestures and the Suspension of Judgment

1. Arne Naess, *Scepticism* (London: Routledge & Kegan Paul, 1968).

2. Ibid., p. ix. See also Chap. I, §1.

3. Cf. ibid., pp. 61 ff.

4. On this point his own characterization of Sextus is illuminating. "Sextus the metasceptic is the same person as Sextus the sceptic." (Ibid., p. 6).

5. Ibid., p. 156.

6. Ibid., pp. 100-102, 108. I use these passages to illustrate Naess's own acceptance of the classical Pyrrhonic suspension of judgment. To the extent that he may depart from ancient Pyrrhonism on matters of detail, I shall not be concerned with his views, for, as I said earlier, my object is to examine the classical tradition in the modernized verbal dress in which it has been clothed by Naess.

7. Ibid., p. 3.

8. Ibid., pp. 28-29. See also p. 38. Students of ancient Pyrrhonism and the writings of Sextus may consider Naess's account here to involve a misconception of the Pyrrhonic view. I shall not pursue this scholarly point, since my interest is in Naess's version of Pyrrhonism.

9. Ibid., p. 29. Naess does continue to refer to the Pyrrhonists as philosophers, on the grounds that the term can be given a much broader, looser meaning.

10. Ibid., p. 15. See also, for example, pp. 37, 110.

11. Ibid., p. 19.

12. Cf. ibid., pp. 3-6.

13. Ibid., pp. 6-7.

14. Ibid., p. 7.

15. See ibid., p. 7. Naess's main discussion of this point appears in §3 of Chapter I.

16. Ibid., p. 9. Naess writes: "That the sceptic does not intend to assert something, to state that something is the case, when uttering his sceptical phrases, is clearly, explicitly, and repeatedly stated by Sextus himself" (p. 9). Unfortunately, the contradiction in this statement is all too obvious; one wishes that Naess had taken the time to explain it away.

17. Ibid., p. 129. Elsewhere he uses the more general but compatible phrase "verbal behavior." See, for example, ibid., p. 46.

18. See above, p. 37.

19. Naess, *Scepticism*, pp. 16-17.

20. Ibid., pp. 39-40.

21. See ibid., p. 44.

22. Ibid., p. 48; italics mine.

23. Ibid., p. 45.

24. Ibid., pp. 45-46. In discussing this example, Naess describes the issue in terms of the question: Can a person *confidently* step into and cross a room with an uncertain floor without committing himself to a belief in the truth of any propositions? Cf. pp. 43 ff. The term "confidently" is important in that it indicates that the illustration is concerned with what I have described as *thoughtful* activity.

25. In the example, the person is described as uttering the words aloud. The essential problem would, however, remain the same even if he were described as articulating them inwardly; i.e., as thinking these thoughts.

26. I find it a bit difficult to articulate these sentences as verbal gestures (like "Honey—m-m-m-m"). But here is a try: "Foot and leg sensations, noises heard, a feeling of confidence, then of accomplishment and relief."

27. Naess, *Scepticism*, pp. 20, 34, 85; ibid., pp. 26, 49, 59-60, 67; ibid., p. 57.

28. Ibid., pp. 2, 66, 67, 80, 102, 129.

29. Ibid., p. 29; second italics mine. It is hardly necessary to point out that Naess, when he writes in the last sentence I have quoted, "the sceptic may support it or fight it with a set of arguments," cannot give the word "support" its ordinary meaning (as he can the word "fight"); rather the sentence should be translated to read, "The sceptic may fight by throwing more arguments at his opponents."

30. Ibid., p. 4. See also p. 32.

31. Ibid., p. 14. His references to Hume later in the same passage are of some interest.

32. Ibid., p. 149.

33. Naess raises this supposition and comments briefly on it. Cf. ibid., p. 60.

34. See above, §2.

35. Naess, *Scepticism*, p. 5.

V Skepticism by Definition

1. Peter Unger, *Ignorance: A Case for Scepticism* (Oxford: Clarendon Press, 1975). The book was preceded by a number of articles in which many of its main themes appeared. Since the book encompasses these and elaborates them in a fuller form, I shall devote my attention in this chapter exlusively to it.

2. Cf. ibid., p. 6.

3. Ibid., pp. 93-94.

4. Ibid., p. 245.

5. Ibid., p. 242.

6. See ibid., p. 198. In several places in *Ignorance* Unger refers to skepticism about rationality as the "wages of ignorance" (see, for example, the title of Chapter IV). It might be of interest to note here a few of the "wages" Unger derives from his conclusion that we are necessarily ignorant about everything (i.e., from his skepticism about knowledge), because they emphasize the extreme nature of his skeptical views. "So, just as universal ignorance will entail that nobody ever sees, or remembers, or notices anything *about anything*, it will entail that nobody ever admits or regrets anything *at all*" (p. 186). "...if nobody ever really knows anything, then nobody will ever be angry, or happy, or surprised about anything" (p. 186). "...if there is universal ignorance, then nobody is ever amazed" (p. 187). "...if nobody knows anything to be so, nobody can ever be happy or unhappy about anything..." (p. 188). "...it is never the case that anyone *ought* to do anything, or that anyone *ought not* to do anything" (p. 243 n.). "In a very general way, then, our ignorance enjoins our silence" (p. 269). "...no one can ever think or believe anything to be so at all" (p. 310). "Nothing...can be asserted or even said to be so..." (p. 311). "...we must conclude, finally, that snow *is* white *and* snow is *not* white" (p. 312).

7. Ibid., pp. 87-88.

8. It should be noted that Unger qualifies his major premise slightly. Since the qualification will not affect our discussion, for purposes of simplicity I shall disregard it. For more on this point see p. 281, n. 24.

9. His main discussion of this point appears in §§2-4 of Chapter II of *Ignorance*.

10. Ibid., p. 66.

11. Ibid., p. 67.

12. Ibid., p. 63.

13. Ibid.

14. Ibid., p. 64; italics are Unger's.

15. Cf. ibid., p. 68.

16. I might mention, in passing, that the impersonal idea of certainty, as Unger describes it on page 63 of *Ignorance*, is a bastard concept. We do not

add anything to the objective content of the statement "It is raining" when we say "It is certain that it is raining." Rather, I think this way of speaking, which is common enough, is simply loose talk. The additional thought we are attempting to convey when we say, usually with emphasis (perhaps after someone has disputed our statement that it is raining), *"It is certain that it is raining"* is really *"I am certain that it is raining."* We use the objective formulation (Unger's impersonal idea) rather than the subjective to give our assertion more weight. But if we were always to speak our thoughts accurately, we should drop the "It is certain that . . ." altogether.

17. Unger does not himself distinguish between these conceptions, which, as we shall see, are quite different from each other.

18. I should note that the label "contingent" certainty is my own. Unger does not himself use it. My reason for introducing it is to give this conception of certainty a distinctive, descriptive title, to contrast it with Unger's third notion of certainty.

19. I have already alluded to this conception of certainty, in my explanation early in the chapter of the distinction Unger draws between absolute and relative terms. However, I did not there pursue the point that it represents a definition of the term *certainty*, different from other definitions he gives. See above, pp. 123-124.

20. Unger, *Ignorance*, p. 67.

21. As with the label "contingent" certainty, this label is my own.

22. Unger, *Ignorance*, p. 68.

23. Ibid., pp. 89, 90.

24. I might note in passing that my interpretation of the major premise of Unger's argument yields a stronger case for skepticism than his own. In his argument he claims only that "there is at most hardly anything" of which we are certain, and elsewhere in Chapter II of *Ignorance* he admits the possibility of our being "logically" certain of some things; e.g., that a few people may be certain that there are automobiles (p. 68). It seems to me that if my understanding of Unger's argument is correct, he does not need to make such a concession. If to be certain that p, it must be logically impossible for one to be more certain that q, and if certainty is a psychological concept, it follows that no one can ever legitimately claim of any p (even the p that there are automobiles) that he (or anyone else) is certain of it.

25. Cf. Unger, *Ignorance*, p. 83.

26. See A. C. Danto, *Analytical Philosophy of Knowledge* (Cambridge: At the University Press, 1968), p. 73.

27. Unger, *Ignorance*, p. 85. Unger's discussion of this argument occurs in §9 of Chapter II, which is entitled "Does Knowing Require Being Certain?"

28. Ibid., p. 85.

29. For purposes of the discussions that follow it must be remembered that certainty, for Unger, is some kind of attitude or state of mind, presumably much like yet somewhat different from a state in which one is completely free of doubt about something.

30. I might claim that my definition is complete because it includes necessary as well as sufficient conditions of knowledge. Certainly I would accept this regarding the "truth" condition it embodies. Whether I would do so regarding the "establishment" condition turns on the question of whether or not such a condition is too severe. At least some epistemologists would argue that it is, holding that we can know more than those things whose truth we can establish. In any event, the important point is that the conditions I state be *sufficient* for knowledge.

31. I shall speak to this issue further in chapter vii.

32. Unger, *Ignorance*, p. 95.

33. Ibid., p. 103.

34. Ibid., pp. 134-135.

35. Ibid., p. 97.

36. Ibid., p. 265. Unger devotes much of Chapter VI of *Ignorance* to supporting this view.

37. Ibid., p. 92.

38. "Fundamentally, the absolute clarity required by knowledge can never be attained"; ibid., p. 147.

39. "S knows that *p* if and only if it is clear to S that *p*"; ibid., p. 137. Unger makes clarity a sufficient as well as a necessary condition of knowledge. However, for the purposes of his third argument for skepticism, its being a necessary condition alone is essential.

40. Ibid.

41. Ibid., p. 141. See also pp. 142 and 144.

42. Ibid., p. 140. Unger elaborates this relationship between clarity and certainty on pp. 140 ff.

43. Cf. ibid., pp. 273 and 284: "Truth . . . is the property of being in agreement with the whole truth about the world" (p. 284). For Unger, this is the *definition* of truth. He writes: "Thus, truth may be defined as agreement with the truth, or as the property of being in agreement with the truth . . . truth is agreement with the truth, that is, with the whole truth about the world" (p. 287).

44. ". . . there really is nothing which is the whole truth about the world. For this reason, there can be nothing either which is any part of the whole truth about the world. . . . the nonexistence of these things is hardly a contingent matter"; ibid., pp. 272-273. See also pp. 308-309.

45. Cf. ibid., p. 309.

46. Cf. ibid., p. 290.

47. Compare the definition of "true" I have just given, as far as its simplicity is concerned, with a parallel definition offered by Unger: "'That is

true' means 'That is in agreement with the truth,' and, there being no qualification, we take what it expresses to be logically equivalent to what is expressed by 'That is in agreement with the whole truth about everything'";
ibid., p. 295.

48. "...when someone knows about something, or knows something to
be so, what he knows is either the whole truth about the world, or, if less
than that, something which is part of that first thing. The former is of
course the far more exotic case, occurring only where there is true omniscience"; ibid., p. 272. This quotation, in admitting that omniscience gives
knowledge of the whole truth about the world, seems clearly inconsistent
with Unger's minor premise, which denies the existence of any such truth.

49. Ibid., pp. 308-309.

50. Ibid., p. 309, n. 8.

51. In §9 of Chapter VII Unger argues that some propositions are neither
true nor false but have some third, intermediate status. See ibid., pp. 306-
308. But any such propositions would be limited to those that either refer
to future contingencies or have vague predicates (p. 312), which is not the
case with the minor premise now under examination.

52. See above, p. 158.

53. Unger, *Ignorance*, p. 242; italics mine. For some other examples see
pp. 136, 137, 196, 198, 209, 210, and 229. Consider also the following:
"This is a good point for me to present an argument for the universal form
of scepticism about knowledge.... Each of the two premisses of this new
argument is put forward as necessarily true" (p. 92).

54. Ibid., p. 310.

55. Ibid.

56. For a longer list of such conclusions, see above, p. 280, n. 6.

57. Unger, *Ignorance*, p. 316. Unger's main discussions of the view
appear on pp. 5-6, 195-196, 246-247, 273-274, 303-304, and 314-317.

58. Ibid., p. 313.

59. Ibid.

60. Ibid., p. 47. Unger repeats this theme on several occasions throughout the book.

61. Ibid., p. 274.

62. By the end of *Ignorance*, Unger's "ancestor language" hypothesis has
become a "hunch" (p. 314). Such, thus, seems to be the ultimate foundation for his skepticism.

VI *Essays in Skepticism*

1. I have myself discussed the issue at some length, in my book *The
Problem of Knowledge* (The Hague: Nijhoff, 1974), pp. 17-47.

2. Lehrer, "Why Not Scepticism?" *Philosophical Forum*, II (1971), 288.

3. See above, p. 65.

4. Lehrer, "Why Not Scepticism?" p. 289.

5. I shall here (and later) often talk in terms of propositions rather than beliefs. This signals no change in the substance of the argument.

6. For purposes of this argument it is immaterial what the precise source and nature of the subversion is; we can assume that, if a belief is false, its falsity results from the subversion of our minds.

7. See above, p. 189.

8. See chapter ii, n. 7.

9. Although the tentative, "nondogmatic" way in which I have just formulated the skeptical thesis offers an apparent way of escaping the "standard objection" to skepticism (see above, p. 22), few skeptics in the tradition have made significant use of it. Lehrer, on one hand, makes a gesture in its direction at the beginning of his paper, "Why Not Scepticism?" (§1), but does not pursue the point any further. Unger, on the other hand, holds a contrary position, arguing that if knowledge is impossible, so too is reasonable belief. The skeptical thesis that knowledge is impossible, therefore, cannot be claimed to be a reasonable belief, for if the thesis were true, there would be no reasonable beliefs. And without reasonable beliefs, there could be no viable hypotheses either.

10. A good example of a dogmatic believer is the religious fideist, who believes without reason.

11. To simplify the text I shall refer to him henceforth simply as a "skeptic," omitting the qualifier unless it is needed for purposes of clarity or precision.

12. If the cognitivist were to attempt to break out of the circle in his argument by trying to justify his claim that he knows that the reasons he has given in support of his conclusion that knowledge exists are true and entail that conclusion, he could do so only by providing reasons that support his original reasons. But these second-order reasons, to be equal to their task, would have to consist of things he both knows to be true and to entail his first-order reasons. So he would find himself again using a circular argument, which assumes that he knows something in order to establish ultimately that knowledge exists. Such a circular argument would continue to repeat at each higher-order level. Thus he would entrap himself in a vicious infinite regress.

VII Skepticism, Cognitivism, and the Foundations of Knowledge

1. Peter Unger, *Ignorance: A Case for Scepticism* (Oxford: Clarendon Press, 1975), p, 198.

2. John Kekes, "The Case for Scepticism," *Philosophical Quarterly* 25 (1975), 38.

3. The statement "I believe that X is Y but X is not Y" is admittedly odd and one that someone would utter only in unusual circumstances. The point I am making, however, is simply that it is not, like the statement "I know that X is Y but X is not Y," logically self-contradictory. The logical difference between the two is retained and the psychological oddness of the first removed if we cast them in the third person: "He believes that X is Y but X is not Y" and "He knows that X is Y but X is not Y."

4. Of course they do not in themselves offer *sufficient* support for the belief, for both of them could be true and the belief, nevertheless, false. (The chair might just be firm, not hard.)

5. It should be obvious, of course, that I am *not* denying the possibility of "irrational beliefs," in one important meaning of that term, for it must, I think, be admitted that we believe many things irrationally in the sense that the reasons we have for believing them fall woefully short of supporting their truth. All I am contending is that we cannot believe anything without any supporting reasons at all. My case is based on logical grounds. If the truth of a given proposition entails that of another, then the affirmation of the first entails the affirmation of the other. Whether, however, the situation is psychologically the same might be questioned for is it not psychologically possible for a person to believe, say, that he is sitting in a chair without believing that he is sitting? Certainly not, if he has reflected self-consciously about his belief. Nevertheless, when we come to consider complex beliefs, it must be admitted that people often believe certain things and at the same time disbelieve other things entailed by their original beliefs. But this is because they are confused, at least to the extent that they are not thinking rationally. In any event, the important point is the logical one. For, if it is logically impossible that anyone should believe anything without reason (in the sense in which we are concerned here), the recommendation that a negative skeptic should carry out the consequences of his skepticism by embracing irrationality is an invitation, on the one hand, to psychological confusion and, on the other more important hand, to a mode of life that he cannot consistently pursue.

6. Bertrand Russell, *Human Knowledge* (New York: Simon and Schuster, 1948), p. xi. With Russell's second statement (about the psychological impossibility of skepticism) I should certainly agree; it is still a bit early, however, to decide whether he is correct in his first (about its logical impeccability).

7. The further argument I gave (see p. 284 n. 12 above), that the cognitivist gets trapped in a vicious regress, is subsidiary and is meant only to show that an apparently possible way for him to avoid circularity is, in fact, blocked.

8. My example is adapted from H. A. Prichard. *Cf.* his *Knowledge and Perception* (Oxford: Clarendon Press, 1950), p. 96.

9. For B even to *state* his view he must accept the law of noncontradic-

tion, for the theory he is offering is one that he holds to be inconsistent with that of A. The possibility of such an inconsistency, however, is dependent on the applicability of the law to the disagreement between the two, for, unless the law applied in this situation, both theories could be true together. And this would be so in any possible disagreement between theories or propositions.

10. Skeptics, as a rule, recognize this. For example, Lehrer makes the following acknowledgement, "the contention [of the skeptic] is that no one knows anything, not even that no one knows anything." Keith Lehrer, "Why Not Scepticism?" *Philosophical Forum*, II (1971), 284.

11. That the proposition, "The skeptic does not know that no one knows anything" is different in meaning from S is clear, for it could be true and S false.

12. Sextus Empiricus, *Outlines of Pyrrhonism*, trans. R. G. Bury, Loeb Classical Library (Cambridge: Harvard University Press, 1933), I, 115-117. Since the question of whether Sextus was a total or only a mitigated skeptic is not at issue here, I shall disregard it.

13. See especially chap. ii, §4 and chap. iv, §§5-8.

14. I don't like to resort to an ad hominem argument, but in this case I think it is justified. I believe that nontheoretical skepticism, as exhibited in the quotation I have given from Sextus, may be described as being, at best, self-deception and, at worst, intellectual dishonesty. The nontheoretical skeptic wants to be able to say things that give the impression that he is denying the existence of knowledge, but when he is confronted with the fact that in doing so he becomes entrapped in contradictions, he wants to have an escape route, so he disclaims making the theoretical statement he appeared to be making. Instead he was only "announcing" or "explaining" his state of mind—an act innocent of all theory. It is hard to avoid the conclusion that such people suffer from intellectual cowardice. Far better the dogmatic but courageous stance of the Academic skeptics.

15. In the next section I shall make an interesting qualification to this conclusion.

16. By "world" here I mean universe. My contention is that the universe cannot lack beings who know something, if for no other reason than that it contains me and I know something.

17. I am not concerned here with the cogency of the Cartesian argument.

18. Further, if it is true, as I believe it is, that thinking entails knowing, the proposition "Knowledge exists" is necessarily true as long as thinkers exist, whatever it may be that they are thinking about.

19. It might be noted also that Descartes's proof of his own existence entails the existence of knowledge, for in his demonstration of his existence, Descartes makes a claim to knowledge which, if his demonstration is cogent, is established as well.

20. I have spoken to the issue elsewhere, in *The Problem of Knowledge*, §§16 and 17.

21. The propositions that concern me here, and in what follows, are, of course, substantive or informative propositions.

22. See above, pp. 217-218.

23. I am concerned here, of course, with beliefs other than those that constitute things we know. In one sense, we are obviously reasonable in believing that which we know, but this remark involves a different meaning of "reasonable belief" from that in which our reasonable beliefs constitute a category distinct from our beliefs that are also things we know.

24. Generally, the literature concerns the question of alternative criteria of *knowledge* rather than of *reasonable belief*; nevertheless the problem remains the same. Furthermore, if my earlier conclusions are correct, the issue in dispute concerns reasonable belief rather than knowledge.

Index

Academic skepticism, 28-29, 82, 88, 90, 112, 114, 207, 212, 235, 237; called dogmatism, 274 n. 22, 286 n. 14; as a form of positive skepticism, 207; and theory, 114

Activity: relationship to thought, 97-98

Aenesidemus, 9, 28, 273 n. 6; as originator of the ten tropes, 30, 273 n. 8

Agrippa, 273 n. 6

Alexander the Great, 27

Announcements: relationship to propositions, 93

Anthropology: relationship to Unger's ancestor language hypothesis, 170-172

Anthropomorphism: in Lehrer's skeptical hypothesis, 175

A posteriori skepticism. See Contingent skepticism

Appearance: and reality, 34

A priori skepticism. See Logical skepticism

Arcesilaus, 9, 26, 28, 272 n. 2, 273 nn. 6, 7

Archetypal skepticism, 1, 3, 268

Argument: circular, 226-239; question-begging, 228-239; self-contradictory, 233; self-reference, 194; throwing, 108-110, 116

Aristotle, 1-3

Augustine, 11, 107

Bayle, Pierre, 10, 26

Belief: basic, 221-223; and judgment, 214-216; and reasonable belief, 264-267; unreasoned, 220-223

Bormann, Martin, 202-203

Bury, R. G., 272 n. 6

Bush, Joseph, 271 n. 7

Carneades, 9, 26, 28, 272 n. 2, 273 n. 6

Certainty: as an absolute term, 123-124, 136-138, 153; Argument from the Necessity of, 122-150; attitude of, 135, 142, 151; contingent personal, 127-130, 133-135; as an empirical concept, 136-137; feeling of, 126, 133-134; ideas of, 125; impersonal, 123-127; logical personal, 130-138; Normative Argument from, 150-154; psychological, 125, 127, 150, 154, 227; relationship to clarity, 157-158; relationship to dogmatism, 151-152

Clarity: Argument from the Necessity of, 122, 154-158; identified with knowledge, 156; relationship to certainty, 157-158

Clitomachus, 28, 272 n. 2

Cogito argument: of Descartes, 44-45

Cognitivism: definition of, 7; logical, 264; use in literature, 271 n. 7

Contingent skepticism, 15-17

Contradiction: feeling of, 141-142

Copernicus, 43
Cratylus, 1-4, 8, 18, 209, 268-269

Danto, Arthur, 139
Definition: nature of, 147
Descartes, Rene, 9, 11, 15, 24, 26, 42-45, 67, 69, 77, 182-183, 246-248, 270, 272 n. 11, 275 n. 25, 286 n. 19; relationship to Lehrer, 67, 69-70
Diogenes Laertius, 272 n. 2
Dogmatism, 5-6; relationship to certainty, 151-152; relationship to cognitivism, 5, 90, 152-153; relationship to nondogmatic skepticism, 201-206; relationship to positive forms of skepticism, 200, 207

Emphasis: alternative arguments from, 142-143; Argument from, 138-144; Principle of, 140
Empiricism: relationship to skepticism, 63
Empiricist assumption, 35, 39-41, 273 n. 15, 274 n. 21
English language: relationship to skepticism, 169-173
Epicureanism, 9, 27
Epistemological skepticism: definition of, 18-19
Ethical cognitivism, 7
Ethical relativism: in the tenth trope, 33
Evil demon argument: of Descartes, 43-45; relationship to Lehrer's skeptical hypothesis, 67-68, 80, 175; relationship to revised skeptical hypothesis, 182
Evolution: relationship to knowledge, 114

Faculty skepticism, 15
Fideism: religious, 10; relationship to nondogmatic skepticism, 201-203
Foucher, Simon, 9

Gassendi, Pierre, 9, 26
Gnosticism, 6
Googolplexes, 62-81, 175-176, 277 n. 10
Googols, 62-81, 175-176, 242, 277 n. 10, 278 nn. 12, 14
Gorgias, 3-4, 8, 18

Heraclitus, 1, 3
Hervet, Gentian, 9
Hume, David, 5, 10-11, 24, 26, 45-61, 63, 215, 219, 275 nn. 30, 31, 37, 276 nn. 41, 44, 279 n. 31; and antecedent and consequent skepticism, 272 n. 9; examination of his case for skepticism, 55-61; statement of his case for skepticism, 46-50; true skepticism in, 50-55
Hypothesis: Lehrer's skeptical, 64, 66-81, 175-177, 198; revised skeptical, 173-199; Unger's ancestor language, 168-173, 283 n. 62

Ignorance: as skepticism about knowledge, 121-122; wages of, 280 n. 6
Incorrigibility: of empirical beliefs, 183; of first-person reports, 184-186; of logically necessary beliefs, 185-186
Intuition: and knowledge, 262-263; in Sidgwick, 263
Irrationality: relationship to intellectual freedom, 219-223; as result of skepticism, 217-218; as skepticism about rationality, 121-122; as a way of life, 217-223

Johnsonian skepticism, 193

Kant, Immanuel, 10-11, 13
Kekes, John, 217-219, 265, 277 n. 2
Kierkegaard, Søren, 10
Knowledge: definition of, 12, 139, 147-148, 150, 170, 262; neces-

sary conditions of, 149, 260, 282
n. 30; partial definition of, 138-
139; Principle of Identifying,
165; proposed alternative definition of, 148-150; range and
limits of, 259-264; sufficient conditions of, 148-149, 260, 282 n.
30

Language: artificial and natural,
172
Law of noncontradiction: and an
alogical world, 240-242; application to the world, 241-245; and
circular arguments, 229-231; as
an eternal verity, 246-248; and
question-begging arguments,
229-231
Lehrer, Keith, 5, 62-81, 175-177,
182-183, 185-187, 195, 198, 242,
277 nn. 3, 4, 9, 12, 278 n. 15, 284
n. 9, 286 n. 10; relationship to
Descartes, 67, 69-70
Leibniz, G. W., 245
Locke, John, 14
Logic: relationship to world, 239-
245
Logical empiricism, 7, 63
Logical skepticism, 15-17, 272 n. 10

Mersenne, Marin, 26
Metaphor: of the ladder, 42, 61;
political, 60-61
Metaphysical nihilism, 4
Metaskepticism: relationship to
skepticism, 82-88
Methodological skepticism: 15, 24,
269-270
Mitigated skepticism, 9, 14, 19;
and logical cognitivism, 264
Modes. See Tropes
Montaigne, Michel de, 9, 26
Moore, G. E., 139

Naess, Arne, 62, 82-118, 278 nn. 6,
8, 9, 15, 279 nn. 16, 24, 29, 33
Negative skepticism, 207-226, 239;
as cryptoskepticism, 208; as no
theory, 224; relationship to positive skepticism, 207, 211; relationship to Pyrrhonism, 207
Nicholas of Cusa, 9
Nielsen, Kai, 276 n. 1
Nondogmatic skepticism, 199-206;
as dogmatic, 205; three options
for, 205-206
Normative ethics, 7

Omniscience: and whole truth
about world, 161
Ordinary language analysis, 63, 84

Peace of mind. See Pyrrhonism
Plato, 1, 11
Platonic Academy, 28
Popkin, Richard, 26, 43
Pragmatism, 63
Prichard, H. A., 285 n. 8
Problem of error: relationship to
skepticism, 20
Propositions: logically necessary,
231, 240-245; self-evident, 238,
261; self-justifying, 238-239; self-
referentially self-refuting, 257;
vacuous and substantive, 251-
258
Protagoras, 4
Pyrrho, 9, 27-29, 37, 83, 115, 272
n. 2, 273 n. 6
Pyrrhonic skepticism. See Pyrrhonism
Pyrrhonism, 28-29, 41, 82-118,
175, 198, 207, 212, 215-218, 235-
236, 274 n. 22, 275 n. 37, 278 n.
8; as a form of morality, 115-
118; Naess's addition to ancient,
83-85; as nontheoretical, 113-
115, 235-237; and peace of mind,
82-118, 175, 215; relationship to
philosophy, 89, 116; relationship to skepticism, 112-115;
stages along the road to, 88-91;
and suspension of judgment, 41,
82-118, 175, 207, 215-216, 218,

278 n. 6, as a way of life, 89-90, 118

Rationalism, 6
Reasonable belief: as epistemological category, 266; as rational belief, 265; and reasons, 201-206; relationship to belief, 264-267; relationship to nondogmatic skepticism, 201-206
Reformation: relationship to skepticism, 9, 43
Religion. *See* Science
Renaissance: relationship to skepticism, 9
Revised skeptical hypothesis, 175-176
Rozeboom, W. W., 277 n. 2
Russell, Bertrand, 225, 285 n. 6

Sanchez, Francisco, 9, 26
Santayana, George, 10
Science: conflict with religion, 43
Scitism, 6
Sextus Empiricus, 4-6, 9, 26-33, 35, 41-43, 61, 82-118, 235-236, 271 n. 4, 272 n. 3, 272-273 n. 6, 273 nn. 8, 16, 17, 274 nn. 19, 22, 278 nn. 4, 8, 279 n. 16, 286 nn. 12, 14
Sidgwick, Henry, 263
Skeptical phrases: in Naess's version of Pyrrhonism, 93-94
Skeptical tradition, 8-12, 25, 26-61
Skepticism: causes of contemporary, 62-63; definition of, 2-3, 12-19; English language, 170; etymology of, 271 n. 8; four periods of ancient, 272-273 n. 6; importance of, 10-12; and nontheory, 269-270; positive, 207; relationship to Pyrrhonism, 115; and silence, 3, 269; standard objection to, 22-23, 29, 88; and theory, 113-115, 235-237; two forms of, 120-122; varieties of, 12-17
Socrates, 1, 268

Specific object skepticism, 14
Stoicism, 5-6, 8, 27, 36, 273 n. 15
Stough, Charlotte, 30
Subject area skepticism, 14
Suspension of judgment. *See* Pyrrhonism

Tautology: logical, 251; and vacuous proposition, 251
Terminal skepticism. *See* Theoretical skepticism
Terms: absolute and relative, 123-124, 136-138, 143
Theoretical skepticism, 15, 269-270
Theory: and knowledge claims, 198-199; lacking in negative skepticism, 224; relationship to Pyrrhonism, 113-115, and skepticism, 235
Timon, 9, 28, 37, 95, 273 nn. 6, 17
Total skepticism, 13, 18-19, 29, 37; in Hume, 46, 50-51; in Lehrer, 64-66; in Pyrrhonism, 88
Tropes, 30-34, 39, 44, 274 n. 19
True skepticism: according to Hume, 50-55
Truth: an alternative definition of, 159-161; Argument from the Impossibility of, 122, 158-168, 173; distinguished from knowledge, 182; as a necessary condition of knowledge, 149, 261; three types of necessary, 245-248; Unger's definition of, 159-161

Unger, Peter, 62, 82-118, 175, 217-218, 265, 268, 276 n. 2, 280 nn. 6, 8, 280-281 n. 16, 281 nn. 17, 18, 19, 24, 27, 282 nn. 29, 36, 39, 42, 43, 47, 283 nn. 48, 51, 57, 60, 62, 284 n. 9

Verbal gestures, 94, 116; and everyday beliefs, 101-106; and philosophical beliefs, 106-112; relationship to propositions, 94-96, 100

Verifiability principle, 7

Verities: eternal, 245-246, 248; existential, 248; theoretical, 248

Wheelwright, Philip, 271 n. 4

William of Ockham, 9

Wittgenstein, Ludwig, 11, 14, 116

World: alogical, 240-245, and appearance, 34, 36-38; possible, 240-245

Zeller, Eduard, 28-29